UNCLE SAM AND
MOTHER EARTH

Uncle Sam and Mother Earth

Shaping the Nation's Environmental Path

Jake Plante

ISBN: 1514368854
ISBN 13: 9781514368855
Library of Congress Control Number: 2015909836
CreateSpace Independent Publishing Platform
North Charleston, South Carolina

To those who threw a lot of the seeds but are no longer here
My parents, Sadie and Sandy, my brother Jerry,
and my friend Jack.

CONTENTS

PREFACE

SPURRED BY GROWING CONCERNS ABOUT climate change, environmental issues have risen to the forefront of public policy. The problems are clear but our ability to solve them requires more skill at bridging environmental science and policymaking. An indispensable but often overlooked part of the equation is how the federal government carries out its environmental responsibilities.

Government actions are fundamental to environmental protection, so understanding the mechanics of government is crucial to effective environmental advocacy. Anyone concerned about the health of the environment and willing to get involved needs to know how environmental laws and regulations are administered, not only in theory, but on a daily basis by imperfect people and institutions.

As someone who spent 30 years in federal service working on environmental issues, I provide an inside look at the environmental role of government and offer new insights for environmental practitioners. The early chapters of the book illustrate the difference that individuals can make by profiling major historical figures of the modern environmental movement—Teddy Roosevelt, Rachel Carson, Stewart Brand, Bill Ruckelshaus, Al Gore, and others—and their unique contributions to raising public awareness. This historical review is supplemented by personal accounts of energy battles in the late 1970s and early 1980s, including a nuclear protest in New Hampshire and the effort to disassemble the fledgling U.S. Department of Energy.

Shifting focus, the book then covers core environmental laws and topics: the National Environmental Policy Act, the Clean Air Act, renewable energy, and climate change as well as other topics like aircraft noise over national parks. It culminates with a discussion of what we as concerned citizens can do to promote a greener and more sustainable world.

The inspiration for the book came from Rachel Carson, who wrote the environmental classic *Silent Spring* at her home in Silver Spring, Maryland, where my family lived for many years. It also came from Eric Redman, who wrote *The Dance of Legislation,* a behind-the-scenes account of how Congress approved legislation to create the National Health Service Corps. Redman took an arcane topic—the process of how a bill becomes a law—and brought it alive with personal narrative.

In this spirit, I've chosen to invigorate the factual and personal reporting by creating five government characters, all of whom are based on one or more real individuals. The characterizations preserve the anonymity of my government colleagues and keep the emphasis of the storytelling where it belongs—on environmental policy and away from exposé. In order of appearance, you'll become acquainted with my respected fictional surrogates, Jack Donahue at the U.S. Department of Energy, Ceci Foster at the Environmental Protection Agency, Everett Williams at the National Park Service, and Audrey Johnson and Dave Simms at the Federal Aviation Administration. You'll also meet one more character, Professor Sam Jennings, who serves as my mentor and sounding board throughout the story. With these few exceptions, every other person and name cited in the book is real.

The fictional dialogue with these characters is noted by a face symbol at the start of a section. While creative in form, the dialogue closely adheres to what was said at various times by actual people. I didn't tape record government meetings and conversations, but I did experience the discussions first-hand, aided by an extensive collection of written records, reports, and personal notes taken along the way. In short, the reported facts, events, topics of conversation, and expressed agency positions in the book are all true and verifiable. I simply let the characters cut to the chase and explain how real events unfolded.

People come to environmental advocacy in different ways. My world view was shaped by a 1950s childhood in a small New England town. Like many kids my age, I spent a lot of time outdoors, which evolved into an interest in protecting natural resources. The 1960s were formative years as well. The Vietnam War taught the need to maintain a healthy distrust of government, but it also taught that policies can change if people make their voices heard.

Because I believe that we have strong voice in shaping the future, I thought it fitting to personify the title—*Uncle Sam and Mother Earth*. All of us can protect the environment in numerous ways, starting with lifestyle changes to shrink our footprint. We can save energy, buy green, recycle, and much more. Beyond personal contributions, however, we must also make our presence felt in the public arena, from city hall to the internet-driven global village, where the environmental stakes are big and the debate is raging.

Hopefully, the book will encourage people to get involved and more young adults to consider an environmental career. It matters little whether your involvement is inside the system or largely independent of it. Eventually, the path to greater change leads you into contact with the government. For those who take the leap into government service, where people are needed with environmental skills, the point is to go in with your eyes open. Government work is challenging in its own right, and asking the bureaucracy to think and act greener is no easy task.

The human species is painting itself into a corner by under-valuing nature. But there is still time to correct the problems and reason to be optimistic. Many signs are pointing in the right direction: increased public involvement, more international cooperation, scientific and technological breakthroughs, and a younger generation that starts out with a much better sense of the challenges and opportunities than my generation ever had.

I hope you'll find the book informative and entertaining. In the process, I hope it will broaden your perspective on environmental issues and what we need to do. While times change and issues morph into new ones, many steps in the environmental dance, like the dance of legislation, repeat themselves. If you learn them, you can master the dance—and move others to dance too.

CHAPTER I

CITIZEN ACTION: THE PROTEST AT SEABROOK

LOCAL ORGANIZERS GREETED US WHEN we arrived and escorted us to our base camp. Hiking down a paved road for less than a mile, we turned onto a trail that soon led to a wooded knoll surrounded by salt marshes. After weeks of training and travel preparations, it suddenly became real as we looked out at our target in astonishment.

Through the late afternoon and evening, hundreds of people unloaded backpacks, pitched tents, and rolled out sleeping bags. We were told that many more people were poised in five other staging areas around the site for a coordinated plan of attack by land and water. Above the commotion, an occasional song could be heard, making the mood surprisingly upbeat despite concerns that tomorrow could turn bloody if the state chose to get tough. As night descended and it grew quieter, the faint rumble of waves in the distance offered a soothing end to the day.

It was Friday, April 29, 1977, just 11 days after President Carter's televised address to the nation on the energy crisis, which he called "the moral equivalent of war." A growing dependency on Middle Eastern oil had left Americans vulnerable to supply shortages and rising prices. Displaying political courage, the president urged Americans to turn down their thermostats and take other measures to reduce energy consumption.

The president's message was focused on energy use, but the environment was the rallying cry now, as people from all corners of New England and 20 other states arrived at the New Hampshire shoreline to fight the construction of twin 1200 megawatt nuclear power plants at Seabrook. Opposition to nuclear energy had been growing steadily in the U.S. in reaction to safety concerns and the industry's ambitious plans for expansion.

The protest was led by the Clamshell Alliance, which originated in 1976 in response to the proposed development at Seabrook. The main organizers of the Alliance were from New Hampshire, but the circle of leadership included energy activists from across New England. The Alliance, which predicted the protest would last three or four days, required participants or "Clams" to prepare for the action by attending six weekly training sessions in nonviolent techniques. They also required each participant to join an "affinity group," a self-governing unit of 10 to 20 people. The term comes from the *grupos de afinidad* used by the anarchists in the Spanish Civil War of 1936. The organizing tactic recognizes that groups must be big enough to get things done, yet small enough to enable friendships and full participation.

Our nonviolence training had included films, discussions, and role-playing that put us in the shoes of the New Hampshire State Police and National Guard and encouraged us to explore what they might feel in the face of mass civil disobedience. We were taught not to de-personalize them as they might do to us—a preventive strategy to lower the possibility of violence. Another concern was unwanted outsiders or so-called provocateurs. To restrain rabble-rousers, we practiced encircling them with arms clasped, then moving inward and squeezing them. The program of instruction was based on earlier Seabrook protests and how the state had reacted. Similarly, the state was familiar with the Clamshell Alliance and its nonviolent tactics. Indeed, the Alliance had even shared its plans for this action with the police and the town of Seabrook, which was on record opposing the power plant and welcomed the protest.

My affinity group began the trip to Seabrook earlier that Friday morning. We rendezvoused at Woolman Hill School, a small Quaker-affiliated private high school in Deerfield, Massachusetts, where I lived and taught. After loading our gear into the large school van, we settled in for the ride across the state to Seabrook. Behind the wheel was Matt Leighton, a friend and fellow teacher at Woolman Hill, who served as our designated logistics person, someone each affinity group had to have. Matt had grown up in England and attended Oxford, and was well aware of how his charming accent and wit endeared him to friends and acquaintances alike. He was in fine form that morning, amusing us with stories, as we prepared to join 2,000 people mobilizing into a peaceful militia.

The call to occupy Seabrook had struck a chord at Woolman Hill and throughout the pockets of counterculture in the Pioneer Valley of western Massachusetts. The northern part of the Valley in Franklin County was home to many former students from the university and colleges in the Amherst area and was a hotbed of anti-nuclear activity. Three years earlier, local resident Sam Lovejoy went for a walk in the woods and unbolted and toppled a large and expensive hilltop weather tower erected for two planned nuclear power plants in the town of Montague. Lovejoy faced five years in prison, but his trial ended abruptly in dismissal due to technical flaws in the prosecution's case. His act of civil disobedience galvanized regional opposition to nuclear power, and it was not long before the electric utility called it quits at Montague. Inspired by the success, Valley residents were eager to participate at Seabrook.

THE OCCUPATION

We were awakened at daybreak Saturday by the throb of menacing surveillance helicopters circling overhead. The repeated sorties drowned out the cries of seagulls but could not spoil the colorful sunrise. After eating breakfast and breaking camp under clear skies, we sat on a grassy bank awaiting orders to move out. When the call came mid-morning, hundreds of people wearing cloth armbands with the logo of a swirling atom inside a clamshell and the words "STOP Nuclear Power" donned their backpacks and started marching single file into the marshlands, snaking along a scouted path to keep our feet dry.

The construction site loomed to the south on a gravel plateau several hundred yards from our base camp and a mile from the ocean. It was an empty landscape except for some small machinery and several huge cement pipes. A few state policemen had dotted the site earlier but were now gone. It was surprising to see no show of force and we wondered apprehensively if the State Police and National Guard were amassed on the main entry road to the west, poised to strike.

As we trod through the marsh and over wood planks to cross streamlets, we saw two Clams up ahead wielding bolt cutters to pry open a section of the perimeter chain link fence that encircled the facility. Cheers went up as the front of the line started to crawl through the fence and scramble up to level ground. Makeshift flags sprung up on the barren real estate and before long, protestors from all sides washed over the site—singing, dancing, cheering, posing for pictures, and filming—spurred by the adrenaline of the moment and a sense of relief that there was no physical confrontation with authorities.

Clearly our easy access to the site was no clever maneuver by the state to sweep in for a quick round-up and expulsion. It was hard to imagine why the state would not defend the site. There was nothing of real value on the grounds, but why would they vacate?

Word soon spread for groups to make camp wherever they wanted, with enough room for walking lanes. Each group was also asked to send a representative to a hastily arranged community assembly, which quickly turned raucous as several strong-willed individuals jostled with group representatives for the opportunity to speak. In the ensuing bedlam of the makeshift democracy, some people wanted to discuss political strategy. But most felt that the first order of business was to build a functioning village. Immediately, work commenced on food and water supplies, sanitation, security, and media communications. Couriers were dispatched to let the outside world know that we were on the site, organizing, and here to stay.

It did not take long that afternoon for the authorities to arrive. First to appear was Colonel Paul Doyon, who was head of the New Hampshire State Police and field general for Governor Meldrim Thompson. Joined by other troopers, Doyon was neatly uniformed, wearing a wide-brimmed Smokey hat and sunglasses, a dark grey shirt, light pants with matching grey stripes down the sides, and spit-polished boots—all in sharp contrast to the scruffy sea of jeans and T-shirts that engulfed him. Doyon greeted our appointed representatives and calmly stated that we were violating the law and that we must prepare to leave. In response, our representatives spoke about the safety hazards of nuclear power, emphasizing that our issue was with the utility, Public Service Company of New Hampshire, not the police. Within minutes, the discussion floundered. Doyon could see the troubling dynamics—an occupation with no controlling leadership and a slow decision-making process, yet the will and resources to hold on for days. To the state's credit, there had been no violent reaction, but its strategy going forward would suffer from the Republican governor's rigid ideology and reputed temper.

Although the encounters with Doyon were brief, he became a likable figure because he listened, asked people's names, and cajoled. However, that softer approach ended the next afternoon when Governor Thompson arrived at Seabrook, walked onto the bulldozed grounds to a polite reception, and delivered a stern message to us: "In America, you certainly have a right to an opinion that is opposite to that of other people. You do have an opinion that is opposite of what I have with respect to nuclear power. So you came as I understand it to let the world know that there is another side and that you represent that other side. Okay, now on the other hand, you understand that you're here against the laws of the State of New Hampshire. You're trespassing here. You have no right under the constitution or our laws to occupy this. We cannot tolerate that and will not tolerate it." With that, the governor gave us half an hour to leave the site or face arrest.

The governor's ultimatum filtered back through the affinity groups. Some protestors chose to leave but most people braced themselves for arrest as the state moved in with a fleet of yellow school buses. My group sat in a circle discussing whether to walk or be dragged to the buses when our turn came. To ease the tension of waiting, we sang and shared stories. Someone quipped, "When the police come, go into your tent, zip it up, and ask them if they have a warrant because this is your home."

The arrest of 1,414 protestors took 14 hours from mid-afternoon on Sunday until 6 am the next morning. My group got hauled away in the waning daylight of Sunday. Going limp to resist passively, we were dragged with our packs to the back door of the waiting buses. At the bus, some of us got up and climbed onto it while others stuck to principle and had to be lifted up by police. We were grateful that the officers maintained professionalism throughout the process and that no one was seriously injured. With young women and elderly people in the mix, and cameras clicking, the police were undoubtedly under strict orders not to hurt anyone.

LIVE FREE OR DIE

When I looked around the bus, I saw familiar faces but no one from my group. Had we been split up on purpose? And where were they taking us? As our bus rolled away from the site, we thought the ride might be a short one to the Massachusetts line, where we would be dumped off and told not to return. As it turned out, our bus rumbled 55 miles in the dark to the state armory at Concord, New Hampshire. Other buses headed to closer armories in Manchester, Portsmouth, Somersworth, and Dover. The unluckiest Clams sat 15 hours in National Guard trucks overnight in Portsmouth without food and water until assigned to armories the next morning. Instead of dampening spirits, the hardship allowed the Clams in the trucks to get acquainted and reconstitute new affinity groups.

Handling legal matters in the Governor's chain of command was David Souter, the State Attorney General, who is best known as President George H.W. Bush's 1990 appointment to the U.S. Supreme Court. Under Souter's direction, we were booked and fingerprinted at the armory. However, the right of due process buckled under the weight of our numbers. We were not read our rights, judges set different bond amounts, and some local New Hampshire protestors were simply told to go home. The state had cleared the Seabrook property, but the legal situation was anything but clear. Clamshell Alliance lawyers immediately cried foul and advised us to maintain "bail solidarity," which meant refusing to pay individual bail until everyone was released together on personal recognizance.

Over 600 people were detained at Manchester Armory, followed by Concord with 276 people and Dover with 265. In the days before cellphones, news about what was happening reached us in a slow trickle. We were unsure of who was where, what the press was reporting, and how long we would be detained. The Guard allowed each of us one call daily and to see family visitors. These personal privileges and visits by the circuit-riding lawyers for the Alliance became the only means of obtaining outside news and maintaining unity among the armories.

The accommodations in the expansive, high-ceilinged armory drill room at Concord were decent. Sleeping was hard with the lights on all night, but the National Guard provided cots and blankets, clean men's and women's bathrooms, three buffet-style meals a day, medical care, and the opportunity to walk around the back parking lot for an hour at noontime. The windowless room was not the Hilton, but it was not Alcatraz either. Many members of the Guard were friendly and sometimes willing to talk with their guests discreetly.

I was fortunate to find a friend from Franklin County, Chuck Matthei. Chuck was 29 years old and known for his activism. He was a Vietnam War resister who had worked for the pacifist organization Peacemakers and the Catholic Workers movement with the renowned Dorothy Day. He was an expert in community development and housing for the poor. But it was not what he knew that mattered, it was who he was. Chuck was Ghandian, with a long monkish beard and soft voice that concealed a steely willpower. He was a committed resister and when he arrived at Concord immediately began a *death fast*, refusing to take all food and water or to cooperate in any way.

My cot was next to Chuck, who would not accept one and made do with his sleeping bag on the cement floor. At the outset, I did not grasp the seriousness of his fast. We discussed our personal convictions and the perils of nuclear power, which resulted in my decision to start fasting on the fourth day of confinement. But while I and several other fasters drank water and a tiny thimble of juice each morning for electrolytes, Chuck took nothing.

As the days wore on, I passed the long hours talking with people, attending meetings, reading, and embroidering the pockets of a denim jacket. "Hotel Concord" was lucky to have songwriter and activist Charlie King, who raised spirits with his folk songs and guitar. Each morning, King led a song circle for the armory, where people shared news and then joined a chorus of Pete Seeger's refrain: "Seek and you shall find, knock and the door will be opened, ask and it shall be given, as the love comes tumbling down."

Meanwhile, Chuck's condition was deteriorating quickly. He was losing energy and his lips were cracking. He didn't walk around, but gladly talked and shared stories with those who came by. Around day five, I wondered if the guards even noticed him. My fear pushed me to approach the guards at the front doorway to see if they knew about his condition. "He's going to die if he doesn't get medical attention," I told them. "You need to do something." I was relieved the next day when a doctor showed up. He listened to Chuck, who said that he did not recognize the laws of New Hampshire and wanted unconditional release. How ironic, I thought to myself—given that the logo on New Hampshire license plates is *Live Free or Die.*

Emotions inside the Armory ebbed and flowed. We said farewell each day to people who had to accept a misdemeanor and fines for criminal trespass in order to leave for pressing work and family commitments. They heard only words of gratitude for holding on as long as they could. Likewise, each day we heard encouragement from outside sources to hang tough. News of the protest was spreading around the world. I remember a huge cheer going up at the song circle when it was announced that the New York Times, staunchly pro-nuclear at the time, carried a detailed report on the protest after days of silence.

Why the state was holding us so long was perplexing. The commander of the New Hampshire National Guard, General John Blatsos, offered a hint in a post-Seabrook interview, "The planning that went into the operation [protest] would put many in military staffs to shame," adding that "... it was too good—overwhelming."

Around New England and in New Hampshire, the press was beginning to tally up the cost of Governor Thompson's discipline. The cost of housing, feeding, and caring for hundreds of protestors in five armories was put at $50,000 a day, the equivalent of $200,000 today. As the days and dollars mounted, the citizens of New Hampshire were beginning to question the governor's unyielding approach. Calls increased on him to end the expensive impasse.

The doctor was visiting Chuck each day. He stayed a long time each visit and the two of them began to form a personal bond. Showing genuine concern, the doctor tried to dissuade Chuck with his diagnosis of growing medical risk. As days seven, eight, and nine rolled by, Chuck's condition looked grievous and he could only whisper. By now his health was of major concern to the entire armory.

On day 11 of our confinement, with Chuck in a perilous state, we watched with surprise as a guard detail came into our area and told Chuck that he could go. "No charges," they said, "we just want you to go." He refused to rise, at which point they lifted him onto a stretcher and wheeled him out of the drill room, into the front lobby of the armory, and down the sidewalk to the parking lot. We heard that Chuck then got up off the stretcher with the assistance of waiting logistics help and was driven away.

We were beginning to hear more talk of a settlement. The American Civil Liberties Union, which jumped into the legal fray after the patchwork bookings, was arguing that our type of confinement for a misdemeanor violated constitutional protections against cruel and unusual punishment. It was beginning to feel like it.

The standoff ended on May 13th with both sides declaring victory. Our side accepted a misdemeanor charge for criminal trespass and waived our right to individual trials in exchange for release on our own recognizance pending appeal. In the days ahead, as things quieted down, the state dropped their misdemeanor charges on all outstanding cases.

After 13 days of confinement, 541 of us left the armories exhausted. I collected my belongings and wearily stepped out of the building and into the open air. I didn't know if anyone would be outside, but sure enough Matt and a few others were there to greet me. "So what do you need?" Matt asked as we climbed into his car. After a life-changing ordeal and a nine-day fast, I only had a simple request, "I'm starved and I've been dreaming about pizza." Later, we headed back to Woolman Hill School.

SAM JENNINGS

"So that's the story," I said, leaning back in my chair at the local coffee shop. "It goes back a long ways, but it still resonates. The system often needs a push from the outside or it stays in neutral."

I could see Sam mulling this over. Dr. Samuel Jennings was my former college sociology professor, and we had kept in touch over the years. Greying now, Jennings was once a flamboyant young teacher on campus with his southern accent, friendly smile, and rapport with students. He was considered among the school's best teachers, known for his thought-provoking class-room performances. He typically started his classes by talking about his days as captain of his college rugby team, using the stories as a warning that his courses would be tough to pass. The rugby also explained his slightly crooked nose as well as his teaching style, which sometimes resembled a coach telling play-ers that their bigger opponents could be beaten if they concen-trated and played hard.

He implored students to challenge conventional wisdom. "Don't trust the media and don't take anything at face value," he bellowed, jutting his finger in the air, "because nothing happens by accident—search for the root causes." Jennings had firm com-mand of many topics, including the environment, and held opin-ions about all of them, but was careful not to stray too far as he prodded and politicized.

Sam and I made a point of getting together every few years in between phone calls and emails. Our friendship grew as the years went by, but his mentoring never changed.

"Look," he said, sipping his coffee, "we know the system is slow to change, never more so than on environmental issues. It often takes a crisis to alter the status quo, like a natural disaster, a war, or economic collapse, but it can also be something inspiring, like an election or a public outcry like Seabrook." Sam raised his eyebrows and leaned forward, "The system is hard to change, but it can change and it does. The real question for me is the role that individuals play in the process. So, let me ask you... do you believe Seabrook was pivotal to public opinion?"

"I'm not sure," I said. "It may have made some difference because only one of the two Seabrook units was built. But historians might say that what happened afterwards was going to happen anyway."

"That's one reason I never became an historian," Sam said. "I find it too hard to discount the role of individuals or to treat history like a predictable line. Let's go back to the 1970s. Do you remember President Nixon's Project Independence? I do. Nixon called for a thousand nuclear plants by 2000. Actually, only about 100 plants operate today with hardly any new ones since the '70s and Seabrook."

"But you can't say Seabrook was the reason," I responded. "What about the partial meltdown of Pennsylvania's Three Mile Island in 1979?"

"Of course a lot's happened since Seabrook," Sam said, "including other protests and TMI as you said, which confirmed people's anxieties about nuclear safety. TMI showed that, yes, there was reason to worry, and public opinion shifted some more. But the earlier confrontation at Seabrook captured the public imagination just at the right moment... when the nuclear industry was riding high and the public was swallowing the propaganda."

Sam's talk of public imagination and timing made me think of Hollywood's incredible fortune with the *China Syndrome*, a movie about a nuclear plant meltdown, which opened in theaters less than two weeks before TMI occurred. As a movie buff, Sam remembered the movie as well as the one in 1983, *Silkwood*, about the murder of Karen Silkwood in Oklahoma. Silkwood allegedly got run off the road trying to deliver a folder of criminal nuclear plant safety violations to a reporter.

"Timing is everything," Sam said, as our conversation swung back from movies to TMI and subsequent nuclear accidents. After TMI, the nuclear industry did its best to recover from the disaster, which took 14 years and $1 billion to clean up. The next catastrophe was Chernobyl in 1986. The Russians failed to contain the massive release of radiation across Ukraine and beyond, a containment effort that is still underway. For the next 25 years, things were relatively quiet and people started to relax again. The nuclear industry sensed an opening with climate change, spinning millennials with the argument that nuclear power is carbon-free. But then the Japanese earthquake and tsunami struck in 2011, destroying four of six nuclear reactors at the Fukushima Dai-ichi complex and laying ruin to a whole region of Japan. Years later, Fukushima remains a deserted wasteland that has experienced subsequent radioactive releases into the Pacific Ocean.

"The place should be called 'die itchy,'" Sam said, "as another reminder about the dangers of gambling with the atom."

"We're also hearing new revelations about the huge amount of radioactive contamination at the Hanford plutonium factory in Washington State," I said.

"All of it matters," Sam continued, "but Seabrook was a moment in space that altered the body politic on nuclear power. Without it, TMI might have been treated like a minor mishap and there'd be more nukes. But here's the real point—individuals can overcome the odds and make changes happen when more of the facts are known."

"The problem with the environment," I said, "is that uncovering the facts about environmental effects can take so long, like climate change, and then you're deep in the hole."

"That's true, but our process demands good science, not just good intentions," Sam said. "And environmental policy has to be balanced with economics, although it's clear that the environment is undervalued today and in dire need of greater protection."

This led us to discuss the value of civil disobedience when change happens too slowly and public consciousness needs to be aroused. The occupation at Seabrook sounded the alarm on nuclear power, forcing a reexamination of national policy and slowing down the feverish nuclear industry. Since that time, the industry has faced an uphill climb to justify its high costs compared with other energy sources, including insurance problems and the need to safeguard radioactive waste for 250,000 years. In addition, the government must weigh the security risks of proliferation, cyber attacks, and terrorism that threaten nuclear power more than other sources.

"Philosophically," Sam said, "every individual thought and action means something and has an effect. These small changes add up eventually, and become the Seabrooks that trigger policy changes."

"Such faith, professor," I said. "But I always take your words to heart—like your advice to me years ago. I'm still jogging today, if you can call it that, because you said that I'd run for the rest of my life if I concentrated on running for 30 minutes and ignored speed and distance."

"Glad you liked that one. It's a small example of approaching things from a different angle, one with sustainability in the mix. Sam paused for a moment and then said, "So now, let me ask you this: If someone wants to be an environmentalist and save the world, is he or she better off working inside the system or outside the system?"

"Well," I said, "that's a hard one. I suppose it's partly practical, like where the jobs are. Political beliefs play into it for sure. But I'd say it mostly depends on people's interests and temperament—how they see themselves fitting in and making a contribution."

"Fair enough," Sam responded. "Keep those thoughts in mind because it played a part in the history of the environmental movement and how certain individuals, inside and outside of government, all of whom mastered the art of government policymaking, helped to move it forward."

CHAPTER II

CHRONICLE OF THE MODERN ENVIRONMENTAL MOVEMENT

UNDERSTANDING TODAY'S ENVIRONMENTAL CHALLENGES REQUIRES a look back at history and some of the gifted people who energized the modern environmental movement in America. What made them effective and how did their understanding and use of government contribute to their success in raising environmental awareness?

The seeds of the modern environmental movement were sown at the turn of the 20th century by President Theodore "Teddy" Roosevelt. The old Wild West was fading from sight and being supplanted by a rush of private claims on large tracts of land and natural resources. Anticipating the consequences of failing to protect the public interest, Roosevelt acted decisively to greatly expand the federal acquisition and preservation of western land. His actions spared many of America's pristine forests, rivers, and wilderness areas from commercial exploitation and contamination, while giving birth to a new national conservation ethic.

The ongoing industrial revolution was producing new jobs, more goods, better transportation, and many timesaving devices. But while

Americans enjoyed the fruits of industry, its adverse effects on the land, air, rivers, oceans, and wildlife received scant attention. For many years, the environmental impacts were unknown, too hard to assess, or swept aside for later. But as industrialization spread, the public health and environmental costs became more visible and incontrovertible. Citizens and public officials spoke up to warn about the perils and to push for greater protection of the natural world.

Several individuals stand out historically because of what their efforts and achievements have meant to the environmental debate and public awareness. Some of these individuals operated from powerful seats in government while others used outside leverage against it. Joining Teddy Roosevelt are Rachel Carson, Lady Bird Johnson, Stewart Brand, Gaylord Nelson, Dennis Hayes, Russell Train, William Ruckelshaus, and Al Gore. Their vision and courage helped make America's environmental awakening a reality.

THEODORE ROOSEVELT: RESOURCE CONSERVATION

The conservation movement of the late 1800s and early 1900s led to the creation of national parks and the protection of forests and wildlife areas from the ravenous intentions of the mining, timber, railroad, and ranching industries, particularly in the West. These large commercial interests met their match in the indefatigable Teddy Roosevelt, a flamboyant personality and amalgam of the great American spirit. Roosevelt defies easy description because of his liberal anti-trust leanings as a Republican and his numerous hats as a public figure: orator, military leader, hunter and outdoorsman, author and historian, world traveler, and naturalist.

To become the youngest president at 42, Roosevelt climbed the political ladder from the New York State Assembly, U.S. Civil Service Commission, and New York City Police Department to the U.S. Department of Navy. As Assistant Secretary for the Navy, Roosevelt thought that America's prestige suffered in relation to its actual military and economic strength. His opportunity to change perceptions arose with the explosion of the USS Maine in Havana and the ensuing Spanish-American War of 1898. To the cry of "Remember the Maine," Roosevelt left his Navy post and recruited a volunteer cavalry of "Rough Riders," leading them into Cuba and a strategic charge up San Juan Hill. Emerging as a war hero, Roosevelt catapulted to higher office as Governor of New York and Vice President of the United States. His final ascent to the presidency in 1901 came unexpectedly, after the assassination of President William McKinley only eight months into his term.

As president, the multi-faceted Roosevelt also demonstrated an aptitude for diplomacy, winning the Nobel Peace Prize in 1906 for negotiating an end to the Russo-Japanese War. His foreign policy motto was "walk softly and carry a big stick," a motto that also characterized his approach to conservation. Some considered Roosevelt belligerent and primitive. "I always believe in going hard at everything," he preached time and again. This was the basis for living what he called the "strenuous life," which he urged for individuals and the nation.

Roosevelt was an avid sportsman and enjoyed hunting trips from an early age, even practicing his own taxidermy as a teen.

At 26, confronted with the tragic loss of his wife and mother on the same day from unrelated illnesses, he left New York for the Dakotas, where he spent the next two years learning to become a cowboy and cattle rancher.

His unassailable standing as an outdoorsman made him extremely effective in the fight over conserving public lands. When he expressed strong sentiments about conservation, and warned about the threats of private development to wilderness areas and migratory birdlife, his words carried weight: "I recognize the right and duty of this generation to develop and use the nature resources of our land; but I do not recognize the right to waste them, or to rob, by wasteful use, the generations that come after us."

Roosevelt's zeal produced an unparalleled record of conservationism during his two terms as president. He founded the U.S. Forestry Service in 1905, overseeing a jump in forest reserves from 43 to 194 million acres. The next year, he signed the Antiquities Act, which allowed him and future presidents to create national monuments for the preservation of historic landmarks and structures on federal lands. Roosevelt took advantage of the Act to establish 18 national monuments including Devil's Tower in Wyoming, the Petrified Forest in Arizona, and a large portion of the Grand Canyon prior to its national park designation in 1919. He also doubled the number of national parks, adding five more, including Crater Lake in Oregon and Mesa Verde in Colorado, and directed a major expansion of Yosemite National Park at the behest of naturalist John Muir. With the momentum from Roosevelt's parkland designations, only a few years would pass until Congress enacted the Organic Act of 1916, creating the National Park Service and centralizing the management of national parks, monuments, preserves, battlefields, and historic places.

Describing the presidency as a "bully pulpit," Roosevelt never hesitated to use the levers of power. When timber interests persuaded Congress to use a Department of Agriculture appropriations bill to tie his hands on forestland protection, Roosevelt outmaneuvered them and set aside another 16 million acres of forests before signing the bill. He also used an Executive Order to establish the first of his 51 national bird sanctuaries, remarking, "Is there any law that will prevent me from declaring Pelican Island a Federal Bird Reservation? . . . Very well, then I so declare it!"

Roosevelt's defense of conservation was not always consistent. For example, only two months after leaving the White House in 1909, he went on safari to Africa. Sponsored by the Smithsonian Institution, the hunting expedition was widely criticized for excessiveness. Roosevelt's entourage bagged a staggering 11,400 specimens, including 1,000 skins of large mammals, 4,000 skins of small mammals, and 5,000 plants. His animal kill included nine rare white rhinos and many duplicate specimens. African ecology was healthier in Roosevelt's time but it was evident even then that African wildlife was threatened by human development, trophy-seekers, and poaching. Roosevelt stoutly defended the hunt in the name of museum science: "I can be condemned only if the existence of the National Museum, the American Museum of Natural History, and all similar zoological institutions are to be condemned."

Roosevelt, who is carved atop Mount Rushmore alongside Washington, Jefferson, and Lincoln, is considered by many historians to be one of our best presidents and the first environmental president. His conservation achievements set a lasting foundation for the rest of the century, especially for the systematic growth of the U.S. National Park System and the U.S. Forest Service. Roosevelt used his charisma, passion, and fist-pounding to get the job done, preserving the American wilderness experience for generations.

⌣⟶

RACHEL CARSON: WEB OF LIFE

Rachel Carson served with the U.S. Fish and Wildlife Service (FWS) from 1936 to 1952, but her greatest achievements occurred after her 17 years in government. Had Carson stayed with the FWS, she most likely would be unknown today. Yet her service was anything but wasted. She gained experience as a biologist, gathered data and documents, and built a network of friends in the scientific community. When she departed government, Carson had the inside knowledge and impeccable scientific credentials to sustain her efforts as an independent writer to expose the great environmental damage being done from the indiscriminate use of pesticides. In this endeavor, Carson left her indelible mark on history as one of the great environmental thinkers and prophets of our time.

Carson's literary and scientific achievements are even more remarkable in light of the personal odds she had to overcome. Born in 1907, Carson grew up near Pittsburgh in Springdale, Pennsylvania, in a family of modest means. She attended a local woman's college with the aid of a loan and needed a full scholarship to attend John Hopkins University in Baltimore where she received a Master's degree in zoology. The Great Depression and the declining health of her father and family finances derailed her plan to earn a doctorate and teach. When her father passed away in 1935, followed by her sister a year later, Carson assumed full care of her mother and two nieces. Now the family breadwinner, she accepted an entry-level job with the FWS as a scriptwriter for a series of radio shows on fish biology.

In the 1940s, woman scientists were rare and Carson was only the second woman to hold a full-time position at the FWS. She considered herself a scientist first and foremost, telling *Life Magazine* in 1962, "I'm not interested in things done by women or by men but in things done by people." During her government service, Carson built a solid reputation around field research in marine biology, devotion to accuracy, and meticulous attention to detail. She also earned praise as a gifted writer about ocean life, with a vivid and entertaining style that led to numerous magazine and newspaper publications and her first book in 1941, *Under the Sea-Wind*. Her time at the FWS was not without periods of disillusionment, however. She once referred to the bureaucracy as "boon-doggling official Washington." But her outlook brightened as her duties expanded in the late 1940s, culminating in the position of chief editor of FWS publications in 1949.

By 1951, Carson had released her second book, *The Sea Around Us*. Her poetic prose describing underwater biology and minerals propelled her onto the New York Times Bestsellers List for 86 weeks, and into the top spot for 31 consecutive weeks. With her success and reputation established, Carson formally resigned from the FWS in 1952 to pursue her twin passions for writing and science.

The title of her seminal work, *Silent Spring*, reflected her scientific concerns and perhaps her personal arc from Springdale,

Pennsylvania to Silver Spring, Maryland, where she wrote the book in 1962. It was an immediate bestseller because of Carson's respected name, its broad ecological theme, and prepublication attacks by a defensive chemical and pharmaceutical industry, including a threatened lawsuit against Carson's publisher, Houghton Mifflin. Her writing brought several serious issues to light, starting with inadequate scientific understanding of the broad dangers posed by the "elixirs of death," including DDT, chlordane, dieldrin, malathion, and other insecticides and herbicides. Carson believed that more needed to be known about how these chemicals accumulated on plants and in soil, persisted in the environment, reacted with one another, and penetrated the food chain. "These sprays, dusts, aerosols," she wrote, "are now applied almost universally to farms, gardens, forests, and homes—nonselective chemicals that have the power to kill every insect, the 'good' and the 'bad,' to still the song of birds and the leaping of fish in the streams, to coat the leaves with a deadly film, and to linger on in soil—all this though the intended target may be only a few weeds or insects. Can anyone believe it is possible to lay down such a barrage of poisons on the surface of the earth without making it unfit for all life?"

Carson wrote *Silent Spring* because she believed that "the public is entitled to the facts." She chided the chemical producers and users for disregarding the mounting scientific and anecdotal evidence against DDT and other toxins. In turn, she criticized the government for its cozy relationship with the chemical and pharmaceutical industries and the government's dereliction of duty to weigh the available data and amend public health regulations. Her scientific revelations and social critique shook public faith in government to its foundation.

Carson knew all about the military's DDT research program of the 1940s from her time in government. In succeeding years, she used her government and scientific contacts to obtain confidential information on pesticide use, including the U.S. Department of Agriculture's misguided 1957 aerial spraying campaign of DDT and other chemicals to eradicate fire ants. This lethal campaign, which blanketed nine southern states and 20 million acres, resulted in serious losses to poultry and livestock, pets, insect populations, mammals, and numerous bird species. Armed with a convincing body of data and testimonials from around the country on the effects of DDT, Carson was well-prepared to blow the whistle on the powerful chemical industry and its allies.

The industry reaction to *Silent Spring* was fierce because companies knew the public relations fallout could harm product sales, turn public opinion, and lead to expensive new regulations. A pesticide trade association, the National Agricultural Chemicals Association, spent more than $250,000—the equivalent of $2 million today—to discredit Carson's research and demonize her. The assault came from all sides. There were charges of sloppy research and amateur science as well as personal attacks. The low point came when Ezra Taft Benson, President Eisenhower's former Secretary of Agriculture, pointedly asked, "Why a spinster with no children was so concerned...?" Then compounding the slur, Benson suggested that Carson was "probably a Communist."

The larger social commentary of *Silent Spring* relates to human self-understanding. Carson warns that human beings with untamed technology may knowingly or unknowingly destroy the delicate ecological balance—the web of life. To make her case, Carson compares pesticides with a better known danger at the time, nuclear radiation, which like the pesticide threat is colorless, odorless, and lethal as a poison and carcinogen. In sounding the alarm, Carson relies on reason and science, not extremism, and avoids social issues like overpopulation. She concentrates on scientific observations and data that show nature's signs of stress, which she assesses methodically—and which others have missed.

In her informative and flowing style, Carson raised American consciousness, which had been preoccupied with world events since Teddy Roosevelt, and shrouded throughout the 1950s by technological advances and subliminal commercial slogans like "better living through chemistry." Carson's message emerges like the sun breaking through the clouds: "The balance of nature is built of a series of interrelationships between living things, and between living things and their environment. You can't just step in with some brute force and change one thing without changing many others."

Carson's route to destiny was anything but orthodox. She was shy, introverted, and mild-mannered and had to cope with challenging family demands. Yet, she developed the knowledge and credentials to write the environmental book of the century, a book that remains poignant today. She not only survived the chemical industry's withering media attack on her professionalism and character, but she defeated it almost singlehandedly in the court of public opinion, ending its misleading approach to pesticides. Obviously, her critics underestimated her courage and integrity as well as her level of preparation, which was built on decades of research and collaboration with scientific colleagues. Most importantly perhaps, they underestimated Carson's moral outrage and her belief that everyone has a public duty to speak up.

Carson only needed to live a few more years to see the extent of her impact. Unfortunately, she succumbed to cancer in 1964 at the pinnacle of her career. Today, her modest brick home in the Quaint Acres neighborhood of Silver Spring has been designated a National Historic Landmark. In 1980, she was honored by President Jimmy Carter with the Presidential Medal of Freedom and in 1981 by the U.S. Postal Service with a Great Americans stamp. But her real honor is the living mantle she holds today as the mother and founder of the modern environmental movement.

LADY BIRD JOHNSON: AMERICA THE BEAUTIFUL

The 1960s brought a cascade of changes in civil rights, women's rights, music and art, lifestyle, religion, and the environment. The underlying force for these movements was the younger generation's opposition to the Vietnam War and military draft. Large numbers of citizens took to the streets to oppose President Lyndon Johnson's decisions to prolong and expand the war, a controversy that overshadowed the president's respected domestic agenda, the Great Society, with its array of War on Poverty programs and the signature 1964 Civil Rights Act. Amid the turbulence, and seemingly unaffected by the president's plunging popularity, the First Lady emerged as an engaging and likable figure with her gracious style and promotion of social causes that appealed to many Americans, young and old alike.

Claudia Alta Taylor Johnson, better known as Lady Bird, graduated from the University of Texas at Austin with two Bachelor of Arts degrees in history and journalism and became a successful businesswoman managing an Austin radio station. She later used her education and skills to advance her husband's political career. When they reached the White House, she was an important partner with him on civil rights and poverty programs, serving prominently as Honorary Chairwoman of the Head Start Program.

But Lady Bird Johnson is best remembered as an environmentalist. Her trademark cause was "beautification," which reflected her lifelong appreciation of nature and the outdoors, beginning as a child growing up in the pines and bayous of East Texas and in the Alabama countryside during summers. Announcing the program shortly after the president's 1965 inaugural, Lady Bird used the banner of beautification to inspire communities and garden clubs across America to preserve beautiful places, clean up spoiled areas, and decorate the landscape with flowers and greenery. But beautification meant far more than planting flowers to her. The universal appeal of beautification created an opening to talk with people everywhere about how their communities could come to grips with problems of urban decay, crime, pollution, mental health, and the need for parks and public transportation. In official Washington, beautification gave her a forum to influence legislation and government programs that addressed historic preservation, park planning, urban renewal, and other social reforms. "Where flowers bloom so does hope," she declared.

Lady Bird's beautification program, in partnership with the nonprofit organization "Keep America Beautiful," confronted widespread indifference to littering and helped to popularize roadway cleanup efforts. In the 1950s and 1960s, American roadsides were eyesores with litter strewn everywhere. People casually tossed trash from their cars, including beer and soda bottles, empty food cans, cigarette butts, and loose papers of all kind. Broken glass was a common sight, especially along wooded stretches of country roads. With her marquee name on the program, it did not take long to see attitudes change, litter subside, and roadside sanitation improve. Within a few years, she had literally changed the American landscape, reinvigorating the nation's self-image in the process.

She also deplored the growth of billboard advertising, which needed to be addressed along with littering to preserve and restore natural roadside views. To meet the challenge, Lady Bird spearheaded the Highway Beautification Act of 1965, which dealt with billboard restrictions and other landscape measures such as screening off roadside junkyards. The bill met stiff resistance from the powerful billboard lobby, the Outdoor Advertising Association of America, as well as labor unions. A billboard in Montana proclaimed, "Impeach Lady Bird." To overcome the opposition, the First Lady phoned Members of Congress while the president worked behind the scenes to round up legislative support.

The Highway Beautification Act passed, but Congress withheld critical state enforcement funds, demonstrating the vital distinction between congressional authorizations and appropriations. Undaunted, the First Lady responded by launching a new pocketbook appeal to the business community. She argued that limiting billboards, planting flowers, and improving the landscape were good for business and tourism. The First Lady gained traction with her appeal, attracting new business supporters, including the National Coal Association to reduce strip-mining, Shell Oil Company to improve gas station aesthetics, and electric companies to increase the use of underground power lines.

The business case for beautification also appealed to the National Park Service, which provided administrative support for the beautification program. Why not encourage Americans to use their vacation dollars touring the National Park System rather than traveling abroad? It would be a win-win for the U.S.

tourism industry and the Park Service. To promote the initiative, Lady Bird and Stewart Udall, the Secretary of Interior, set out on a series of colorful "Discover America" trips to national parks. Together they hiked, white-water rafted, camped under the stars, strolled beaches, explored ancient forests, and visited American Indian reservations—all of which received in-depth domestic and international coverage. Lady Bird traveled over 100,000 miles on about 40 tours, which also served to advertise the Administration's legislative achievements on conservation, land and water reclamation, air quality, wilderness preservation, and park acquisition.

The First Lady also left a lasting imprint on the nation's capital, where the Interior Department planted about 2 million daffodil and tulip bulbs, 83,000 flowering plants, 50,000 shrubs, 137,000 annuals, and 25,000 trees. The plantings brightened White House gardens, the National Mall and Smithsonian grounds, Pennsylvania Avenue, and the Virginia banks of the Potomac, an area later enshrined as Lady Bird Johnson Memorial Park.

Lady Bird made an enormous contribution to awareness and appreciation of natural surroundings and the role that natural beauty plays in the quality of life. Unfortunately, she does not receive the environmental acclaim befitting her achievements. Perhaps it is because she was First Lady and worked entirely inside the system, unlike the more independent voice of Rachel Carson. Perhaps it was her style of operating behind-the-scenes, avoiding public confrontations, and using her personal charm to persuade. In her unique way, Lady Bird fought insistently for the environmental benefits of beautification and its crossover effects on urban renewal and community development. Her dedication and accomplishments, which were admired globally, are even more remarkable given that they helped bring people together during the tumultuous era of the 1960s.

⟵⟶

STEWART BRAND: THE BLUE MARBLE

On December 7, 1972, Apollo 17 blasted off from Cape Kennedy in Florida on the last manned lunar mission by the National Aeronautics and Space Administration (NASA). The three crew-members, Eugene Cernan, Ronald Evans, and Harrison Schmitt, took the opportunity on the first day of the voyage to look back and photograph the Earth from 28,000 miles away. Their photo-graph captured the exquisite beauty of the planet in juxtaposition to its dark suspension in space. The meditative "Blue Marble," as it is known, became the symbol of a more holistic view of the human condition. More than words, the photo revealed the fragile nature of our planetary home and beckoned the human family to tran-scend its differences to become better environmental stewards. As Astronaut Cernan observed years later, "We went to explore the Moon, and in fact discovered the Earth."

The iconic 1972 image of the Blue Marble appeared just when writer and publisher Stewart Brand decided to end publication of the *Whole Earth Catalog*, which featured earlier Earth photographs on its covers. For four years, the popular catalog had offered an eclectic mix of information, tools, and advertising on new age topics such as windmills, shelter design, beekeeping, weather forecasting, growing and preserving foods, and much more. Brand's inspiration for the catalog came from futurist Buckminster Fuller's concept of Spaceship Earth and from the successful mail order business of

L.L. Bean. The oversized 11"x14" Whole Earth Catalog sold over 2 million copies in its first three years, offering hard-to-get information in the days before the internet.

Brand used an early satellite picture of Earth for his first cover of the *Whole Earth Catalog* in 1968. It had not been easy for Brand to obtain the NASA image and he could not understand why. His quest had begun two years earlier on a rooftop in San Francisco with a vision of being in outer space and looking back toward Earth. The epiphany led Brand on a crusade for Earth photos, which he believed would transform human consciousness. To publicize his suspicion that NASA and the 10-year-old space program were intentionally suppressing the photos, he walked around the University of California Berkeley wearing a white jump suit, top hat, and Day-Glo sandwich board selling buttons that read, "Why haven't we seen a photograph of the whole Earth yet?" He chose the question carefully, as he put it, to "use the great American resource of paranoia."

Brand was delighted with the outcome of his Berkeley performances. "It went perfectly. The dean's office threw me off the campus, the San Francisco Chronicle reported it, and other newspapers picked up the story." With newfound notoriety, Brand took his show on the road to other prestigious universities, including Stanford, Columbia, Harvard, and MIT, and he mailed his buttons to every influential person he could think of, including U.S. Senators, scientists, United Nations officials, and international leaders.

Whether because of Brand's lobbying campaign or not, NASA's attention to earth photography improved. The cover of Brand's second Whole Earth Catalog in the spring of 1969 featured the startling blue "Earthrise" image taken from behind the moon in December 1968 by the crew of Apollo 8.

Brand believed that if people saw a color photograph of the whole earth, "no one would ever perceive things the same way."

In describing the impact later, he said, "It is no accident of history that the first Earth Day, in April 1970, came so soon after color photographs of the whole earth from space were made by homesick astronauts on the Apollo 8 mission... Those riveting Earth photos reframed everything. For the first time humanity saw itself from outside. The visible features from space were living blue ocean, living green–brown continents, dazzling polar ice and a busy atmosphere, all set like a delicate jewel in vast immensities of hard-vacuum space. Humanity's habitat looked tiny, fragile and rare. Suddenly humans had a planet to tend to."

Satellite imagery of Earth jolted our perspective and the Blue Marble has become a universal symbol for a world increasingly dependent on global cooperation. Former Vice-President Al Gore used the photograph as the opening slide in his popular climate change slideshow, underscoring the necessity for international cooperation to solve the climate crisis. The modern international realities of war and peace, the internet, jet travel, economic trade, and public health all point to an emerging global village in the words of author Marshall McLuhan. Whether civilization matures fast enough to survive as a global village remains to be seen, but we now had a full sun-draped planetary image to light the way.

GAYLORD NELSON AND DENNIS HAYES: EARTH DAY

Since 1970, the annual observance of Earth Day on April 22 has been a reminder of the need to care for the environment. All across

America, communities, schools, churches, government agencies, and civic-minded businesses celebrate Earth Day with a myriad of inventive activities, including rallies, exhibits, art projects, field trips, and tree plantings. Like a rite of spring, the local traditions surrounding Earth Day reinforce environmental responsibility and enlighten each new generation of children in how to think globally and act locally.

The founders of Earth Day showed the potential power of a simple idea. Using Earth Day to elevate environmental issues, they set larger societal wheels in motion, infusing environmental values into the mainstream of American culture and education. Before long, behaviors that were once considered novel, like the "3 Rs" of reducing, reusing, and recycling, became the norm. Commenting on the social acceptance of environmental ethics, William Ruckelshaus, former head of the U.S. Environmental Protection Agency, remarked in 1993, "Today, society is full of environmental advocates; virtually everybody in the *country* is an advocate for the environment. That whole argument is over. The question is—what is the *intelligent* thing for society *to do* about the environment?"

Earth Day was the brainchild of Wisconsin Democratic Senator Gaylord Nelson, who pondered the idea for years. Nelson wanted to show that environmental issues had widespread support and belonged in the national limelight. He correctly surmised that a national forum on the environment, organized loosely to accommodate many different interests, would unleash the public's desire for more government candor and action. He also recognized that the grassroots energy surrounding Vietnam anti-war protests and teach-ins could be tapped constructively for the planned forum and whatever spin-off activities might evolve. With this enthusiasm and his senatorial status to lend respectability, Senator Nelson struck the Earth Day match and it caught fire.

Indeed, it was a real blaze that influenced Nelson's announcement of Earth Day in September 1969. Decades of industrial contamination had led to the deterioration of the Cuyahoga River in Cleveland. Although the river had experienced more than a dozen fires over the previous century, a fire that June on the river reportedly burned five stories high. The story caught the eye of *Time Magazine*, as Americans read in disbelief that our rivers were turning into lethal cauldrons. The Cuyahoga wake-up call came on the heels of another environmental disaster in 1969—the oil spill in Santa Barbara, California. The rupture of a Union Oil platform six miles to sea washed 100,000 barrels of crude oil into the Santa Barbara channel and along the California coastline. It ranked as the worst oil spill in U.S. history until 1989, when the Exxon Valdez ran aground in Alaska, and 2010, when the BP Deepwater Horizon oil well blew out in the Gulf of Mexico. The Santa Barbara spill caused the death of thousands of sea birds, dolphins, seals, and sea lions and offshore drilling in the Pacific is more controversial to this day because of it.

A few months after Nelson's invitation for all to join a "nationwide grassroots demonstration," his Senate staff could not keep up with the interest. To manage the mounting organizational needs, Nelson hired Dennis Hayes as national coordinator to oversee nine staff and a $125,000 budget. Hayes was a bright and articulate 25-year-old graduate student at Harvard's Kennedy School of Government. His resume included student body president at Stanford University and anti-war activist, just the right combination that Nelson wanted. With no time to waste, Hayes left Harvard to organize the event.

The first Earth Day in the spring of 1970 attracted some 20 million participants from 2,000 colleges, 10,000 elementary and secondary schools, and numerous communities. The impact was immediately felt in Washington hallways. For example, one week after Earth Day, President Nixon's Advisory Council on Executive Organization gave its blessing to the proposed creation of a U.S. Environmental Protection Agency.

Although Earth Day was enormously popular, it was not without detractors, including some traditional liberals. NBC News reported that 2,000 Philadelphia residents boycotted the city's Earth Day events because they believed that "the nation's newfound infatuation with the environment has distracted attention from the misery of the poor." Similarly, Senator Jacob Javits (R-NY) addressed the Earth Day rally on Wall Street and warned against letting the popular environmental movement siphon interest away from other pressing national issues such as poverty, racial tensions, health services, education, housing, population control, and ending the Vietnam War.

But the environmental movement was here to stay and it continued to grow into the new millennium. In 1990, Earth Day reached 200 million people in 3,600 communities and 140 countries. In recent years, participation has grown to 500 million people representing 175 countries. And in many schools and communities, Earth Day has evolved into Earth Week.

As the years went by, Nelson and Hayes stayed active in Earth Day to keep it relevant and expand it around the world. For his part, Hayes organized the Earth Day Network to promote year-round environmental education and service projects here and abroad. He also became a leading proponent of solar energy and served for two years in the Carter Administration, directing the

Solar Energy Research Institute in Golden, Colorado, now known as the National Renewable Energy Laboratory. In 1990 and 2000, Hayes returned to Earth Day to chair anniversary activities built around their respective themes of recycling and global warming/ clean energy.

Gaylord Nelson received the Presidential Medal of Freedom for Earth Day in 1995 and lived another 10 years. In the beginning, Nelson could not have imagined that his Earth Day dream would generate such a large constituency for the environment. His legacy is also shaped by his clear and consistent advocacy: "All economic activity is dependent upon [the] environment and its underlying resource base of forests, water, air, soil, and minerals. When the environment is finally forced to file for bankruptcy because its resource base has been polluted, degraded, dissipated, and irretrievably compromised, the economy goes into bankruptcy with it."

How long can the Earth Day tradition survive? The novelty of Earth Day wore off long ago and its message has morphed from one of change to one of common sense and daily life for most Americans. In education, for example, environmental lessons have become a regular feature of elementary and high school instruction. And in higher education, most four-year colleges and universities are offering majors or minors in environmental science or environmental studies.

Despite its age, Earth Day has staying power because it flows with the times. It remains a creative grassroots expression, a favorite event for the media, and a convenient way to recognize people and organizations for their environmental achievements. Also, because our environmental problems are not shrinking or becoming less urgent, we need Earth Day for its reminders, recurring education, and updated warnings about the hazards that lay ahead. Whatever else the event may bring in the coming years, we can look back and see that the first Earth Day shattered the old paradigm by demonstrating widespread public sentiment for environmental action. In so doing, Gaylord Nelson and Dennis Hayes paved the way for what came next: the environmental legislation of the 1970s.

RUSSELL TRAIN AND BILL RUCKELSHAUS: LAW OF THE LAND

The 1970s was a prolific decade for environmental protection as Congress expanded federal jurisdiction over the environment by enacting comprehensive new laws and tougher compliance measures. Lawmakers took steps to protect the air we breathe and the water we drink, improve safe disposal of hazardous wastes, preserve historic buildings, and save endangered species. In addition to these and other special purpose laws, Congress established a whole new procedural system for investigating environmental impacts.

What explains the environmental breakthroughs of the 1970s? It was the perfect storm, beginning with the contributions of environmental leaders like Rachel Carson with *Silent Spring,* Lady Bird Johnson with beautification, and Gaylord Nelson and Dennis Hayes with Earth Day. In addition, a post-Carson genre of environmental literature was emerging. Influential articles and books like *Tragedy of the Commons* by Garrett Hardin and *The Population Bomb* by Barry Commoner, both written in 1968, raised disturbing new questions about resource limits. Most important perhaps was the growing public outrage over environmental mismanagement, culminating in the Santa Barbara and Cuyahoga River calamities.

The government struggled to catch up with public opinion in the 1970s and to deal with the rising costs of environmental cleanup. In the divisive Vietnam era, environmental issues offered a welcome oasis of bipartisanship. Russell Train, an environmental advisor to President Richard Nixon, spoke with the president-elect just before his 1969 inauguration, "I emphasized that concern for the environment cut across geographic boundaries and across economic groups and suggested that an environmental agenda could be a unifying political force." Nixon took Train's advice, seized the moment, and discovered that passing new environmental legislation was not as difficult as they had thought.

Russell Train was a moderate Republican in the mold of Teddy Roosevelt when resource conservation was part of GOP genetics. His career progressed from a legal advisor on Capitol Hill, to an assistant to the Secretary of the Treasury, to a U.S. tax court judge. His interest in the environment arose from two safaris into the African wilderness and what he learned about its imperiled state. Acting on his concern, Train founded the Wildlife Leadership Foundation to help Africans establish and manage wildlife parks and reserves. In 1965, his career took another turn toward the environment when he became president of the Conservation Foundation, an organization devoted to environmental research, education, and public involvement.

In 1968, Train chaired President-elect Nixon's transition task force on resources and the environment and was rewarded with an appointment as Under Secretary of Interior. At Interior, he championed sound environmental construction of the 800-mile Alaskan oil pipeline, fought successfully against a second Miami airport in Everglades National Park, and helped create the federal Coastal Zone Management Act to balance coastal land and water issues for better state protection of coral reefs, beaches, estuaries, and undersea life.

However, Train's most far-reaching accomplishment was the National Environmental Policy Act (NEPA), which was signed into law by President Nixon on January 1, 1970. It was a fitting start to the new decade. NEPA, which is often described as the umbrella of environmental laws, requires federal agencies to take a systematic hard look at potential environmental impacts prior to project approval. In laying out the procedural steps for federal agencies, NEPA sets the terms for public participation, scientific evaluation, and report documentation for potential areas of impact.

Train used Interior Department cases to road test environmental procedures and to build the working knowledge that Congress needed to craft NEPA. Leading the charge in the Senate was Henry Jackson (D-WA), Chairman of the Senate Interior Committee, and Edmund Muskie (D-ME). In the House, NEPA was managed by John Dingell (D-MI), Chairman of the House Energy and Commerce Committee. Some 40 years later, Rep. Dingell reflected on NEPA and the times, "In the 1970s, we recognized that we owe it to future generations to protect the world, which is our only home. The laws we passed were not revolutionary, they were common sense, and were passed on an overwhelmingly bipartisan basis. One could even say that these environmental laws were so important that they were, in fact, nonpartisan. The National Environmental Policy Act passed the House with only 15 votes against it, the Endangered Species Act with only four, and the Clean Air Act Amendments of 1990 with only 25."

Train envisioned NEPA as part of a larger overhaul of government. He convinced President Nixon that the environment deserved more prominence with the creation of a White House environmental policy office and a national environmental agency. Both ideas came into being, respectively, as the Council of Environmental Quality (CEQ) and the Environmental Protection Agency (EPA). The CEQ was chartered under NEPA to advise the president and to ensure that federal agencies interpreted NEPA correctly and consistently. The EPA, which opened its doors several months later in December 1970, was established under a Congress-approved White House reorganization plan to consolidate federal environmental research, standard-setting, and enforcement functions.

The first EPA administrator was William "Bill" Ruckelshaus, another moderate Republican and lawyer, whom President Nixon recruited from the Justice Department where he managed federal civil cases. Ruckelshaus had strong Indiana political ties and enough environmental experience during his early career with the Indiana state attorney general's office to make him a credible choice for the EPA. Although Train was also a candidate to lead the EPA, Nixon kept him in place as the first CEQ Chair.

Ruckelshaus quickly built a reputation for integrity, organizational ability, and toughness during EPA's formative years when the agency was defining its mission, setting priorities, and staffing up. Until now, states had managed environmental compliance loosely without meaningful federal oversight. Ruckelshaus strengthened federal authority and used his legal and state background to demand more state accountability.

Ruckelshaus and Train worked well together and set a good example, shielding the public from Nixon's skepticism about the environment and environmentalists. Ruckelshaus described his relations with Train: "We became quite close friends. There was a potential, obviously, for becoming rivals after EPA was formed.

I thought, and I think he concurred, that it would be a waste of time for us to engage in that sort of activity. This wasn't exactly an administration brimming over with environmentalists, so to the extent that we needed some strength in the counsels of the White House or the cabinet, we decided to stick together."

Ruckelshaus respected Train's knowledge and the caliber of his lean 35-member staff at CEQ, which managed everything the White House said and did on the environment. In divvying up responsibilities, the two leaders agreed that Train and CEQ would take the lead on international affairs while Ruckelshaus and his thousands of EPA employees would concentrate on domestic affairs. Ruckelshaus had more than enough to do. He had to create an agency, support a legislative agenda, and establish public credibility. With respect to the latter, Ruckelshaus set out at once to put teeth into EPA enforcement and to show that gross polluters in industry and local government would be stopped. As Ruckelshaus observed, "it was important for us to *advocate* strong environmental compliance, back it up, and *do* it; to actually show we were willing to take on the large institutions in the society which hadn't been paying much attention to the environment. The private sector polluters, like the big steel companies who hadn't paid much attention to the problem, needed to be pushed very hard for compliance. The cities also needed to be pushed to move forward."

Ruckelshaus fought hard for the fledgling EPA, winning the political battles that shifted power to Washington. The industrial and wealthy interests that attacked Ruckelshaus and the EPA misjudged his political prowess, his integrity, his effective compartmentalization of lawsuits, and his support from the American people. Ruckelshaus parlayed the attacks into public examples of how the EPA was serious about enforcement. Nothing exemplified growing EPA confidence more than the 1972 EPA ban on all domestic use of DDT. One decade after *Silent Spring*, on the shoulders of Ruckelshaus's reputation and power, Rachel Carson's salient warning finally prevailed. With EPA on its way, Ruckelshaus departed in 1973 to become acting director of the Federal Bureau of Investigation (FBI), leaving the agency in the capable hands of the new EPA Administrator, Russell Train.

The sweeping environmental reforms of this period were remarkable by any measure, including longevity. Much of our subsequent lawmaking has been in the form of amendments to the original bills. One piece of enduring legislation has been the Clean Air Act, with its major amendments of 1970, 1977, and 1990. The Act identifies nearly 200 harmful air pollutants and establishes standards for the most pervasive ones like ozone and particulate matter. In 1972, Congress turned its attention to water with the Coastal Zone Management Act for protecting coastal ecology, and the Clean Water Act, which sets standards for surface water and discharges of pollutants into navigable waterways. In 1973, Congress added the Endangered Species Act, a landmark effort to classify extinction threats to wildlife and make it illegal to hunt or harm species on "threatened" and "endangered" lists. Had the Endangered Species Act existed earlier, our nation could have averted the excessive hunting of species like the great auk, a penguin-like bird that perished in the 1800s and passenger pigeons, which met their demise in 1914.

Further legislative progress on the environment was interrupted in 1973 by world events. The Organization of Petroleum Exporting Countries (OPEC) used its control of the world oil market to impose an oil embargo on the United States. The embargo had a major impact on U.S. oil supplies, gas prices, and public concern about the economy. Among the ripple effects was President Nixon's controversial action to save fuel by lowering the national speed limit to 55 mph.

In 1976, a revival of environmental lawmaking occurred in the field of waste management. Passage of the Resource Conservation and Recovery Act (RCRA), which amended the 1965 Solid Waste Disposal Act, became the nation's primary law for the safe disposal of solid and hazardous wastes from municipal and industrial sources. The main tenets of RCRA are state plans to improve the handling of nonhazardous solid waste, including the elimination of open dumping in landfills, cradle-to-grave management of hazardous wastes, and more durable underground storage tanks to hold petroleum and hazardous products. Complementing RCRA with preventive measures, the 1976 Toxic Substances Control Act included restrictions on the manufacture and sale of PCBs, asbestos, and lead-based paints.

Congress enacted another vital piece of hazardous waste legislation in 1980, the Comprehensive Environmental Response, Compensation, and Liability Act, also known as the Superfund program. Superfund, which taxes chemical and petroleum industries for major hazardous site cleanups where liability is unproven, was triggered by widespread news coverage of the 1978 catastrophe at Love Canal in Niagara Falls. Since the 1920s, Love Canal had been a dumping ground for the city, the U.S. Army, and Hooker Chemical Company. Inexplicably, the city school district needed land and bought the property from Hooker in 1953 for $1 dollar knowing that the grassed-over site was contaminated. As time went by, the poisonous deposits of dioxins, benzene, and other toxins at Love Canal caused widespread illnesses in the community, including cancers, birth defects, nervous disorders, asthma, and chromosome damage. The remediation effort included the costly evacuation of approximately 950 families and the demolition of their homes.

Like the environment, energy was an ongoing concern in the 1970s. The 1973 energy crisis generated a wave of legislation to increase U.S. energy independence, including the 1975 Energy Policy and Conservation Act, the 1976 Energy Conservation and Production Act, and the 1978 National Energy Conservation Policy Act. The new laws set the foundation for long-term energy security, but in 1979 it was déjà vu as the political revolution in oil-rich Iran led to a second energy crisis and another painful round of spiking U.S. gas prices and lines at the pump.

The 1970s also saw new environmental policies and legislation for specific industries. In aviation, for example, the Federal Aviation Administration (FAA) issued its first Noise Abatement Policy in 1976 to address growing community noise complaints. Three years later, Congress passed the Aviation Safety and Noise Abatement Act, which authorized the FAA to soundproof homes, and in the most serious cases, to buy out affected homeowners located too close to an airport.

Russell Train and Bill Ruckelshaus continued to play a significant role for many years. Train served as EPA Administrator until 1977, supervising the implementation of new solid waste programs and shepherding amendments to the Clean Air Act, such as the required use of catalytic converters in cars to reduce emissions. After EPA, Train had a long association with World Wildlife Fund, serving as its president from 1978 to 1985. He finished his memoirs, *Politics, Pollution and Panda: An Environmental Memoir*, in 2003 and lived until 2012 and the age of 92.

Bill Ruckelshaus served briefly at the FBI and the Department of Justice before entering private practice and taking a job with the Weyerhauser Company. In 1983, Ruckelshaus accepted a plea from President Ronald Reagan to return to the EPA to replace the controversial Ann Buford Gorsuch. It had been a rocky environmental road for the Reagan Administration, starting in 1981 with the president's gaffe, "Trees cause more pollution than automobiles do." His poorly qualified appointments to lead three key agencies with environmental responsibilities only confirmed the public's worst fears: dentist James Edwards at the Department of Energy, business confidant James Watt at the Department of Interior, and Gorsuch, a state's rights advocate, at the EPA. Under congressional fire for mismanaging the high-profile Superfund program, the embattled Gorsuch resigned less than two years after taking the job. Ruckelshaus rode back into town on a white horse with a mission to restore the integrity and scientific principles of the EPA.

Looking back on his two terms at the EPA, Ruckelshaus noted the difference that time makes. Recalling his first stint wistfully, he said, "by and large everybody thought they were attached to a cause larger than themselves. I found when I went back to EPA ten years later, the challenge certainly was still there—as well as the interest and excitement—but it was hard to recreate that sense of joy in creating something brand new. *'By God, we're going to do something about this terrible problem afflicting society! Isn't it wonderful we're all banded together to do it!'* There was a real sense of camaraderie and joy about what we were doing. The rush of youthful enthusiasm you sense in a brand new institution is really something to experience. It was fun."

In addition to his political savvy and principled stands on environmental stewardship, Ruckelshaus was authentic on the need for public involvement: "Public opinion remains absolutely essential for anything to be done on behalf of the environment. Absent that, nothing will happen because the forces of the economy and the impact on people's livelihood are so much more automatic and endemic. I don't conclude that it's either a strong economy *or* a clean environment; this is what ... people in the country sometimes tend to think of as the central issue to the environment. But I do think you've got to have public support for environmental protection or it won't happen. That's what shifted between the early 1960s and the time EPA was formed."

When Ruckelshaus departed the EPA in 1985 for the second time, the agency budget contained more funding for enforcement actions, solid waste management, research on acid rain and radiation, and a new program to clean up the Chesapeake Bay. In addition, funding for the Superfund program was 50 percent higher. The EPA was on its way again.

AL GORE: GLOBAL REALITY

Elected to the U.S. House of Representatives in 1977 at the young age of 28, Al Gore wanted to distinguish himself from the other 434 members. One way was to join the Congressional Clearinghouse on the Future, a small in-house think tank that Congress had just formed a year earlier. His active participation in the Clearinghouse was a sign of Gore's proclivities as a futurist. Annie Cheatham, the first director of the Clearinghouse, remembered that Gore asked lots of questions at Clearinghouse events, consistent with his background as an investigative reporter in Tennessee: "He was young, clearly eager to learn, and trying to define areas where he could make a difference." Within a few years, Gore was the natural choice to lead the Clearinghouse, becoming its second chairperson from 1979 to 1983.

The Clearinghouse arose from a 1974 House Rule called the "foresight provision" that required all committees and subcommittees except Budget and Appropriations to continuously undertake future-oriented research. Although Congress spent a great deal of time on its traditional oversight responsibilities, it spent hardly any time on emerging issues and their legislative implications. The Clearinghouse helped fill the gap by supplying House members with information on major trends, recommending hearing witnesses and questions, and providing a speaker series and newsletter. In doing so, it endeavored to serve the House in a nonpartisan manner, which was important to building institutional trust, especially among the small Republican minority at the time. One young Republican who found the Clearinghouse appealing was Newt Gingrich of Georgia, who entered Congress in 1979 and whom some likened in style and personality to Gore.

Gore used his soapbox at the Clearinghouse in the early 1980s to highlight future-oriented issues such as biomass plantations, the internet, and robotic warfare. He urged congressional colleagues to take a longer view despite the inherent uncertainties. Gore lamented, "There are powerful institutional incentives in the Congress to adopt a short-term horizon: the budget cycle, the end of the fiscal year, the next election. Our daily schedules are so cram-packed with meetings on one short-term problem after another, we scarcely have time to even consider the long-term future."

Two decades later, Al Gore emerged as the world's foremost spokesperson on the issue of climate change and the need to monetize and reduce carbon emissions. His career path included eight-year stints each in the House of Representatives and the U.S. Senate, where he concentrated his efforts on arms control, the new information superhighway, and the environment. In 1992, Gore published his first book, *Earth in the Balance*, which described the global ecological crisis and international strategies to address it. The book, which became a New York Times bestseller, coincided with his successful campaign for vice president, making him the first dedicated environmentalist to cross the White House threshold since Teddy Roosevelt.

Gore's interest in climate change grew during his vice presidency. In 1997, President Clinton asked Gore to represent the United States at the United Nation's climate change conference in Kyoto, Japan. The resulting Kyoto Protocol broke new ground with binding national targets on greenhouse gas emissions. Although Congress refused to ratify the agreement for economic and political reasons, the agreement has been signed by more than 190 countries. The only holdouts besides the U.S. are Andorra, South Sudan, and Canada, which withdrew from the agreement in 2012.

After his razor-thin loss in the presidential contest of 2000, the disappointed Gore assessed his options and decided to reincarnate as a spokesman for the drifting environmental movement. He established the Alliance for Climate Project and circled the globe with a climate change slideshow that later became the subject of the Academy Award-winning film, *An Inconvenient Truth*. Gore gave his climate change slideshow about 2,000 times, opening it with the ever-striking Blue Marble and Earthrise photographs from the Apollo missions. He used the images to emphasize the earth's thin biosphere and its susceptibility to human activity, magnified over the past century by a 400 percent increase in world population and a technological revolution. Echoing Rachel Carson, Gore professed, "If we do not see that the human part of nature has an increasingly powerful influence over the whole of nature—that we are, in effect, a natural force just like the winds and the tides—then we will not be able to see how dangerously we are threatening to push the earth out of balance." Gore's transformation from political defeat to prophet on climate change culminated in 2007, when Gore received the Nobel Peace Prize for his environmental achievements, sharing the honor with the U.N. International Panel on Climate Change.

Gore's special contribution to environmental awareness has been to make the Blue Marble a conscious reality by communicating the scientific case for climate change and its primary cause—human activity. His passion and intellect, clever use of media, and continued influence in Washington and around the world made him extremely effective. So effective, that the attacks of his critics were visceral, reminiscent of the Roman inquisition of Galileo in the 17th century for debunking a flat earth.

In *Earth in the Balance*, Gore warns of "horrific consequences" for failing to recognize and respond to the growing signs of ecological crisis. Like the successful Marshall Plan that rebuilt post-World War II Europe, Gore recommends a similar global commitment for the environment that would restructure the world economy around cleaner fuels and technology. To succeed, he boldly surmises, the environment must become the leading societal value over others such as democracy and market economics, "I have come to believe that we must take bold and unequivocal action: we must make the rescue of the environment the central organizing principle for civilization."

Because climate change is a global problem requiring global solutions, Gore puts his short-term faith in international agreements like Kyoto. In supporting such agreements, Gore sees no inherent conflict between environmental protection and economic growth. To him, we can be cleaner and more efficient simultaneously. However, he does acknowledge the "inconvenient truth" about climate change, which is that average American lifestyles must change, as Jimmy Carter also professed in relation to energy. And while Gore applauds people for doing their part to reduce, reuse, and recycle, he says that this is not enough. Everyone is needed in the public square. "I'm a big advocate of changing the light bulbs and buying hybrids. ...I have put 33 solar panels on our house and dug the geothermal well and done all of that other stuff. But as important as it is to change the light bulbs, it's more important to change the laws. And when we change our behavior in our daily lives we sometimes leave out the citizenship part and the democracy part. ... In order to solve the climate crisis we have to solve the democracy crisis."

Gore continues to do more than his share as a concerned citizen, author, and businessman. He remains a formidable environmental figure on the national and international stage, combining his ability to convey the big picture on climate change with his command of the technical issues. As a futurist, Gore has frequently been a step ahead. His bold environmental proposals for promoting clean energy and carbon pricing on a global level have cast the environmental debate in a new light and given it new urgency. And whether or not the details of his proposals are adopted, Gore has succeeded in challenging our complacency.

MAKING A DIFFERENCE

The modern environmental movement has benefited from the accomplishments of many people, among them leaders from Teddy Roosevelt to Al Gore. Their calls to do the right thing environmentally influenced the public debate and shifted more of the government's vast machinery toward environmental protection. In every case, their specific contributions were magnified by their success in capturing public attention, raising environmental awareness, and providing an enlightened view of the future.

We can be grateful that Teddy Roosevelt protected large tracts of wilderness and scenic areas that helped to foster new American values and traditions surrounding environmental stewardship. Rachel Carson taught us about the fragile underlying connectedness of nature and the urgent need for better environmental science. We listened to Lady Bird Johnson's heartfelt appeal for beautification, which transformed the American landscape and made environmental responsibility something personal and local. In the other direction, Stewart Brand expanded the notion of home and opened the American psyche to a planetary perspective. Gaylord Nelson and Dennis Hayes then brought the environment into mainstream American life and ensured its place in American education. As public consciousness coalesced, the foundation was set for revamping the nation's environmental laws. Behind the legislative push were Russell Train and William Ruckelshaus, who together revolutionized U.S. environmental protections across the board and helped to rebuild public faith in government. Following the climax of congressional victories in the 1970s, the next two decades were relatively uneventful. However, the new millennium brought renewed enthusiasm when defeated presidential candidate Al Gore turned his full attention to environmental issues. Gore applied the vision of Brand, the science of Carson, and the government spirit of the 1970s to launch his international crusade to address climate change.

All of these leaders overcame industry criticism or government resistance to achieve their goals. Regardless of the stiff headwinds they faced, each of these individuals used their power and intellect to persuade the public of the need for greater environmental action. Today, we enjoy a cleaner and healthier world because of their efforts.

CHAPTER III

EARLY DAYS OF DOE AND LOCAL ENERGY CONSERVATION

⌒

EXITING THE CROWDED SMITHSONIAN METRO station, I walked down Independence Avenue toward the U.S. Department of Energy (DOE) for my first day of work. It had been just two weeks since Ronald Reagan's decisive victory over Jimmy Carter. Washington, D.C. was in the throes of the transition, made more tumultuous by the enormous swing in ideology. A new brand of Republican was taking over and Democrats, along with many Independents and establishment Republicans, were scrambling to find new jobs.

It had been a gamble to accept a job with the DOE amid the 1980 presidential campaign because of Ronald Reagan's repeated pledge to abolish the three-year-old department. Even if the pledge was merely overheated campaign rhetoric, it was clear that Reagan wanted to shrink government and reduce the federal workforce. But regardless of who won, I was eager to see how government worked on the inside and how the progressive energy and environmental lawmaking of the 1970s was being put into practice.

My job in local government relations was situated in the Office of Congressional, Intergovernmental, and Public Affairs, a headquarters operation of 65 employees. The Office's division of Intergovernmental Affairs was split into three branches specializing in state, local, and tribal relations. Our role in local affairs was to keep city and county officials apprised of new federal programs and funding opportunities, mainly in the area of conservation and renewable energy. We also kept a pulse on municipal activities, relying on energy conferences and workshops sponsored by the National League of Cities, National Association of Counties, and U.S. Conference of Mayors for information. What we learned at these forums and elsewhere made its way up the chain of command and into briefing papers for the Secretary of Energy.

It was all I could do to get my bearings during my first few months at the department. There was a lot to learn in an agency of more than 21,000 employees and five times that number of contract personnel. Most DOE employees served in large administrations for fossil fuels, nuclear power, and conservation and renewable energy, or in one of the roughly 25 national labs and research facilities scattered around the country.

Despite its enormity, DOE felt congenial. It also had a markedly diverse workforce, mirroring national demographics. Workers in Intergovernmental Affairs represented a broad mix of gender, race, education, geography, and political affiliation. There was a Ph.D. nuclear scientist from the state of Washington, a former aide to President Gerald Ford from Michigan, and people with cultural ties to every corner of the country. It was nice to see the mixing bowl in action and how little the differences seemed to matter.

The pure enjoyment of the new job and surroundings did not last long though. Immediately following President Reagan's January inauguration, rumors began to swirl about a major reorganization. A month later, Secretary of Energy James Edwards, the former governor of South Carolina and a dentist by profession, announced

sweeping reforms. His primary target was conservation and renewable energy programs, which he slated for severe cuts. What this
meant for our work in intergovernmental relations was unclear.

Meanwhile, the Reagan revolution was stirring the passions of
conservative coworkers who supported supply-side economics and its
heavy emphasis on energy production. It was becoming easy to be
tagged as a nonbeliever. When a senior staffer heard me speak up on
behalf of local energy conservation efforts, he chided, "You guys from
the Northeast don't know how liberal you sound." Compounding
the political changes, it was apparent that the DOE still suffered
from lingering institutional crosscurrents. The department was in its
infancy as an organization and its assimilation of more than 10 former
energy-related offices and agencies, each with a separate culture, was
still unfolding. DOE integration was further slowed by the lack of a
well-defined mission for the department, a reflection of the fractured
national and regional politics of energy that had influenced the presidential election. In this unsettled state, the department's major energy
interests openly competed for attention and resources.

QUICKSAND

All of this made interesting fodder at Jack Donahue's morning coffee
klatch. Donahue ran the State Affairs branch of Intergovernmental
Affairs and was a respected manager who had come to Washington during the Kennedy Administration. He was tall and distinguished-looking

with neatly combed shocks of salt and pepper hair. People were drawn to Donahue because he had an encyclopedic memory and was fast on his feet whether the topic was agency business, personal advice, or a timely quip. He was also one of the few remaining people that could dictate a letter and get it exactly right the first time.

Donahue held court every morning at 7:30 for half an hour before the normal workday started. Regular attendees included members of his staff and a few others like me who enjoyed the storytelling and commentary.

"Come on in and sit down," Donahue said to me when I first started the job. "Another poor bastard from Massachusetts—you picked a great time to come to the party. I hate to tell you, but it's going to get ugly around here and I don't think you're in good shape. Are you a veteran?"

"No," I said, as the others in the room leaned back, amused by Donahue's stiff going-over of the new guy.

"Well, I gotta say then," Donahue deadpanned, "with no seniority or veteran's preference, you might want to start looking for something else. Jim Edwards, the mouth-from-the-south, is planning a major root canal."

FRANKLIN COUNTY ENERGY CONSERVATION TASK FORCE

The road to Washington had begun three years earlier in western Massachusetts. At the end of Woolman Hill's summer term, I left the school's idyllic setting above the Connecticut River Valley and moved to the nearby town of Greenfield, the county seat, to look for better paid work. It was the worst time to find another teaching position, but several energy jobs were being advertised by the local Community Action Agency, the delivery arm for government low-income programs and services. The jobs were intended to complement the county's winter home heating fuel assistance program by helping to organize local wood dealers, start a county recycling program, and coordinate a county energy conservation task force.

The agency's case for the new energy positions was relatively easy to make on the heels of President Carter's national TV address of April 1977, in which he urged "strict conservation" to reverse the nation's growing dependency on foreign oil. In addition, the agency could utilize the federal Comprehensive Employment and Training Act (CETA) to fund the jobs. Patterned after the 1930s Work Progress Administration, CETA provided low-income people with one-year public service employment or classroom training to gain marketable private sector skills. Created by the hardworking Senator Gaylord Nelson, the founder of Earth Day, and Senator Jacob Javits, CETA was signed into law by President Nixon in 1973, when a downturn in the economy pushed national unemployment to the then-unacceptable level of 5 percent. The program would serve close to a million low-income people before being swept away a decade later in the anti-government tide of the Reagan years.

The advertised job that appealed to me was coordinating the Franklin County Energy Conservation Task Force, whose genesis was a local citizen's initiative to ban the shipment of nuclear waste through the county. Unable to pass the controversial resolution at annual town meetings, local organizers returned a year later with a milder proposal to establish volunteer town energy conservation committees, which voters approved in 14 of the county's 26 towns. The Community Action Agency watched the process unfold and convinced the three county commissioners to jump on the band-wagon with a county energy conservation committee that could assist the town committees.

I was crestfallen when the agency informed me that someone else had been selected for the job. But as luck would have it, the agency called me back a week later to ask if I was still interested—their first choice had had a change of heart.

It did not take long to get going. Within a month, the new task force came to order around a long rectangular table in the county courtroom in Greenfield. Initial membership consisted of town representatives and 10 selected at-large members from local businesses, utilities, fuel suppliers, nonprofit groups, and housing agencies. As the task force gained visibility over the next few years, more towns approved energy conservation committees and task force membership swelled to 39 members, including 22 town representatives from Franklin County, two town representatives from neighboring Worcester County, and 15 at-large delegates.

While the task force would go on to make important contributions to the community, none of it was clear at the outset. The political landmines appeared at the first meeting, when a couple of town representatives used the session as a platform to criticize the electric utilities over nuclear power. If the criticism continued, it would jeopardize our goal of working with the business community and divert attention away from energy conservation, an issue that united us all. In fact, the Community Action Agency had instructed me to avoid the subject of nuclear power, honoring a quiet ground rule laid down by the county commissioners in consenting to the task force. For this reason, I never mentioned my involvement at Seabrook. Better not to be typecast, I thought, and to stay focused on helping families and businesses save energy and keep more money circulating through the local economy.

Another pitfall to avoid was letting our meetings turn into rap sessions about the energy crisis. This concern led us to tighten up our monthly agenda by leading off with a guest speaker, which encouraged members to arrive on time and provided our local newspaper reporter with his or her story for the night. Next, we went around the table for member reports. As time went by, we heard about town committees organizing energy audits of town buildings and schools, weatherization workshops, wood coops, ridesharing and recycling projects, and new library bookshelves devoted to energy.

Citizen involvement can be unwieldy, but when harnessed, can produce remarkable results. Few other places in New England or the country could match the region's interest in energy issues, the network of committed volunteers, or the degree of institutional support. Much of it could be attributed to demographics. Only 65,000 people lived in Franklin County at the time, mostly working and middle class, and they wanted more information about how to conserve energy to reduce fuel costs. The County is also one of the state's largest counties geographically, sandwiched between Vermont and New Hampshire to the north and the college towns of Amherst and Northampton to the south. In this rural farmland environment, small-town government thrived, people knew their elected leaders, and they felt empowered.

Many county residents were also curious about the county's abundance of renewable energy and how it could help to lower home heating bills. Franklin County was 73 percent forested and many families owned wood stoves, purchasing their supply from among 40 independent cordwood dealers. In addition, hydropower had a rich history in the county along the south-flowing Connecticut River and its major tributaries to the east and west. Modern hydroelectric technology might make some of the old dam sites profitable again. The exposed ridges of the western Berkshire Mountains offered opportunities for wind power. And plentiful solar energy might prove feasible because of the high cost of heating oil. Besides renewables, the county had the Yankee nuclear power plant in the town of Rowe and the world's largest hydroelectric pump storage station of its day on the Connecticut River in Northfield. With all of these energy assets, county residents liked to joke about being "the OPEC of New England."

The local press loved covering the task force experiment in democracy and its unusual intermingling of town volunteers, energy aficionados, business leaders, and county officials. But to sustain the program over time, we had to produce something tangible. Energy research seemed to be the best way forward. Over the next few years, we produced a countywide survey of residential energy use, a fact book on local energy, an inventory of unused dam sites, and a comprehensive energy policy, all relatively innovative at the time.

From the energy survey, we discovered, for example, that one-third of county homes lacked adequate insulation and that a similar percentage of people were commuting over 100 miles a week to work. From doing the fact book, we saw exactly what each town was consuming by energy sector and fuel type, and what it cost annually. These types of findings helped the task force and town committees identify where new initiatives were needed.

There was also much to discover from the county's history of hydropower. After rummaging through county dam inspection papers, searching old reports, and doing an aerial inspection of abandoned and overgrown sites, we identified 137 dams in the county with ten or more feet of elevation drop. Of this total, twelve sites—seven owned by the utilities and five privately—were generating 450 megawatt hours of electricity per year, which was 12 percent *more* electricity than the county's annual consumption.

When the local newspaper reported the story, residents were amazed to learn that Franklin County was a *net producer* of electricity from conventional hydropower alone. They also learned that the potential for home-grown power was even greater. Engineers determined that the 125 unused sites, if redeveloped, would generate an additional 95 megawatt hours of electricity, or another 24 percent of annual county usage.

The research set the stage for developing county energy policy. Working several months together, the task force and county planning board produced a 42-page statement of goals, policies, and action items for county building codes, recycling, transportation, and agriculture. The policy favored more use of renewable energy and less reliance on petroleum fuels. It even contained agreement on the elephant in the room—nuclear power. As approved by the commissioners, the stated policy was "to reduce and to minimize dependence on nuclear generation" and to "discourage any further planning and development of nuclear power in Franklin County until all safety precautions and ancillary services such as evacuation, community health, radiation monitoring, and waste disposal are satisfactorily resolved." The policy went on to "discourage the transportation of out-of-county nuclear wastes through Franklin

County" and the "expansion of temporary waste disposal capacity" at the local nuclear power plant. While the carefully chosen grammar of "discourage" was not a "ban," the County was now squarely on record against further development of nuclear power.

Building on these efforts, the University of Massachusetts in Amherst was awarded a DOE grant to conduct a new wide-ranging energy study of Franklin County. DOE hoped the study would serve as a national blueprint for how communities could become more self-reliant through energy conservation and renewable energy use. With all that was going on, county residents were beginning to believe that something special was happening and that Franklin County, usually one of the least influential jurisdictions in Massachusetts, had become the state leader on energy.

After my year of CETA funding expired, the county commissioners agreed to carry my position temporarily in the county planning department. The only hitch was that the director of the planning department believed that the task force should be a subcommittee underneath the county planning board. Despite successful coordination between his office and the task force on energy policy, he grew increasingly agitated with the independence of the task force. Each story about it in the local newspaper, *The Greenfield Recorder,* seemed to make matters worse. Nor did it help when the university published its 600-page Franklin County Energy Study, drawing national attention, including from an unexpected source—former California Governor Ronald Reagan. In his August 1979 syndicated column, prior to his presidential run, Reagan wrote that communities "like Franklin County ... do not have to sit by while bureaucrats and politicians in Washington tie up the nation's energy in red tape. They can act in their own communities to take charge of their own future. That's a spirit worth bottling and spreading around."

Increasingly frustrated by the task force and its full claim over my time, the planning director urged the commissioners to install an executive committee over the task force. When the plan went public, it elicited a strong reaction from task force members who defended their grassroots charter and direct access to the commissioners. In a quandary, the commissioners decided that the management concerns of the planning director were eclipsed by the continued enthusiasm over energy issues, good press, and an offer by the Massachusetts state energy office to pick up my salary for six months. In an unexpected turn of events, they announced the creation of a new county energy office. Within days, I was packed up and moved into a small room of an old house across from the county building to begin my third year staffing the task force.

Franklin County benefited from the groundswell of national interest in energy during the Carter years, and from the president's belief that states and local communities needed to play a larger role in American energy security. Within this context, the DOE called the county to see if we would be interested in preparing a guide-book on the county energy program and sharing our experience with other communities in New England. With the encourage-ment of the commissioners and the addition of a writer, conference planner, and university representative from the energy study, we organized and conducted six major energy conferences in the early spring of 1980, one in each New England state.

The momentum continued courtesy of TV journalist Bill Moyers. Script writers and camera technicians for the PBS *Bill Moyers Journal* descended on the county to portray the renewable energy path outlined by the university energy study. They interviewed residents and filmed local events, including a task force meeting, culminating in a one-hour broadcast that aired in May 1980.

Although the year was going well, it was not without setbacks. Several solar grant proposals failed, including a plan to assess solar opportunities for low-income housing and another to install a rooftop system at the county jail, replete with architectural drawings for inmates to use in mounting the panels. When we did reel in a grant, this one to evaluate the restoration of a large hydropower site, the reconstruction costs turned out to be too high for the paper mill owner. But bigger problems loomed around the corner. From the earliest days, task force membership included a small but vocal group of determined activists. Although most task force members urged continued focus on conservation and renewables, a strategy with proven appeal, the activists were restless again and wanted to use the task force as a springboard to their dream of municipalizing the private electric utility and moving it toward renewable energy, especially wind power, and away from oil and nuclear.

Despite pleas to consider the political and legal ramifications, and the siphoning of task force time and energy, the group could not be dissuaded from pursuing their plan. Meanwhile, the majority of task force members concentrated on a fall weatherization initiative that brought the task force and town committees together with 12 community sponsors and 16 local hardware stores to offer three weeks of training classes and store discounts for home weatherization materials. All county citizens needed to do was to pick up one of the 20,000 printed brochures, clip the coupon signed by a county commissioner, and present it to the store at time of purchase for a sizable discount. Everyone saw it a common sense way for government and business to work together.

Going to DOE

It was around that time that I got a call from a DOE representative asking if I would be interested in working at the department. I decided to contact Sam Jennings, my old professor and mentor, a couple of days later. After a few minutes of exchanging pleasantries and family news, I told Sam that I was considering a job offer in Washington.

"Franklin County is great because it's small enough to get things done," I said, "but it's been harder lately."

"How so?" Sam asked.

"Well, to make a long story short," I said, "our task force is being sidetracked by a few people who think the county should seize the private electric utility. They see it as a fast track to wind and solar, and a way to prevent more nukes. The commissioners haven't heard the idea yet, but when they do, the shit is going to hit the fan. We're supposed to be apolitical and this is as political as it gets."

"It does sound controversial," Sam remarked.

"Some of us have been trying to talk this group off the ledge—but they don't realize how fragile things are. We need every ally we can get, *including* the utilities."

"Well, look," Sam said, "there comes a time when you have to move on, and it sounds like you're ready. Besides, an opportunity to go to Washington might not come again."

"That's true," I said.

"Listen, I know you well enough to know that you'd make a better teacher than a bureaucrat," Sam said, "but getting a taste of Washington can't hurt—and the city's got a lot to offer." He cautioned however that Washington is a tough town and that the federal bureaucracy is a labyrinth filled with dead-end jobs and ways of trapping and pigeon-holing people. To underscore his point, he said, "You might want to watch the new low-budget zombie flick, *Hell of the Living Dead*—they can rob your soul."

"I'll take your word for it," I said.

"So, what's the worst that can happen?" Sam asked rhetorically. "You work there a few years, it doesn't pan out, and you find an honest job teaching. It can't hurt to give it a try. But, let me ask you something," he said pausing, "what happens if Reagan wins the election? He's vowing to abolish Energy."

"It's funny," I said. "Reagan wrote a newspaper column a year ago praising Franklin County and local energy work. So, I'll just have to keep my fingers crossed—I'm feeling lucky."

"Remember," Sam said professorially, "luck is the convergence of preparation and opportunity. Let me know how it goes."

After accepting the new job, I gave my notice to the commissioners, handed off my work to a new coordinator, and said good-byes to my friends on the task force. Months later in Washington, I heard with consternation that the county energy program was faltering. It was a bad omen when President Carter, during his final days of office, honored the county with a presidential award only to have the White House invitations to the commissioners arrive *after* the ceremony. Then it happened. The advocates of municipalizing the utility went public with their idea and the commissioners lost confidence in the task force. Within a few months, as local resources dried up and the national dialogue shifted, the task force collapsed and faded into history. Pondering the news miles away, I was struck by the lack of common sense about the government role on energy, whether in progressive Franklin County or in the increasingly regressive and politicized hallways of the U.S. Department of Energy.

REDUCTION IN FORCE

Signs of an impending layoff were growing as tidbits of information crept out about the arcane procedures for a federal Reduction in Force (RIF). The process starts with a department looking at employee position descriptions to see which ones are similar in nature and can be fenced off as a group. Next, management walks everyone on paper into his or her new group in the new and leaner organization, ranking each person by seniority, veteran's status, and qualifications. More seniority, for example, earns bumping rights over those less senior. Like musical chairs, the game leaves a certain number of people without a position and the recipients of a RIF notice.

The subjectivity in the process kept everyone on edge. The angst about being "RIF'ed" was made worse by the palpable sense of entombment in the DOE Forrestal building. The Forrestal was called the Little Pentagon when it was built in the late 1960s for the Department of Defense. Its grey uniform cement construction and waffle iron window pattern could have been designed in Siberia. The main section of the building is suspended on large pillars five stories high. Reportedly, the elevated design was to protect employees and defense secrets from the hordes of Vietnam War protestors that might someday storm the building. Cement also engulfed the facility's entranceways, which lacked any greenery and the gentle rolling waterfall that architects envisioned for the street-level promenade. The inside looked like the outside, void of art or color that might give the eyes some relief from the long and monotonous hallways. As an employee, it was easy to see that if this country wanted more inspired energy thinking, it should build DOE a new facility and hand over the Forrestal to a better suited tenant, like today's U.S. Department of Homeland Security.

Our 1-month RIF notices arrived in August 1981. With less than a year on the job, my fate was sealed by a lack of seniority or veteran's preference. But as I was literally walking out of the Forrestal, the management offered me a part-time job for three months. I never found out how it happened, or who may have put in a good word, but I was glad to have a job and the benefit of the object lesson—despite what upper management says, they hold a hidden set of keys in their back pocket.

When my three months expired, the office quietly converted me to permanent part-time status as a GS-9 on the General Schedule, a salary ladder that extends to the top grade of GS-15. This grade is reserved for senior managers, who are outranked only by an elite corps of Senior Executive Service administrators in the civil service and by the president's handpicked political appointees, called "Schedule Cs."

GOOD ADVICE

I went in to see Jack Donahue on the early side one morning to ask him about a government relations meeting with state and local officials the day before. "How's it going?" he asked looking up, crouched over his chair, in a morning ritual of polishing his shoes.

"I happened to overhear your conversation with the governor's aide yesterday," I said. "You were pretty tough on him."

Donahue responded at once. "I had to be. These guys think they run the federal government and they don't. Sometimes they need a little reminder. There are 50 governors and 535 Members of Congress and they all want the money. Someone has to tell them to get in line. Besides that, they don't always understand our limits. Let me put it this way, we're not here to change the world, we're here to stop fraud and abuse and make sure that the public's money is spent correctly—and that's usually on things that the private sector can't do for a profit, like storing nuclear waste—or you name it: feeding the poor, building the interstate highway system, repairing bridges, or basic research."

Donahue saw me digesting his comments. "So, I know what you're probably thinking," he said, as he turned and sat upright. "Yes, Kennedy said, 'Ask not what your country can do for you.' But those were different times and Kennedy had the charisma to make us feel good about public service. So my advice to you right now is—do your job well but don't take initiative. That's right, don't take initiative."

I couldn't help smiling, "Oh yeah, that'll work on my annual evaluation."

"Seriously," Donahue said, "no good deed is going unpunished these days, so best to keep a low profile. This is a great show. The pay is good and gets better, especially the benefits. So don't screw it up."

⌣⌢

Dusk 'til Dawn

In May 1982, President Reagan renewed his assault on the Energy Department by submitting legislation transferring most of its functions to the Department of Commerce. The proposal received little support on the Hill, but it clearly showed no softening at the White House. Meanwhile, DOE continued to retrench, significantly slashing conservation and renewable energy programs, and thus the need for government relations. In the spring of 1984, more dark smoke signals from the White House foretold another round of DOE personnel cuts. Knowing my odds of survival had not improved, I decided to write a personal letter to my Senator, Charles Mathias of Maryland, to suggest that retraining and reassigning DOE staff made more sense than layoffs.

I should have listened to Donahue's advice. A couple of weeks later, the director of Intergovernmental Affairs called me into his office. He had received a copy of my constituent letter from Senator Mathias's office for a DOE response. After politely complimenting my writing form, he proceeded to chew me out for the letter and told me never to do it again. When I left his office, I looked for the nearest hole to climb into, knowing the story would get around. I silently cursed the Hill and muttered to myself, "How could Mathias' staff be so lazy or inept as to disregard confidences and send my letter to DOE for reply?"

My ricocheting letter did not earn any points, but it made no difference. The severity of the new RIF far surpassed the earlier one in 1981. In the end, DOE energy conservation and renewable energy programs were devastated. In Intergovernmental Affairs, where the staff was reduced to less than 10 people, a few resourceful co-workers found jobs in other parts of the agency. One of them was a friend, who pulled me over in the hall one day and whispered, "I can get you a job where I'm going—nuclear is hiring." In an instant, my mind flashed back to Seabrook and Franklin County and a voice inside asked, "What is this place doing to you?" My friend must have noticed the hesitation as I stumbled to construct a safe reply. "Thanks so much," I said, "but I don't think nuclear would be a good fit." A puzzled look crossed his face, as he was unable to fathom why I would not accept his lifeline to stay with the agency.

On September 25, 1984, I departed the DOE for good, angry at the administrative people who were smiling at the exit meeting, the Federal employee unions for ineffectiveness, Senator Mathias' nameless flunky, and the whole world in general.

In the ensuing weeks, I decided to limit my job-hunting to morning hours, volunteering in the afternoons to keep busy. Ironically, I landed a job with a "beltway bandit" in Maryland that supported DOE's remaining conservation programs. But I really wanted to return to federal service. I could not imagine living in a company town like Washington and not working for Uncle Sam.

Following several months of looking, my wish materialized. Exiting Metro onto Independence Avenue once again, I walked past the Forrestal Building and next door to the headquarters of the Federal Aviation Administration to begin a new career involving the National Environmental Policy Act and the two largest environmental impacts in aviation—aircraft noise and airport emissions.

CHAPTER IV

THE NATIONAL ENVIRONMENTAL POLICY ACT

⟵⟶

THE 1970 NATIONAL ENVIRONMENTAL POLICY Act (NEPA) is our country's most important piece of environmental legislation. It transformed government by infusing the environment into everyday decision-making and setting a higher standard for project planning and design. NEPA also boosted the principle of open government, giving Americans the right to review federal actions and to comment on their potential impacts to the environment, communities, human health, and quality of life. By allowing more time for public input and debate, NEPA has ensured a more rigorous look at the facts.

This is not to say that the government has to treat all public comments equally or to select the best alternative from an environmental standpoint. On the contrary, the government may opt for the worst alternative environmentally. But it cannot do so until the public has spoken, it has disclosed environmental impacts, and it has weighed all relevant information. In effect, NEPA requires the government to listen before it decides what to do and puts a shovel in the ground.

The NEPA process is typified by Environmental Impact Statements (EISs), which are required for federal projects that cause significant environmental impacts or are highly controversial. As an environmental advocate, it is important to know how EIS studies are performed because they embody the core principles of the environmental process and the broad responsibilities of the government to manage and protect the environment. One of the first things to know about EISs is that they can take years to complete, giving project opponents time to organize, sway elected officials, and affect the final outcome. One such case with lasting repercussions was the EIS conducted by the U.S. Air Force and the Federal Aviation Administration (FAA) at Homestead Air Force Base in Florida.

⌐⌐⌐

HOMESTEAD HURRICANE

Hurricane Andrew slammed into the south Florida coast in the early morning of August 24, 1992, with sustained winds of 145 mph and gusts of 175 mph. The sudden strengthening of the hurricane in the preceding hours surprised meteorologists, causing massive traffic jams as thousands of people tried to flee the upper Florida Keys and Miami-Dade County.

South of Miami and midway to the Keys, the 32,000 residents of Homestead experienced the full brunt of Hurricane Andrew. Several people died and thousands of homes in the city and surrounding area were severely damaged or destroyed, including all but nine of Homestead's 1,200 trailer homes. The devastation extended to farmlands, businesses, schools, water supply, electricity, and other infrastructure. The two national parks on either side of Homestead—Biscayne National Park to the east and Everglades National Park to the west—also suffered major blows. The parks lost 70,000 acres of mangrove trees, a fourth of what had been there. In wreaking $25 billion worth of damage statewide, Hurricane Andrew was one of the largest and costliest hurricanes in U.S. history.

A few miles northeast of Homestead and closer to the shoreline, Homestead Air Force Base, which played prominently in the 1962 Cuban Missile Crisis and was supporting two F-16 fighter wings and U.S. Customs Service regional anti-drug operations, sat squarely in the storm's bulls-eye. The 5,000 airmen and 70 aircraft on the base were evacuated before the storm hit, but most of the facility's 2,000 buildings were demolished or seriously damaged.

In the aftermath of Hurricane Andrew, the U.S. Air Force looked at the costs of rebuilding and decided to close Homestead Air Force Base and transfer most of the facility to the FAA for a new commercial airport. When the Air Force completed its EIS two years later, local residents and an Everglades coalition of 15 environmental organizations hotly criticized the environmental study as incomplete and inaccurate.

Feeling the legal and political pressure and needing more civil aviation expertise, the Air Force asked the FAA in December 1997 to help them with a major do-over of the EIS, technically called a supplemental EIS. The FAA agreed to the request and to assume the technical lead for the new study. In addition, the National Park Service (NPS), the U.S. Fish and Wildlife Service (FWS), and the U.S. Environmental Protection Agency (EPA) joined the new study as cooperating agencies, exercising their right to be closely consulted on the work because of their expertise and regional management of natural resources and parklands.

While the new EIS took on added dimension, the purpose remained the same—to assess the advantages of the new airport for regional capacity and congestion relief at Miami International Airport. The main environmental issue was aircraft noise. It was clear that if Homestead Air Force Base became a commercial airport, south Florida would experience more noise from additional operations and altered flight patterns.

Citing noise and other environmental concerns, the federal cooperating agencies strongly opposed the airport plan, preferring that the former base be redeveloped as a conventional mixed-use residential and commercial property. The NPS was particularly worried about the project's potential effects on wildlife and visitor enjoyment of Everglades and Biscayne National Parks, Big Cypress National Preserve, and Crocodile Lake National Wildlife Refuge in the Upper Keys. Moreover, the NPS did not trust the FAA to keep its pledge to deactivate one of the two runways at the base.

Such policy differences and tensions permeated the new environmental review for Homestead. Given the sensitivities, the FAA Office of Airports, which was directing the new study, asked my branch in the Office of Environment and Energy for support on noise modeling and analysis. We agreed to help knowing the technical challenges we would encounter, including the enormous size of the study area, which encompassed most of southern Florida and extensive areas of parkland. Sampling ambient or background sound levels at the NPS park units would require 29 field monitoring sites. Calculating noise over the large stretches of water, a hard acoustic surface like pavement, would require new software development. Responding effectively to park concerns would require new and more sensitive noise impact criteria that were consistent with park values. All of this led to a robust and innovative effort to investigate noise effects, including daytime and nighttime levels of exposure, the loudness of each planned flight, and the amount of time that aircraft would be heard. In the end, the noise study provided government decision-makers with a wealth of information by which to compare and judge the proposed alternatives.

The FAA and the Air Force published the draft of the new EIS on schedule in December 1999, exactly two years after the study began. The document elicited a wave of more than 8,000 written public comments and large turnouts at public hearings. At the first hearing, a thousand people showed up at the high school in Homestead, including 100 concerned residents of the exclusive Ocean Reef Harbor community of north Key Largo in neighboring Monroe County. Although the "Ocean Reefers" traveled a long distance to attend and arrived early, pro-airport officials controlled the speakers list and put them at the bottom. Frustrated by hours of waiting, the group left the meeting in disgust, more determined than ever to organize against the airport.

Meanwhile, the presidential election of 2000 between Vice-President Al Gore and George W. Bush was gaining steam and the July target date for the final version of the EIS was starting to slip. Inside the FAA, we knew that the brewing controversy over the study was roiling the White House. Homestead redevelopment aroused passions on both sides. The majority of Florida business interests and politicians, including Miami Mayor Alex Penelas and Democratic Senator Bob Graham, lined up with the Air Force, the FAA, and the aviation industry in favoring the new airport. The opposing environmental community drew heavyweight support from the cooperating agencies: the NPS, FWS, and EPA.

The authority of the Air Force to make the final decision under NEPA had long since dissolved into a technicality. Everyone within the Departments of Defense, Transportation, and Interior, not to mention the entire state of Florida, knew that the buck stopped at the White House and President Bill Clinton.

As the presidential election entered the home stretch in the fall of 2000, the White House fell silent on Homestead. Whatever conversations President Clinton was having with Vice-President Gore, Council of Environmental Quality (CEQ) Chair Kathleen McGinty, and members of his cabinet and political team, the rest of the world could only wonder. Clearly, the White House wanted to avoid angering those on either side of the issue. The White House was also constrained about what it could say. Any public statement before a final EIS decision could put the whole study in legal jeopardy. As a result, President Clinton chose the safest path and deferred the Homestead verdict until after the election.

The ploy would have succeeded but for one thing—the Green Party candidacy of Ralph Nader. Polls showed the presidential race tightening, with Florida as a key toss-up state. Nader was making inroads there and in other states with broad left-wing attacks on Clinton's environmental policies and other issues. As reported in the Miami press, Nader used "... the Homestead air base issue in his stump speeches around the nation as proof there was no real difference between (Democrat) Gore and Republican nominee George W. Bush." Concern about Nader within the Gore campaign was growing. To fend off Nader on Homestead and to shore up his support on the left, Gore sent Kathleen McGinty, the CEQ Chair, to southern Florida three weeks before Election Day to reassure the environmental community that he was on their side.

McGinty met with a select group of environmental and elected leaders at the Audubon Society Tropical headquarters in South Miami. She reportedly opened the meeting by stating "… how important it was for environmentalists to rally around Gore in the closing days of the campaign." She stressed that throughout Gore's career in public life, "protecting the environment had been one of his highest priorities [and] now it was time for the environmental community to come to his aid."

In response, McGinty heard harsh criticism of Gore's public neutrality on the Homestead airport study. Audubon representatives reported that their 3,000 south Florida members were extremely upset about Homestead and unwilling to volunteer for the Gore campaign, a sign they said that people were moving toward Nader. When McGinty proposed a Gore visit and environmental rally in southern Florida, she was told that if the event were held, it would be disrupted by large protests—an embarrassment the Gore campaign could ill afford.

The electoral goal of the Nader campaign was to reach 5 percent of the national vote, a threshold that guaranteed federal funding for the Green Party in the next presidential cycle. But in the final days of the campaign, against his staff's advice to concentrate on vote-rich states like California and New York, Nader opted to spend his time in Florida and other battleground states where votes were getting hard to find.

Gore lost Florida and the presidency by a razor-thin 537 votes out of almost 6 million votes cast in Florida. Most attribute the loss to voter confusion over butterfly ballots, uncertainty over dimpled and hanging chads on the punch cards, and the 5-4 political finale at the Supreme Court that ended the recount. While many voting and campaign factors could have made the difference in such a close race, Homestead ranks at the top of the list. White House postponement of the Homestead decision during the election season sowed uncertainty in the minds of environmentally supportive Floridians. They voiced their dissatisfaction by casting protest votes for Nader and sending a message to Gore, the Democratic Party, and the pro-airport establishment. Nader fueled the fire, as his late campaign tactics underscore, and the environmental community vented its anger with a vengeance.

Nader received 97,488 votes in Florida, or 1.63 percent of the state total. In Monroe County, home to the concerned citizens of Ocean Reef Harbor and the Keys, Nader received 1,090 votes out of 33,895 cast, or 3.22 percent of the total. The Monroe County percentage for Nader was the fourth highest among Florida's 67 counties and reflected the siphoning of environmental votes from Gore statewide. If Monroe County alone had followed the state average of 1.63 percent for Nader, and the remaining balance of 538 Monroe County voters had pulled the predictable Democratic lever, Gore would have picked up the 537 votes to tie plus *the one vote to win*!

The Air Force signed the Homestead EIS Record of Decision two months after the election on January 15, 2001. Acting on behalf of the White House, the Air Force *rejected* the proposal to use Homestead Air Force Base as a commercial airport in favor of the plan for mixed-use development of housing, retail business, and industry. With this, the NEPA controversy that engulfed the 2000 election in Florida was laid to rest.

THE NEPA PROCESS

As the Homestead experience showed, community involvement and public information disclosure are considerable forces in federal environmental decision making. Indeed, the openness of the NEPA process can have implications that go beyond the proposed project—in Homestead's case to a presidential election.

NEPA is referred to as a procedural law and was the world's first law demanding a holistic and interdisciplinary approach to environmental problem solving. It requires all Executive Branch departments and agencies to take a systematic hard look at environmental impacts early in the planning process before committing to a course of action.

NEPA has been battle-tested since 1970 and has survived intact. Its resiliency is a tribute to the foresight of its founders. One visionary who helped craft the law was Dr. Lynton Caldwell, a professor of government at Indiana University. Caldwell published an influential article in 1963 called, "Environment: A New Focus for Public Policy?" Foreshadowing NEPA, Caldwell wrote, "Fragmented action and policies affecting natural resources and human environment have brought waste and confusion in their train and are a result of the lack of recognition of environment as a general subject for public action." His solution was a "new policy focus" to integrate planning and action and to foster agency coordination on the environment.

Caldwell served as an advisor to Sen. Henry Jackson, Chairman of the Senate Interior Committee, during the drafting of NEPA and is credited with the idea of an EIS as the "action-forcing mechanism" for environmental compliance. Caldwell also helped to draft the goals of NEPA, which declare that "... each person should enjoy a healthful environment" and that government has a responsibility to create conditions "... under which man and nature can exist in productive harmony, and fulfill the social, economic, and other requirements of present and future generations of Americans."

NEPA assessments are required for all federal actions, including approvals, licensing, and funding, even if the federal share of funding is small. The assessments fall into one of three basic levels of NEPA documentation. The first and simplest level is Categorical Exclusions (CATEXs), which applies to small projects that rarely cause environmental concern, such as minor facility maintenance work. Each federal agency compiles its own individual list of CATEXs. If a proposed project fits a category on the list, an agency simply documents this fact, stores it in the file, and moves on with the project, assuming there are no "extraordinary circumstances" that require more analysis.

Occupying the ubiquitous middle ground of NEPA, between the simple CATEX and a full-blown EIS, is the Environmental Assessment (EA). The extent of an EA can range from a simple checklist or screening analysis all the way up to a complex undertaking that mimics an EIS. If the EA shows no serious environmental outcome, which is often the case, the agency writes a Finding of No Significant Impact to fulfill NEPA requirements. However, if the EA evaluation does discover potentially significant effects, the agency must proceed to an EIS. The only option is going back to the drawing board and designing a "mitigated EA" to eliminate any potential for significant impact by downsizing the project or introducing new environmental measures.

The least common and most complex NEPA action is an EIS. It begins with public notification of the proposed federal action and a community scoping process to elicit public comments and concerns. Based on this feedback, agencies revise the project plan and move forward with their analysis. The format of an EIS always includes a purpose and need statement, followed by chapters on project alternatives, the affected environment, and the environmental consequences, which is the heart of the document with its study data and findings.

When a draft EIS is complete, the agency must make it available to the public and hold a public hearing. Draft EISs are also reviewed by the EPA, which grades the document on how well it identifies environmental impacts and presents information. A critical review from the EPA can mean costly revisions or added legal risk. In the end, the project agency makes the corrections it deems necessary, states its preferred course of action from among the studied alternatives, and publishes the EIS. The process is ultimately completed with a Record of Decision, a separate document that summarizes the EIS findings, declares the agency's approval or denial of the project, and describes mitigation measures that may be a condition of approval.

Under the broad umbrella of NEPA and its three levels of documentation, agencies comply with all of the special purpose laws on the environment, which cover about 30 different environmental impact areas and their respective mandates. On air quality, for example, the Clean Air Act specifies the pollutants of concern, technical standards, assessment methods, compliance requirements, and other factors. Other areas of environmental concern may include endangered species, energy and natural resources, compatible land use, floodplains and coastal zones, wild and scenic rivers, solid and hazardous wastes, farmlands, parklands, and climate change. Social impact areas may include historic properties and environmental justice, which addresses the possibility of disproportionate impacts on minority and low-income populations.

The government watchdogs for all of this environmental activity are the EPA, CEQ, and U.S. Justice Department. The lead agency for NEPA is the CEQ, which sets government-wide policy for its administration and enforcement. For instance, the CEQ approves every agency's categorical exclusion list and is always on the lookout for questionable categories that are written too broadly or lack convincing justification or specificity. The CEQ also plays an important role as mediator. When federal agencies cannot agree, as happened at Homestead, the CEQ calls the parties together to resolve the differences. If the issues are intractable, the matter gets elevated to the White House.

The CEQ is a small organization and has to manage its workload judiciously. To do this, the CEQ delegates the bulk of NEPA guidance development to federal agencies, giving them leeway to interpret and apply the law to their respective operations, for which they are the experts. At the U.S. Department of Transportation, for example, NEPA guidance is produced on several levels: first by the department, second by individual agencies, and third and most detailed in form, by the major organizations within agencies. It can be a long and painstaking process to develop new or updated NEPA guidance. Agencies can spend months or years engaged in the process. During this time, the CEQ stays above the fray like a factory floor manager, overseeing the agency's working efforts until it grants final approval.

EPA INSIGHTS

Duke University offered a series of popular NEPA training courses for many years. The courses typically lasted a week and attracted an interesting assortment of professionals from different federal agencies and private companies. One course that I attended was called the "Law of NEPA," which presented the finer points of environmental case law. During the class, I met Ceci Foster, a senior analyst with the EPA government affairs office. Foster was in her mid-thirties but a relative newcomer to the EPA, having spent much of her young career working for a state air quality agency. A big part of her job at the EPA involved NEPA and the evaluation of agency EIS drafts, so I was curious about her impressions of the course.

"The message I'm getting," she said, "is how much room there is for judgment and the high price for mistakes. Like thinking an EA is the right level, only to have the court say it should be an EIS—wasting months, maybe years."

"Fortunately, that doesn't come up often," I said, "but we've occasionally gone straight to an EIS just for insurance. Our biggest problem most of the time is how much analysis to do in various impact areas."

"That's a good question and better to get it right early because the back-end repairs can be expensive," she said, citing re-evaluation requirements if new scientific data comes to light or having to do a supplemental EIS if the problems are more deep-rooted.

"Speaking of supplementals, the Air Force asked us for help on a big one at Homestead Florida several years ago."

"I heard about it," she said, "I'd say they went to the right place for help because EPA considers your EISs pretty good compared to a lot of other agencies."

"Glad to hear it," I said, "because the law can get complicated."

"For sure," she said. "There are plenty of nuances and the environmental science is constantly changing. As our instructors say—'it's the art of NEPA.'"

"Maybe it's human nature to resist change," I said, "but our agency would stick with the status quo forever if we could on environmental issues—we're great at deferring things with phase two studies and research roadmaps. But then, *bang*, something unexpected happens, like an adverse court ruling, and the wheels finally start moving."

"That's exactly why we need to be here," she said. "Somebody's got to keep management up-to-date. I only wish more agencies would send their people to training like this."

"Can't complain there," I said, "plus we spend a lot of time each year on in-house training with our regional staff. Our management is also good about guidance. They know the more that's written down, the less chance of error."

"It's a lot about reducing mistakes, isn't it?" she said. "That's why I'd always take my medicine early. Why not fix a study, or go the extra mile on analysis, rather than suffer a poor rating from us or a bad court decision? However—and you won't hear this from me in class—from our perspective, a sister agency losing litigation isn't so bad if the ruling leads to better environmental policy for everybody."

⌐‿⌐

NEPA-LIKE STATES

Seeing the benefits of NEPA, a number of states have enacted state environmental laws that are patterned after it. These so-called "NEPA-like" states include: California, Hawaii, Montana, and Washington in the west; Indiana, Minnesota, South Dakota, and Wisconsin in the Midwest; Georgia, North Carolina, and Virginia in the south; and Connecticut, Maryland, Massachusetts, New Jersey, and New York in the northeast. The list also includes the District of Columbia and the territories of Guam and Puerto Rico.

NEPA-like states have stronger environmental protections than their counterparts, particularly with regard to information disclosure, public participation, and assessment quality. A few years ago, I learned how much weaker environmental protections can be in states without NEPA-like procedures.

The Maine Department of Inland Fisheries and Wildlife is interested in removing dams throughout the state to restore streams and saltwater habitat. I got to know the Department because they wanted to remove an earthen dam for a small man-made pond that is close to our property and about a mile from the ocean. By removing the 70-year-old dam, the state hoped to restore the area to tidal marsh and enhance the habitat for smelt and eels.

The proposed project is a good example of what can happen when environmental interests compete with each other. Although stream restoration has obvious merit, the pond's freshwater habitat supports bald eagles, blue herons, cormorants, buffleheads, and many mammals including coyotes, foxes, and fishers.

Because Maine has no NEPA-like law, the state was not obliged to follow customary NEPA protocols. We and our neighbors near the pond received no notice of the intended action. When we did find out, we discovered that the project analysis paid no attention to the affected environment or the trade-offs between freshwater and saltwater ecology. In addition, the analysis did not consider possible alternatives to dam removal like a spillway or revised fishing limits.

The project was supported by a $425,000 grant and had the backing of state and regional environmental organizations. Federally, the U.S. Fish and Wildlife Service wrote a letter of support for the project and the U.S. Army Corps of Engineers guided the wetlands permitting process. Despite the engagement of federal agencies, NEPA was not applicable because the Corps of Engineers delegates small permitting actions to the states. At the same time, state project planners took advantage of Maine's Permit by Rule program, which streamlines state approvals of wetland projects that "should not significantly affect the environment." As a consequence, public notice and involvement was bypassed at both federal and state levels, resulting in a fully streamlined process.

It all unraveled quickly when word of the grant award leaked out in a small weekly newspaper. What was efficient for the project planners looked underhanded to the local community, including town officials—a case of ends justifying the means.

Interestingly however, the pivotal factor was not the public controversy or the state's weak environmental analysis. The state probably would have fought and won eventual approval under Maine environmental law. Rather, it was a careless deed search on the property that brought the project to a halt. The state had overlooked our covenant on the pond, which protected the dam and the height of the water. A critical fact like this would have come to light quickly with public notice, as NEPA requires, and spared the useless expenditure of thousands of dollars and a mark against efficient government.

SIX AREAS FOR REFORM

Environmentally, the government wields enormous power by virtue of its procedural advantages, funding resources, and large professional pool of scientific, legal, and support staff. This power can manifest for better or worse. Oftentimes, the government is the public's strongest advocate for environmental protection, aggressively upholding environmental standards. But there are also times when the government will do whatever it can to control or circumvent environmental regulations that it thinks are an impediment to its own projects or favored private development.

Opposing Uncle Sam is never an easy task for communities and individuals. NEPA has been likened to a chess match with both sides knowing how to play the game. Over the years, however, the board has tilted more and more in favor of the federal government at the expense of local communities, quality of life, and the environment. The following six factors help to explain the government's increased mastery over NEPA, why we need to be concerned, and where reforms are needed.

The first factor is the growing size and complexity of NEPA studies. NEPA documentation has grown exponentially in response to improved science and methodology and a more astute public. Pressure also comes from agency lawyers who want to bulletproof the government's case. If any uncertainty exists in the environmental record, general counsel will automatically recommend more data and analysis. While more information is good, volume for its own sake is not. The trend in NEPA documentation is universally lamented because it adds significant time and cost and reduces the odds that readers can sift through the mountains of data to make any sense of it.

NEPA founders did not intend for this to happen. The CEQ regulations state, "The text of final environmental impact statements shall normally be less than 150 pages and proposals of unusual scope or complexity shall normally be less than 300 pages." Yet, it was not long before EISs were so big that they were being portrayed by their height and weight, not page numbers. The electronic age has rendered printing moot, but EISs continue to grow in volume and cost. Thus, when the CEQ added climate change to NEPA requirements in 2010, it felt compelled to issue a "rule of reason" to keep the analysis and documentation from getting out of hand.

To manage its burgeoning NEPA workload, the FAA Office of Airports employs about 75 full and part-time environmental specialists around the country. Department of Transportation records indicate that the average EA takes about 18 months to complete, while the average EIS requires four to six years. On the high end, the total EIS effort at Homestead took a whopping eight years to complete, with a price tag that reached into the millions.

Increasing EIS times and expense are making agencies more hesitant to commission them if there is a choice. The EPA reports that federal agencies completed about 1,000 EISs each year during the rollout of NEPA from 1970 to 1974. The next decade saw a dramatic decline of EISs into the 300 range annually. From 1987 through 2011, the yearly totals were consistently in the 200s. And in 2012, that barrier broke as the number fell to 198.

The corollary to size is growing complexity. For example, a few years ago, communities near airports could verify FAA environmental analysis by paying a nominal fee to acquire and run the agency's noise and air quality models. However, the FAA has spent the last decade integrating the models into a high-tech system, which was designed mainly for international noise and emission trade-off studies to help the U.S. and Boeing Corporation fend off European environmental regulators. Consequently, the only people left who can model airport noise and emissions are a few elite consulting firms. The issue also extends to FAA use of proprietary software for designing airspace and flight procedures. Not even the FAA has access to the source code to inspect the core logic. While these new systems provide more analytical horsepower, their use boils down to the fact that the public can no longer recreate or verify how the agency gets its numbers.

The government's desire to control workload leads to the second factor of concern: overzealous efforts to streamline the environmental process. Most NEPA practitioners would agree that more streamlining of the process is needed. But they also know that streamlining carries the potential for abuse and that NEPA already provides built-in mechanisms for easing the burden. For instance, most of the tens of thousands of environmental actions processed each year by the government are handled routinely and quickly as categorical exclusions and short EAs. Moreover, agencies are allowed to delegate some technical tasks to project sponsors, like the FAA does with airports and draft EA documentation.

Another sensible streamlining tool is called a "programmatic EIS." It begins with a set-up study of generic technology or project site considerations that are common to a whole group of planned projects. This study is then later cross-referenced on individual project applications. An illustration is the U.S. Department of Interior's 2012 programmatic EIS that established 17 solar energy zones in six western states. By having preapproved areas for solar development, the project-level documentation was significantly reduced. This is streamlining at its best—a common sense approach to eliminating redundancy.

But streamlining can go too far. For example, agencies might be tempted to stretch project descriptions to fit existing CATEXs or to delegate environmental duties more than they should. Another temptation might be to segment large projects into smaller pieces for the purpose of avoiding significant impacts and an EIS. While segmentation is strictly prohibited under NEPA, it is hard to substantiate because any project area or phase of construction with independent utility can be analyzed separately.

One of the most flagrant overreaches on streamlining was a new interstate highway that the Federal Highway Administration and state of Maryland built in 2011 called the Intercounty Connector (ICC). The six-lane east-west highway stretches 18 miles across Montgomery County, north of Washington D.C. and only a few miles from the home where Rachel Carson wrote *Silent Spring*.

The ICC was first planned in the 1950s and rejected repeatedly over the course of five decades because it would plow through established neighborhoods, consume precious open space, induce sprawl, and require 11 major bridges to traverse sensitive tributaries and watersheds of the Anacostia and Potomac Rivers that flow into the Chesapeake Bay. The extraordinary government measures used to overcome longstanding issues with the ICC illustrate how streamlining can sometimes be a code word for pernicious attempts to clear away environmental opposition.

A telltale sign of a bad project is a muddled EIS purpose and need statement. On transportation projects, a statement that confuses public transportation needs with prospective business development is a tip-off about project weakness. The opening words of the ICC purpose and need statement had just this problem:

> *"The proposed Intercounty Connector (ICC) project is intended to link existing and proposed development areas between the I-270 and I-95/US 1 corridors within central and eastern Montgomery County and northwestern Prince George's County..."*

Federal highway and state transportation planners did their best to downplay the commercial interests behind the project, led by well-known Washington real estate mogul Kingdon Gould III. Gould needed the ICC to realize his field of dreams, the new city of Konterra that is now under construction south of Laurel, Maryland, near Interstate 95.

The stumbling fortunes of the ICC turned around with the election of President George W. Bush and conservative leaders at the state and county levels. Seeking to neutralize the opposition, they engineered a pivotal piece of U.S. Department of Transportation legislation in 2003 that supplemented a 2002 Bush Executive Order for expediting big transportation projects stalled for environmental reasons. The streamlining act mandated greater deference to lead federal agencies, concurrent federal and state permitting, and strict adherence to project schedules. It also had a chilling effect on dissent within federal and state resource agencies.

Trying to avoid the appearance of an all-out assault on NEPA, the Bush Administration limited its initial round of fast-tracked projects to 13, including the ICC highway.

Rarely do politics infect the NEPA process as they did on the ICC. Besides the blatant use of special streamlining legislation to override public and scientific concerns, local government officials began limiting public debate too. An example of this was the Montgomery County ICC Citizens Advisory Committee, which was established to support the county planning department. For four years, the 10 appointed members of the committee met monthly with planning officials to discuss the project. Despite the committee's dedication and hard work, the first time a majority of the committee voiced opposition to various alignments for the highway, the committee was summarily disbanded.

Following Federal Highway Administration approval of the ICC EIS, the Audubon Naturalist Society brought a lawsuit against the project on the grounds of deficient air quality analysis. Despite its merit, the suit lost in large part because of the traditional deference that the courts give to the government on scientific matters. With that, the ICC was finally constructed.

A third worrisome factor about NEPA effectiveness is the diminishing quality of public involvement. While the government has to guard against delaying tactics, it must also be careful to give all sides and viewpoints ample opportunity to be heard. NEPA often stands for "Not Every Person Agrees" and that can be the key to more enlightened government decision-making in the public interest.

Public hearings are common at the start of an EIS and when the draft is complete. The government has learned the hard way about their risks. Some of the early public hearings featured open-mike formats that turned into shouting matches. At one controversial FAA public hearing in New Jersey, someone dressed as Bozo the

Clown showed up throwing clocks to express how some residents felt about the late night aircraft noise expected from the proposed rerouting of east coast traffic. At another memorable event, an FAA employee refused to provide enough chairs for an overflow crowd. The story hit the local newspaper, prompting a mea culpa by the FAA. The employee later explained, "NEPA says that you have to accommodate the public, but it doesn't say that you have to make them comfortable." To put matters to rest, the FAA Airports Office required its environmental staff to attend a special session in sensitivity training.

With the passage of time, federal agencies have learned to manage public events more tightly to control the message and reduce the risks. A popular technique today is the walk-around workshop where the public comes in and circulates around the room, stopping at various poster displays to talk with project staff one-on-one. The chance of unflattering press is minimized and people with concerns can only write them down and place them in a box. The event is personal and civilized but the big winner is the government, which has punched its NEPA ticket, gotten its message across, and avoided open criticism that might expose a feeble planning assumption or a flaw in the analysis.

The parallel to less meaningful public involvement are the growing hurdles to public opposition. Concerned citizens can sometimes succeed at the margin and shape elements of a project, or they can try to slow a study down in the hope that the project eventually gets canceled for some reason. Another strategy is to conduct an independent analysis that challenges agency assumptions. But barring these limited strategies, the only true recourse for stopping a project is litigation, which is the fourth factor of concern—the government's legal advantages. Litigants under NEPA have to prove that a federal agency has been "arbitrary and capricious" in failing to take the requisite hard look at environmental impacts. This burden of proof goes well beyond other legal standards like "clearly erroneous findings of fact" and is virtually impossible to prove.

The most effective legal strategy is built around procedural errors. Perhaps an agency is doing an EA that should be an EIS, or it has failed to address a relevant impact area altogether, such as environmental justice, climate change, or hazardous air pollutants. Without a procedural weakness to attack, challengers must find a scientific or technical weakness. This is a harder route because the courts, as noted, are highly deferential to the government. In a courtroom standoff of scientific experts, the court is obligated to favor government agencies in light of their jurisdiction and expertise. In addition, judges look at the *totality* and *reasonableness* of an agency study to determine its legal sufficiency and will not flyspeck the analysis. Thus, in order to win in court, litigants must prove more than imperfections in government work. They must show whole gaps or omissions.

The FAA happens to enjoy a legal rabbit in the hat that is unavailable to other agencies. Based on the FAA Aviation Act of 1958 and its amendments, the FAA can bypass the lower District Courts and petition the appellate Circuit Court system to hear cases involving orders by the FAA Administrator, including Records of Decisions for EISs. By extension, if the FAA suspects a pending lawsuit over a controversial EA, it can cleverly create an EA Record of Decision and tack it onto a regular EA finding so that the case goes straight to Circuit Court. This strategy has several advantages. In District Court, one judge presides and witness testimony is allowed. This adds time-consuming trial preparation and discovery, and exposes government witnesses to cross-examination that might uncover mistakes or inconsistencies in the government case. In Circuit Court, the case is restricted to the FAA-managed administrative record for the project. And questioning by the usual three-judge panel is limited to the lawyers for both sides, which for the government are always experienced environmental trial attorneys from the Department of Justice.

The fifth factor is technical in nature: NEPA's soft treatment of project baselines, which are the business-as-usual conditions that proposed projects are judged against. The relative silence of the law in this area has allowed federal agencies to use more favorable assumptions. Specifically, agencies are permitted to look beyond the present and into the future to contemplate two visions: one with the project and one without it, which is the baseline or in NEPA parlance, the "future no-build scenario." The math is simple—the more growth and pollution assumed in the baseline each year, the smaller the impact differential caused by the project. On the west coast, the state of California imposes a tougher standard. It defines the baseline as the present condition only—what actually *exists* here and now—and all future project years are evaluated against this one benchmark.

The ramifications of allowing the federal government to float the baseline cannot be underestimated. It lowers the estimated severity of environmental impacts and enables more incremental growth in the system for years to come. It is the main reason why the FAA has never lost a project due to air quality. All the FAA has to show is that without its new project horrible problems will arise with aircraft delay, airfield congestion, and passenger access, which directly translate into increased baseline emissions—game over.

The final factor working against the public on NEPA is the lack of government accountability on mitigation, which is often a late-breaking compromise in the NEPA process. The CEQ strongly encourages agency monitoring of mitigation measures, such as wetlands restoration, but it lacks the authority to insure that agencies keep their promises. Between lax oversight and the lack of budgeted resources for mitigation monitoring, few agencies stay on top of their long-term environmental commitments.

Mitigation enforcement will remain a weak link in NEPA until agency reporting and notification requirements are strengthened. A glaring example of inadequate public notice involves mitigated EAs, which enable agencies to modify projects to avoid significant impacts and EISs. Yet oddly, agencies are not required to clearly define the mitigation commitments they make for a mitigated EA. To the extent that these promises are ambiguous or hidden from view, agencies may do less than they should to follow through on their commitments.

The lack of accountability and transparency on mitigation is a long-standing issue. The CEQ has suggested several solutions to the problem such as making mitigation more measurable through new performance standards and by forcing agencies to declare which of their commitments are binding. The CEQ also advocates agency Environmental Management Systems, which are databases that track a wide range of energy and environmental information, including agency milestones on mitigation. While a step in the right direction, it remains to be seen whether the new systems will be effective and sustainable.

It is important for the public to understand the lack of clarity surrounding mitigation. It is hard to imagine how the government's written commitments on environmental measures, often technically or politically essential to project approval, can sometimes be little more than words on paper.

PUTTING IT IN PERSPECTIVE

Despite NEPA's slow weakening over time, the law remains vital to national environmental protection. It has become indispensable to the advancement of open government, environmental education, and comprehensive planning, all of which contribute to improved federal decision-making. In addition, it provides quality control to inhibit ideas and projects that cannot stand up to scrutiny. If an agency fails to kill a poorly conceived project internally, the NEPA process is right there to expose its shortcomings in public.

Perhaps the biggest testament to NEPA's value is the periodic backdoor attempts in Congress to bypass its requirements by proposing special legislation to exempt a project from NEPA. This was tried in 2015 by the oil industry and congressional supporters of the controversial Keystone XL tar sands pipeline project, a tactic that failed.

While NEPA never guarantees a green outcome, agencies definitely feel the procedural push of NEPA toward more balanced choices and greater investment in the environment. By having environmental consequences considered in the analytical mix along with economic, safety, engineering, and other factors, federal decisions rarely result in the worst alternative environmentally.

On the other hand, NEPA has been around for a half century and is showing signs of age. After decades of practice, federal agencies have learned how to manage NEPA to their maximum advantage. They have figured out how to navigate and compartmentalize the law to exploit its weaknesses and to obtain the projects they want, which may not necessarily be good for the environment.

Unless updated, NEPA will fail to provide the same level of environmental protection in the coming years as it has in the past. More agency accountability and transparency is needed and the technical and legal loopholes in the law need to be closed. However, making our environmental laws work is a delicate balancing act, and any major reforms to NEPA carry risk. Environmental laws are a favorite target of shortsighted politicians and businesspeople who ignore what our environmental laws have done for breathable air, clean water, and the protection of other natural resources that help sustain healthy economic growth. They peddle the myth that our environmental laws are too stringent, when the reality is that many of our environmental safeguards are weak and getting weaker.

The environmental community understands that some groups would like nothing more than to gut NEPA and other environmental mandates. Thus, attempting to reform NEPA through new legislation is precarious and could end up losing more ground than is gained. If NEPA is amended in the foreseeable future, it is likely to happen slowly and on a piecemeal basis, through executive actions within the friendlier confines of the EPA, CEQ, and other agencies.

CHAPTER V

COMPETING PUBLIC INTERESTS: QUIET PARKS VS. OPEN SKIES

⟨⟩

ECHOES OF THE CANYON

MANAGING AIRSPACE OVER NATIONAL PARKS changed forever on June 18, 1986. A mid-air collision of a de Havilland DHC-6 Twin Otter and a Bell 206 helicopter at the Grand Canyon killed all 25 people aboard the two sightseeing aircraft. The accident occurred below the rim of the Canyon in an era when park air tours were lightly regulated and 40 small companies flew hundreds of seasonal air tours at the Canyon, many along the same popular routes.

Following the accident, the FAA instituted special flight procedures at the Grand Canyon with traffic corridors, no-fly zones, and altitude restrictions to increase safety. The U.S. Congress also weighed in with the National Parks Overflights Act of 1987, instructing the National Park Service (NPS) to study the effects of park overflights on public safety and visitor enjoyment. The resulting NPS Report to Congress on the Effects of Aircraft Overflights on the National Park System took seven years to complete, but the scope and quality of the study justified the wait.

The Park Service dedicated most of the Report to Congress to noise management issues and how to make parks quieter. Aircraft noise had become a major problem at the Grand Canyon and it was spreading to other national parks where tourists were willing to pay for a bird's-eye view. But as the popularity of park air tours increased, so did noise complaints from park rangers and visitors on the ground. It didn't take long for matters to reach Washington and escalate into a full-fledged dispute over who represented the loftier public interest: the Park Service, defending the serenity of national parks, or the FAA, defending the freedom of the skies.

The 325-page Report to Congress broke new ground by prioritizing national parks with overflight problems, developing new noise assessment methods, and recommending the use of noise control strategies such as no-fly zones, curfews, and quiet aircraft incentives. The report also altered the political landscape, providing a catalyst for bold lobbying efforts by the Park Service to seize control of park airspace and noise standards from the FAA. Anything less, they contended, would prevent the agency from upholding the NPS Organic Act of 1916 and its decree to make parks enjoyable and leave them unimpaired for future generations.

The public often wonders why it takes the federal government so long to act. By setting ambitious goals for "natural quiet," the Park Service opened up a classic struggle for power between two federal agencies, each trying to guard its cherished principles and lines of authority. The process of sorting out the sensitive issues and formulating a balanced policy between park management and national airspace is still going on today.

THE CULTURAL DIVIDE

"So what's the solution?" asked Sam Jennings, who had called me to catch up and see how things were going at the FAA.

"Not sure yet," I said. "We're at an impasse."

"But you're only talking about air tours, right?"

I explained that air tours were the crux of the problem because they tend to fly lower and louder, creating more complaints from park visitors who expect tranquility and only the sounds of nature. But because noise is noise, the contribution of general aviation, passenger jets, and military training flights could not be ignored. Consequently, the problem had grown into a thicket of issues over protecting the entire national park system without undermining aviation as a whole.

"Most of the debate is inside the beltway," I said, "but public perceptions are important, and the Park Service has the clear edge."

Sam wasn't surprised, "Many of us enjoy the convenience of flying, but we love our national parks. And don't take this personally, but who is more likeable, the friendly park ranger escorting us on a nature walk or the faceless FAA, which can't stop the airlines from mangling our luggage?"

"I confess, we're helpless on luggage, and we have no illusions about losing the popularity contest with the Park Service and their Smokey the Bear ranger hats. We get it—fair or not—we're considered aloof and too chummy with the airlines."

"It seems like there should be an easy fix," Sam said.

It was a normal reaction, especially because aircraft noise is man-made, impermanent, and can always be adjusted or eliminated. And in the case of park noise, the offending levels are far below anything that might harm a person's hearing—the measure of impact is simply visitor annoyance. Moreover, park problems do not affect the whole country or even all national parks, just top tourist destinations like the Grand Canyon.

But standing in the way of compromise are deeper issues about quality of life. Everyone agrees that parks should be a place to get away, enjoy the peace and quiet, and experience nature. But just as beauty is in the eye of beholder, so is sound. Some people are undisturbed by low-level aircraft noise, while others perceive it as intrusive. These differences are mirrored in our institutions. The Park Service worries that concessions to the FAA would be condemned by the public and the environmental community as a violation of their sacred trust to preserve the parks. The fear at the FAA, which is amenable to restricting air tours—a tiny segment of the aviation industry—is that the restrictions will spill over into other areas of aviation.

Complicating matters is the large cultural divide separating the two agencies. The arguments put forward by the NPS are part philosophical, which tends to puzzle and exasperate the engineering-minded FAA. For example, the NPS insists that because every national park is unique, every park superintendent should be in charge of determining how much noise is too much for his or her park. At the FAA, the thought of delegating airspace management to hundreds of park fiefdoms is untenable. If you are going to clip the wings of aviation, it has to be done objectively and consistently across the board. In addition, the FAA is fearful of the legal consequences. If national park superintendents are granted the right to restrict overflights, how can the government deny the same privilege to other national properties, state and local parks, or the outdoor recreation industry?

"So what's next?" Sam asked.

"Right now, we're planning another round of field studies. Everyone agrees more research is needed, even if we don't know where it's headed exactly."

"Enjoy the work," Sam said, after we finished catching up on other news.

ACOUSTICS AND ANALYSIS

Most people assume that noise impacts from aircraft and other transportation sources are regulated by the EPA. But that authority belongs to the Departments of Defense and Transportation and its member services and agencies. Inside the FAA, noise policy and research are housed in the Office of [Aviation] Environment and Energy (AEE), including park overflight issues and relations with the NPS.

FAA research on park overflight noise fell to my branch in AEE, which developed the agency's airport and airspace noise models and was the designated nerd squad for in-house analysis. Our first park assignments in the early 1990s focused on the Grand Canyon. We evaluated alternatives for reducing noise on Dragon Corridor, a north-south flight zone in the eastern quadrant of the park. We also rated the certified noise levels of operating tour aircraft and how to use possible noise limits and fees at the Canyon to stimulate the acquisition of quieter technology.

Our work on the Grand Canyon climaxed in December 1996, two years after the NPS Report to Congress. Earlier in the year, the president had issued a memorandum directing the FAA to implement proposed noise regulations for the Grand Canyon before the year was over. However, FAA management had gotten bogged down, forcing us to scramble with only a few weeks to go on the calendar. Three actions were needed immediately: one addressing long overdue reporting requirements on air tour activity, one modifying flight paths, and one incentivizing quiet aircraft. FAA staff is rarely summoned to sacrifice evenings, weekends, and holiday leave, but there was no other choice—we had 10 days to do what would normally take a year or more for each action.

The AEE director quickly set up three task forces and asked me to manage one of them, an EA for quiet technology called Noise Limitations for Aircraft Operations in the Vicinity of the Grand Canyon National Park. As I began to assemble a 12-person team from AEE, Air Traffic, and contract organizations, the director pulled me aside and said, "What do you need to get the job done? I'll do everything I can." It took a few seconds for the offer to register, and then it came to me. Our legal staff was stretched thin and we needed somebody to roll up their sleeves full-time. Within days, an attorney from the Federal Highway Administration was on detail to us. Our group worked feverishly to meet the deadline and produce a complex 100-page analysis of quiet aircraft alternatives. During this time, no one ever complained about the extra hours without pay or the monotonous nightly diet of pizza and soda. It was public service at its best.

As the dust settled, the take-home message for the agency was clear—park issues were going to require more resources and better internal coordination. Immediately, senior management set up weekly meetings to manage park issues across the big FAA offices of Air Traffic, Airports, and Flight Standards and the smaller head-quarter support offices of AEE, General Counsel, Government and Industry Affairs, and Public Affairs. The meetings lasted for more than three years, while our hard-earned regulatory actions for the Grand Canyon were bottled up by industry lawsuits and our conflicts with the Park Service metastasized to other national parks, including Rocky Mountain in Colorado and Grand Teton in Wyoming.

As contentious as the Grand Canyon was, noise issues else-where were even harder to resolve. The reason stemmed from the National Parks Overflights Act of 1987, which limited the NPS mandate to "substantially restore natural quiet" to the Grand Canyon. Thus, the NPS standard devised for the Grand Canyon—no aircraft noise over 50 percent of the park, 75 per-cent of the day—only applied there. Every other park remained case-by-case.

With no universal standard and more and more parks register-ing visitor complaints about overflight noise, the FAA and NPS agreed in 1997 to pursue a joint national rule that would establish a framework of noise policies and procedures that park manag-ers, tour operators, and nearby communities could use to negotiate air tour limits at national parks. Yet to realize the vision for the national rule, a number of underlying scientific issues had to be resolved, including the best way to measure ambient sound and how to define park noise impacts. Settling these issues, both agen-cies agreed, would entail more research.

To jumpstart the effort, the FAA drafted a Noise Research Plan in early 1998 and sent a few of us to Denver to discuss it with the Park Service. The meeting went well, resulting in specific IOUs for both agencies, including the development of new guidance on ambient sound monitoring and noise zoning of parks. In addition, the FAA agreed to conduct more visitor field studies, which the NPS had been pressuring the FAA to do for many years to supplement NPS's earlier ones.

Visitor field studies for noise are expensive and pose numerous logistical challenges, starting with the location of good test sites that have a steady convergence of aircraft overflights and park visitors. Collecting the "dose-response" data at these sites is labor-intensive, involving two teams of personnel. One team, dedicated to noise monitoring, is hidden from view and uses interactive software to record natural and human sounds, including wind, wildlife, cars, voices, footsteps, and aircraft. Simultaneously, a survey team is strategically stationed at the end of a trail or on an overlook, where visitors are asked if they heard aircraft noise, and if so, whether it was annoying.

When the data are processed back in the lab, technicians merge both sets of time-stamped data to compare the amount of aircraft noise that each visitor received (dose) with his or her level of annoyance (response). The dose is evaluated using more than a dozen metrics that capture the number and loudness of aircraft events, the amount of noise exposure over selected intervals, and the amount of time that aircraft are heard. The ultimate aim is to find the best noise metric for predicting visitor annoyance. With that information, it becomes a straight shot to the creation of noise standards.

The FAA conducted its first dose-response study at Bryce Canyon National Park in the summer of 1997, prior to the research meeting in Denver. Over a 10-day stretch, our 10-person team collected 900 visitor interviews on the Queens Garden Trail, considered a typical short hike. The next summer, we turned our attention to five visitor overlook sites at Grand Canyon and Bryce Canyon—a two-week effort that yielded another 700 visitor surveys.

Having sufficient data on these front country conditions, both agencies now wanted to test the hypothesis that backcountry hikers and overnighters were the most noise-sensitive. With that purpose in mind, I arrived at the Grand Canyon in November 1998 with a colleague from the Volpe National Transportation Systems Center in Cambridge, a research organization that provided noise measurement and modeling support to my office. Our mission was to scope the Hermits Rest Trail for suitability as a backcountry test site. November was well past the ideal time to be hiking the Canyon at an elevation of 7,000 feet, with sub-freezing temperatures and snow on the ground. The NPS had tried to discourage the late expedition, but we felt compelled to squeeze it in to make our tight schedule for the spring roll-out of the study.

The trailhead for Hermits Rest is at the terminus of the West Rim Drive about 10 miles west of Grand Canyon Village. We had trouble finding the trail in the snow but eventually located the markers. At 1,000 feet down, the snow had melted, but it took us the entire day to negotiate nine miles of switchbacks and the last mile of descent to the Colorado River. Our knees ached from the strain of carrying 60-pound backpacks filled with camping supplies and noise monitoring equipment. After a cold night in a pup tent, we completed our work in the morning and ascended the Canyon.

The scoping trip confirmed our suspicions—a backcountry dose-response study was going to be virtually impossible. Besides the small number of estimated hikers, we found more branching of the trail than expected, a major hurdle to pinpointing the location of hikers and their noise exposure. Coupled with the challenges of canyon wall echoes, we concluded that this site, and perhaps any backcountry site, was unsuited for the rigors of dose-response testing.

Despite the disappointment at Hermits Rest, the survey research program represented a bright spot in FAA and NPS relations. It led to several improvements in park noise assessment and a compromise on a definition for ambient sound. Initially, the FAA preferred the "existing ambient," a data set consisting of all background sounds, including human voices, footsteps, and vehicle traffic. The NPS preferred the "natural ambient," a quieter data set stripped of all human and mechanical noise. Over time, the FAA came around to the NPS approach as a way of supporting NPS natural quiet goals. But the FAA still took exception in parks where noisy human activities were permitted, such as snowmobiling in Yellowstone National Park or boating at Biscayne Bay National Park in Florida. It was not fair, the FAA maintained, if aviation was held to a higher standard than louder park-approved activities.

While natural sounds are largely masked in urban areas, the natural ambient is a dominant feature of low-level sound environments like parks. In order to understand how dominant, it helps to know the common decibel (dB) sound pressure scale weighted to human hearing. The scale ranges from zero, the quietest level our ears can detect, to 120 dB, a highly painful level. Normal breathing is about 10 dB, while soft whispers are 20 dB. In parks, the data indicate that natural sound levels and aircraft noise from higher altitude flights generally fall in the range of 25 dB to 30 dB. The everyday equivalent would be a quiet library or a bedroom at night. Higher up the scale, the hum of a refrigerator is approximately 40 dB, normal speech is between 60 and 65 dB at 3 feet, and a vacuum cleaner is about 70 dB at 10 feet. Still higher, a gas lawn mower is 90 to 100 dB at 3 feet, while a rock band might play at 110 dB.

Ambient sound levels provide the baseline for park noise evaluations. If this analytical floor is lowered, then more aircraft noise is computed above it, which translates into greater impacts. Despite the FAA concession to use all-natural levels that subtracted out human noise, the NPS maneuvered for even lower baseline levels through the use of special metrics. One proposed metric was a statistical cut of existing ambient data at the *quietest* 10 percent line, inversely called the $L_{90.}$ The metric was originally developed for urban environments to estimate the contribution of wind and other natural sounds. But because of its scientific coarseness and irrelevance to parks, the FAA refused to use it.

For its part, the Park Service rejected its share of FAA noise methodology too. Since the 1970s, the FAA's primary noise metric has been the Day-Night Average Sound Level (DNL). DNL represents an amalgam of factors related to annual aircraft operations—number, duration, and loudness—that are condensed into an average day of noise exposure. It is particularly well suited to the metropolitan airport environment because it levies a hefty noise penalty on aircraft operations at night, when sound carries and people are sleeping.

But while DNL makes sense for airports and community land use planning, the metric is a poor fit for parks. One reason is that it generates an average, not what people actually hear. The FAA often tries to compensate for this by using supplemental metrics to identify the loudest flights and times of the day. Another DNL drawback for parks is that the 65 dB level of significance for airport noise impacts, a threshold that corresponds with speech interference, makes little sense in quiet park settings.

DNL results are generally depicted using contour lines, which are overlaid onto residential street maps to identify affected homes and neighborhoods. Noise contours follow runway geometry, bulging or contracting in response to runway activity, aircraft types, and departure flows, which are typically louder than arrivals. Contour accuracy is critical because the FAA spends approximately $300 million a year soundproofing homes within 65 DNL contours and acquiring and disposing of homes in more severely affected 70 and 75 contour ranges. While thousands of homes remain eligible for mitigation, airport noise contours have shrunk dramatically over the past 50 years due to quieter aircraft engine technology.

But noise contouring is also ill-suited to parks. Lower aircraft activity over a large area causes contours to balloon artificially because the plotting software lacks sufficient data points. For parks and other regional analyses, a standard x-y coordinate system is the preferred alternative. Noise values are computed at each grid point, typically spaced one or two miles apart in park studies. These values can then be color-coded to produce regional maps that have a familiar appearance to contours, but without the implied accuracy of a contour line.

The most appropriate noise measure for parks, according to the Park Service, is the amount of time that aircraft can be heard. Seeking greater precision in this regard, the NPS designed a sophisticated new metric in the 1990s called "time audible" or audibility for short. Audibility distinguishes the noise source, in this case aircraft, from ambient sounds by their respective frequencies or tones, as opposed to pressure-related decibel levels. Audibility originated with signal detection theory used by the Navy in anti-submarine warfare, and when applied to parks, assumes that all visitors are actively listening for aircraft.

Audibility is comparable to the octaves on a piano keyboard. It analyzes 24 bands in the sound spectrum from a low frequency band centered on 31 Hertz to a high frequency band centered on 8,000 Hertz. Using these bands, the NPS asserted that any detectable or audible aircraft sound represented a potential park impact. It was a powerful assumption when coupled with a highly sensitive metric that started counting if any one of the 24 frequency levels was higher for aircraft than the ambient.

While detecting audible sounds is a simple matter for the human ear, it is extremely difficult to mathematize. How we hear airborne sounds is subject to complex atmospheric physics, weather conditions, aircraft orientation, local terrain and vegetation, and the state of the listener. Given the unproven accuracy of audibility and its greater cost of data collection and interpretation, the FAA preferred the standard method of measuring average 3 dB changes in the sound environment, a delta that acousticians consider barely perceptible. Moreover, the FAA wanted to put more of the focus on visitor and wildlife behavioral effects, all of which the research suggested were at levels well above the quiet depths of audibility.

RANGER TALK

It had been a while since Denver, the last time Everett Williamson and I had spoken together personally. He had spent many years as a park ranger in the field before moving to Washington D.C.

to become the NPS noise policy expert and manager of the 1994 Report to Congress. Friendly, easily approachable, and passionate about wilderness, no one loved his job more than Williamson, which was readily apparent by how often he wore his olive green uniform and ranger hat to meetings.

A list of concerns, audibility atop them, prompted me to seek out Williamson in early 1999. As I walked up the Mall toward the Washington Monument and the Department of Interior, I thought about where we might find common ground on noise methodology.

"I'm glad you came by," Williamson said. "There's a lot going on and the research doesn't get enough attention."

"It's interesting," I responded. "We've both had a string of office directors and special assistants who thought their glowing personalities would solve everything. Their charm offensives set a good tone, but charm doesn't fix technical issues."

"Are you implying that I'm not charming?" Williamson smiled. "So, where should we start?"

"I wanted to tell you about our visitor survey results—they're textbook," I said, reporting that the two noise curves for short hikes and overlooks were virtually identical in shape, illustrating the consistent relationship between more aircraft noise and more annoyance. The findings also confirmed that visitors on short hikes were about 15 to 20 percent more sensitive than visitors at park overlooks with their busier traffic scenes. Also, we had identified the best predictor of annoyance: as it turned out, a combination of two metrics, one for sound level and one for time. "This is exactly what we've been waiting for," I said to Williamson. "Let's suppose we drew a line on the curves at 10 percent visitor annoyance—say that's our policy. Then the limit would be crossed at overlooks when aircraft noise exceeds the ambient by 8 dB, or 30 percent of the time. The limit would be proportionately tougher for short hikes, and tougher again for backcountry."

Choosing his words carefully, Williamson said, "Well, let me say this. We wanted these studies and we thought they'd be useful, but we're having second thoughts. In many ways, visitors aren't the best judge of how to protect the parks. Our job is to provide the best experience possible, whether it's daytime visitors or wilderness groups—both carry expectations for solitude. Besides that, we don't think the visitor surveys address all of the issues, including protection of viewscapes and wildlife."

I was stunned. "Everett, we've come so far, and we know that humans react before wildlife—our pressure point is merely annoyance. If we don't use the data, we're going to end up in a qualitative morass."

"It wouldn't be qualitative to use audibility, which we believe is the best way to protect natural quiet," Williamson said.

"Except that detection is far below the known effects," I said. "That's why we did the dose-response studies. Besides, it's a stretch to call something as quiet as breathing an impact or to suggest that the whisper of a 737 at 37,000 feet is worse than an ear-piercing military flyover because it lasts longer?"

"However, it does serve to sensitize people," Williamson responded. "We understand it's not perfect—like any other metric. I guess it comes around again to our differences over averages and minimums. The FAA needs to understand that we manage to goals, not averages. Our parks wouldn't be pristine otherwise. Say you were crossing a fast-moving river that you knew was three feet deep on average, you'd drown crossing it. In the same way, if you're at a park for a few days in the peak summer months, and it's loud because of aircraft, it's little comfort to know that the park is quiet *on average*."

I acknowledged the importance of seasonal differences and that parks are unique in many ways. On the other hand, the research was showing that many park conditions are similar and disposed to averages. We had found remarkable consistency in visitor responses across different parks, different studies, and different years.

"Have you ever read Edward Abbey?" Williamson asked. "He was a seasonal NPS employee in his early career and a wilderness advocate, some say anarchist. One of his best books was *Desert Solitaire*." Williamson got up from his chair and went to his bookcase, pulled out a book, and flipped to a marked page. "Let me read you a paragraph of his."

> *"A civilization which destroys what little remains of the wild, the spare, the original, is cutting itself off from its origins and betraying the principle of civilization itself. If industrial man continues to multiply its numbers and expand his operations he will succeed in his apparent intention, to seal himself off from the natural and isolate himself within a synthetic prison of his own making. He will make himself an exile from the earth."*

"That's the big picture for me, but don't get me wrong," Williamson said. "We're willing to compromise. But there's only so much I can do. Likewise, I know you've got to deal with the flying interests at FAA."

"We're trying to meet you more than half way, but the hang-up is audibility," I said, volunteering more new findings. These findings showed that Time Above, the standard metric that uses average aircraft and ambient sound levels to estimate the time that aircraft are heard, predicted visitor annoyance better than audibility. This made it particularly hard for the FAA to understand why it would want to pay for development and use of audibility.

"That's why we're building our own audibility model," Williamson replied.

"In my opinion, we're wasting a lot of time on noise metrics. Audibility is great in theory but extremely hard to apply. We should be spending our time looking at park land use and how visitor data fit into it."

Williamson and I spent a few moments discussing the concept of "acoustic zoning." Overlooks and roadways, the loudest park areas with more people and vehicles, would carry the fewest flight restrictions. Short-hike trails, campgrounds, and some backcountry areas would have moderate restrictions. And the most sensitive backcountry and wildlife areas would be the most restricted, with possible no-fly zones. Zoning for each park would be unique, providing park superintendents with the flexibility to protect their prized natural and cultural assets. It would also establish a formal basis for park participation in airspace management while eliminating the quagmire of noise metrics.

I suggested to Williamson that we could do acoustic zoning now at the Grand Canyon, an idea that piqued his interest. All it would take, I said, is an easy adjustment to the average ambient sound levels in different areas. The byproduct would be two acoustic zones, one across most of the park and a more sensitive one predicated on approved park management plans and vegetation characteristics.

"You'd be willing to do that?" Williamson said, disbelievingly.

"That's what I'm saying. And it'll have the desired effect of keeping aircraft away from the areas you really want to protect."

"It might work for the Canyon, but I can't promise elsewhere," Williamson said.

"I understand. We'd just be showing that zoning could be win-win. And elsewhere for us would require your development of national guidelines. There'd have to be consistency in how parks manage acoustic zoning. But we'd show the benefits—you'd get flexibility and we'd get a system that works with conventional metrics."

"Good talking with you," Williamson said as he pushed his chair back. "I'm late to my next meeting, but let's talk some more."

THE PLAN UNRAVELS

After years of research and development, the outline of an agreement on noise standards appeared to be emerging. Ideally, its general principles would be ratified in a joint national rule. Yet even without the rule, the FAA could move ahead and implement new standards based on what it had learned and the expectation that both agencies would view the changes as constructive.

On the verge of taking our research public—and tantalizingly close to the development of national park policy—the program came to an abrupt halt. In the winter of 1999, the White House launched a Reinventing Government Initiative championed by Al Gore, who claimed that the new government-wide program would save taxpayers $137 billion in reduced waste. The biggest thrust was the elimination of branches, the ground-floor of management. As a result, the smallest management unit would be divisional, with a minimum ratio of one manager to 10 staff.

The reforms hit the FAA like a meat cleaver and the White House seemed unperturbed by the collateral damage. For years, it had been an uphill battle inside the FAA to convince management of the need for park noise research. We had conducted the program quietly, hoping to see if it bore fruit. Now, just when it did, the program fell victim to a reorganization that wiped out the unit that ran the program, had the knowledge to recommend well-balanced policy, and could stand up to critics inside and outside of the agency.

"How ironic," I thought, "that it was Al Gore's program," recalling an earlier time in 1992 when I had complimented Gore's new book, *Earth in the Balance.* "It's remarkable," I had said at a staff meeting, "that a vice president was an expert on the environment." A senior manager at the meeting, who saw climate change and the book as a threat to aviation, remarked "You're reading that crap?" His tart reply got a good laugh around the room and I learned another embarrassing lesson about openness in the bureaucracy.

After losing my branch and management role, I left AEE for the FAA Airports Office to become a special assistant on the environment. Although my new duties were less technical, there was no shortage of park issues in Airports, including the ongoing EIS noise analysis for Homestead Air Force Base. In addition, the AEE director, a strong park research advocate, resigned soon after, compounding the loss of institutional interest and memory. The noise research program began to disintegrate. Indeed, it would take AEE until 2005 to publish the final report for the 1998 field research at overlooks.

Meanwhile, the Park Service, which seemed less affected organizationally, quickly took advantage of the vacuum at the FAA. Within a matter of months, the Park Service had released sweeping new noise guidance, maneuvered to gain FAA acceptance of audibility, and successfully lobbied the Hill on new legislation to help it seize airspace control.

In the first instance of guidance, the NPS issued a strategic directive in 2000, called Director's Order #47 on Soundscape Preservation and Noise Management. The order constituted a bold power grab. It granted park superintendents virtually unlimited authority to make agency noise decisions, proclaiming their "special expertise and jurisdiction ... to determine the nature, extent, and acceptability of impacts on park resources and visitors" as well as the "significance of noise level or impacts" under NEPA. On methodology, the order instructed park superintendents to consider all aircraft noise, not just air tours, and to use qualitative methods, not just quantitative ones, including the controversial L_{90} statistic for ambient data.

Despite its hardening stand, the Park Service continued to cooperate selectively. In the fall of 1999, for example, the NPS was anxious to run an audibility validation study with the FAA and U.S. Air Force. The NPS was confident that its model for predicting audibility was more accurate than either the FAA or Air Force noise models. The final validation report was issued in 2003, but the agencies knew the results well before then. The extensive data from field testing showed that all three models were poor predictors of audibility. However, endeavoring to put a positive spin on the findings, the agencies agreed to say that the models performed "equally well" on a comparative basis.

AEE feared that the validation results could lead to endless debate with the Park Service. What if the NPS challenged every FAA park study with its own independent analysis? Worse yet, what if there was a spill-over effect on all FAA noise modeling? Would it invite new legal challenges at airports? AEE felt compelled to act.

Sidestepping coordination with the Airports Office and Air Traffic, AEE convened a meeting with the NPS in the FAA Administrator's 10th floor conference room, dubbed the Round Room, to consummate a grand bargain: AEE would incorporate audibility into the next public version of the FAA airport noise model if the NPS shut down its model development. The deal enabled the NPS to declare victory on audibility, the FAA to get past the validation study, and both agencies to conserve financial resources.

Perhaps the most striking postscript to the Reinventing Government Initiative was passage by Congress of the National Parks Air Tour Management Act of 2000, a reconstituted vision of the abandoned joint national rule. The Act called for the creation of Air Tour Management Plans (ATMPs) to facilitate a systematic and scientific approach to restricting air tours and the new licensing of start-up companies. For the next decade, this joint NPS and FAA program would consume the lion's share of growing federal resources devoted to park noise issues.

The NPS claimed that 110 national park units needed ATMP studies to help manage existing or future air tour problems. Yet, in 2005, four years into the new program, no management plans had been completed and the FAA had burned through $20 million in planning and data collection at roughly 15 parks. Budgeting for the program was supposed to be shared equally but the NPS constantly pleaded poverty. Even after both agencies signed an interagency agreement in 2004 establishing a 60-40 split, the NPS reneged on its 40 percent commitment. The FAA found the funding imbalance even more irksome because the NPS reaped the only tangible benefit from the program—an expanding cache of ambient data that would help the Park Service track long-term changes to park soundscapes. Still, the FAA plodded ahead, unwilling to throw in the towel.

In 2006, the needs assessment for the program was revised downward to 93 national park units involving 99 air tour operators. However, it did not bode well when the FAA announced that its annual goal for 2006 was to complete just *one* ATMP. The lack of production was blamed largely on program architecture. In a rather unique step, Congress had granted "joint agency authority" over ATMP studies and associated NEPA documentation. But putting both agencies on equal footing, with no incentive to compromise, was comparable to putting two scorpions in a bottle.

The downhill slide continued for the next eight years, until the FAA finally refused to pump more resources into ATMPs, each of which carried an estimated price tag of half a million dollars. It was astonishing that the FAA had not pulled the plug on the ATMP program sooner. In the end, the agency had paid out $32 million dollars for the program, with little to show except scoping trips, work plans, public and tribal meetings, and ambient data. In comparison, the former research program had been conducted for under $1 million dollars and produced two large dose-response studies, national ambient measurement guidance, improved assessment tools, and a detailed plan to convert these building blocks into national policy.

Lessons learned from the park noise research experience are not black and white. But it is clear that the ATMP program, an outgrowth of government restructuring, failed to fulfill its goals for air tour management and the development of national park noise standards. It was a poorly conceived program from the start and clearly needed more congressional and agency oversight. As a result, Congress and the two agencies wasted millions of taxpayer dollars and set park noise policy back more than a decade.

THE AIRPORTS OFFICE FLIES DIRECT

During the ATMP era, the FAA Airports Office was finding it increasingly difficult to complete its environmental requirements at airports in the vicinity of national parks. At every turn, no matter how small the airport or project, the NPS was demanding more park noise analysis that jeopardized our timelines and budgets.

Unable to wait any longer, the Airports Office arranged a meeting with AEE in April 2003 to discuss the need for agency park guidance. The Associate Administrator for Airports began the meeting by citing current airport studies involving parks: St. George near Zion National Park in Utah; Mesquite near Lake Mead National Recreation Area in Nevada and Arizona; Flagstaff near Grand Canyon National Park in Arizona; Cal Black near Glen Canyon National Recreation Area in Utah; and Taos near the Taos Pueblo in New Mexico. She complained that the Park Service was applying pressure on our regional offices to adopt experimental ATMP procedures, despite the fact that ATMP legislation did not apply to airports. NPS demands included the use of audibility and study areas that extended a half mile outside of park boundaries. She declared that whatever the NPS and AEE agreement on modeling and audibility had been, the Airports Office would not be bullied into using a metric that no one could say worked correctly.

As the agency's lead environmental office, AEE listened politely and assured us that they were doing everything possible. It was a constructive dialogue but the meeting simply confirmed what we suspected—AEE was bogged down with the Grand Canyon and

ATMP issues and unable to devote attention to our problems. We would simply have to make do.

The first opportunity to create our own park guidance for airports came at Pulliam Airport in Flagstaff, Arizona, on a small runway extension project. Until now, a highly controversial aspect of every park-related study was how big to make the study area. At Flagstaff, we devised a method that worked so well it became standard practice. The method took the slowest jet aircraft operating at the airport and calculated its ground distance at the point it reached a cruise altitude of 10,000 feet, a transitional level in air traffic control. In Flagstaff's case, the technique produced a 25-mile radius and circumference around the airport, encompassing two park properties, Walnut Canyon and Sunset Crater Volcano National Monuments, located 8 miles and 17 miles from the airport, respectively. In addition to these parks, we honored a Park Service request to evaluate the Grand Canyon, 55 miles away, on the theory that any new operations over the Canyon, even at high altitude, might be "the straw that breaks the camel's back" on restoring natural quiet. In the end, the noise analysis showed that the airport's 20 scheduled flights a day, including a few new regional jets, would have negligible impact on all of the parks.

Although we refused to use audibility at Flagstaff, it was not long before the Airports Office succumbed to the pressure. In 2006, the St. George airport project in southwestern Utah became a major park battleground, second only to the Grand Canyon and Homestead. The city needed to replace its unsafe, antiquated airfield situated on a hillside plateau overlooking the city. The chosen site for the new airport was a few miles southeast of town at an abandoned military airstrip in the desert, which the local kids used for drag racing. The NPS was concerned about the potential noise effects of the new airport on Zion National Park, located 26 miles to the northeast.

The headquarters of the Airport Office led the study and used everything in its analytical arsenal, including field measurements, acoustic zoning, seasonal effects, and a complete accounting of Zion overflights, including commercial, military, general aviation, and air tour operations. Despite the monumental effort, the NPS demanded that we also use audibility, which led to a protracted fight inside the FAA. The Airports Office argued that using the experimental metric would cost $240,000 to implement and set a binding precedent, while General Counsel and AEE, which had long since given up, argued that refusing to use audibility would invite legal challenge. The dominos fell when the Airports regional director for the study sided with the majority.

Immediately, our scientific doubts about audibility were confirmed as the calculations went haywire. The analysis of all overflights showed that audibility exceeded 1,440 minutes or 24 hours a day over the entire park. At some park locations, the over-prediction reached as high as 300 to 400 percent. In other words, the audibility analysis was saying that, if the new airport was built, park visitors would hear aircraft noise 70 to 80 hours a day!

When we told the NPS about the results, they insisted that we cap the daily findings at 100 percent and not report the actual minutes computed by the model, which had buckled under the complex mechanics of audibility and overlapping aircraft events. Feeling vindicated, we denied the request for reasons of public disclosure.

The use of audibility also delivered an amazing twist. Every conventional metric for noise exposure, loudness, and time showed that flights to and from the proposed St. George airport would cause more noise over Zion. But to our surprise, audibility predicted just the opposite. Having never implemented the metric before, it took us awhile to unravel the mystery. As it turned out, audibility was not only hypersensitive to the long crossing times of high-altitude overflights, but to local operations. Because larger and faster aircraft were scheduled to operate at St. George, it meant fewer operations over Zion than before and less crossing time per flight—therefore less audibility.

We could not believe our damn luck. It was the ultimate irony. Audibility alone was showing that the new airport would make Zion National Park quieter! Not willing to look a gift horse in the mouth, we reported in the EIS that audibility was the preferred metric of the Park Service and that our audibility findings supported the project without the need for mitigation.

The NPS fumed and set out to build a statistical quick fix for audibility. Meanwhile, the Airports Office decided it was high time to develop its own parks guidance for airport projects.

CAL BLACK

Audrey Johnson, my boss, called me into her office to discuss our park guidance. Johnson was a long-time FAA employee who started her career in the Air Traffic organization, known for its blue-collar culture and Type A personalities. She had not been a controller but she was quick and to the point, and knew the air traffic business from years of planning and designing airspace. She had no trouble making the jump to Airports and assuming leadership of the environmental division. Well-respected around the agency, Johnson had good instincts and interpersonal skills, key ingredients to effectiveness.

"Congratulations! Management signed our guidance this morning," Audrey said. "The process took some time, but now the regions know what to do and what not to do, and NPS won't be hearing 10 different stories from us."

"It would've taken a lot longer," I said, "if Las Vegas and Clark County hadn't complained."

"I can't blame them," Audrey said. "If you were Clark County, you'd be crazy to risk a new billion dollar airport project with draft guidance. Once they discovered the holdup was upstairs with AEE concurrence, they broke the logjam fast. I suspect AEE thought our guidance might ruffle Park Service feathers."

"But it offers NPS earlier consultation and more of it. What's there not to like?"

"Well, I can think of a few things," Audrey said, "including our footnotes on ATMPs and audibility."

"By the way, even those might not be enough," I said, "because NPS is rumored to have another new metric in the works."

"I'll tell you," Audrey said. "I'm losing patience with their thinly-veiled obstructionism. Which reminds me, what's the latest on Cal Black?"

"I think we're going to have to go out to Utah to take the pressure off the region. NPS is leaning on them for a lot more work."

Trying to finish the EIS for Cal Black Memorial Airport, located near Glen Canyon National Recreation Area in Utah, was a sore point with Johnson and her patience had worn thin. It had been years since the Sierra Club, National Parks and Conservation Association, and Southern Utah Wilderness Alliance had successfully filed suit against the FAA for inadequate noise analysis. The Park Service supported the plaintiffs, despite wanting the new airport in order to close the old one inside the park. In an unusual decision, the court held in 1993 that the new airport could be opened immediately, while at the same time instructing the FAA to do more noise analysis to complete the administrative record.

"This is the strangest NEPA case I've ever seen," Audrey said. "And no one cares about it anymore because the airport is operating. I wouldn't either, except people wouldn't be happy if they knew we were still spending money on it."

"We've just got to remember," I said, "in all these years, the park hasn't received a single noise complaint about the airport. So, we *know* that aircraft noise isn't a problem. Number two, Lake Powell is a popular place for boating and that can be loud."

"The real kicker," Audrey added, "is that Cal Black has only *four* operations a day, and two of these operations are NPS aircraft. Excuse my French, but goddammit, if the NPS wants less noise at Cal Black, let's bar their flights!"

"The region is going slow to avoid another lawsuit," I said.

"Maybe we can't stop the Park Service from encouraging the environmental groups to sue us again," Audrey said. "But in my opinion, it's all bluff this time given the facts: a tiny airport that's been operating without a problem for decades. This is not Chicago O'Hare. Why the NPS continues to fight this one is beyond me."

⌣⟶

ANALYTICAL INTEGRITY

After our experience at St. George, we tried to avoid further use of audibility. We succeeded on small actions, including a runway extension project at Mammoth Yosemite Airport in California that was found to have no impact on Yosemite, Sequoia, and Kings Canyon National Parks located 25 or more miles away. However, we were not as fortunate on two proposed replacement airports, one for Mesquite, Nevada, and one for Sun Valley, Idaho.

At Mesquite, our audibility analysis showed weirdly similar effects to St. George. In addition to all-encompassing overpredictions, locating the new airport 10 miles closer to Lake Mead National Recreation Area would effectively *reduce* aircraft noise at the park. We found the same thing at Sun Valley, Idaho, and Craters of the Moon National Monument. With astonishing results like this, our office was beginning to rethink its opposition to audibility. The Park Service's beloved noise metric was making a convincing case for the use of larger aircraft and moving airports closer to parks. By embracing audibility, we might never lose a new airport project again.

In trying to diagnose the mechanics of audibility, we approached AEE and requested a quick model run using a single aircraft. AEE hand delivered the numbers to us, typed on a blank piece of paper. We were incredulous. The complex frequency algorithms for audibility were literally ignoring the ambient data and using a constant baseline of zero decibels, adding another source of error to resolve.

The NPS had peddled audibility theory for many years and knew that policy development is sometimes driven by advances in modeling and analysis capabilities. But now we were seeing actual data and the signs in every direction pointed to a metric that was not ready for prime time. With FAA scientific integrity at stake, straight talk was needed. The first opportunity came in 2008 at a jointly sponsored FAA and NPS noise criteria workshop for agency staff, contractors, and the academic community.

In coordination with AEE, the Airports Office delivered a prepared statement at the workshop appealing for common sense:

"Audibility analysis is showing that new airport projects are making national parks quieter, quieter surprisingly, contrary to every other [noise] metric. We're getting over 500 percent overprediction of audibility in our second major application of the metric for the Mesquite EIS." We also stated our unwillingness to hide the problem by using a cosmetic fix for audibility—shoehorning the exaggerated data into a 100 percent cap. In response, Park Service representatives showed no willingness to budge on audibility. They simply repeated their claim of sole authority over park noise criteria and the right of each park superintendent to judge what is good for his or her park.

An exchange later in the day symbolized the deadlock. The FAA made a simple request to standardize the descriptive label for visitor response to aircraft noise. All of the statistical data showed that it makes no difference whether it is called "annoyance" or "interference with enjoyment." The Park Service immediately rejected the request, saying, "We need a group of factors that we can consider when we make our decisions. If it gets complicated, so be it."

The great recession of 2009 quelled the controversy over audibility for the next several years. Like a tsunami, the recession swept away the economic basis for new airports at Mesquite and Sun Valley as well as other major projects like the proposed international airport at Ivanpah, located 30 miles southwest of Las Vegas. It also threatened a large new heliport planned for Las Vegas.

The purpose for the new heliport made sense—to improve safety in downtown Las Vegas by relocating helicopter operations from McCarran International Airport and North Las Vegas Airport. The FAA western regional office was fully behind the project, but FAA headquarters had reservations about its potential environmental impacts. Building the world's largest heliport with 100 helipads carried the likelihood of public controversy, which would require an EIS, not a lower-grade EA as initiated.

Headquarters also urged the region to provide more detailed analysis of alternative heliport sites, the number of expected operations, and where they were going to fly.

Another weakness of the regional analysis was a failure to cite the relevant literature on psychoacoustics, which shows that people object to noise from helicopters more than fixed-wing aircraft because of its comparative loudness, forward projection, penetrating low-frequency, and pulsating blade slap. An example of this was on Long Island, New York, where North Shore residents of Suffolk and Nassau Counties complained for years that their houses were shaking because of helicopter noise, comparing it to a war zone. As the problem festered, the New York congressional delegation threatened legislation to establish mandatory flight paths and altitudes to reduce the noise, much of it coming from corporate activity. The issue was resolved in 2012 when the FAA relented by installing a new set of helicopter flight procedures that shifted local operations out over the Long Island shoreline.

In conventional airport studies, helicopter noise is often dismissed as a small and insignificant portion of airport activity. But this was going to be the world's largest heliport. A steep price will be paid, we warned our regional office, if the analysis is not improved, especially when the Park Service weighs in and demands audibility analysis. Inexplicably however, the Park Service never did submit comments on the study and FAA headquarters lost its leverage with the region, which completed the EA in 2008 without any changes or improvements.

But the story did not end there because Clark County also needed FAA headquarters approval to spend $176 million dollars on the first phase of heliport construction. The approval stalled in 2010 when the Airports financial division uncovered the fact that Clark County had been overcharging passengers on ticket fees for helicopter tours since 1992. The FAA immediately ordered the

County to desist and would have forced the County to repay the money, but as a staff member at headquarters confided, "we have no way to find the people who took the tours."

Despite continued lobbying, the economic tide was turning and the FAA regional office had exhausted its goodwill at headquarters. The Airports Office is a relatively small organization with only about 500 employees nationwide, many of whom know each other. In an organization that values collegiality and even calls itself a family, going it alone can be risky. In the end, the heliport project was mothballed.

⌒

NO TIME TO WASTE

Our national parks and National Airspace System are two prized public resources. As challenging as it is to balance their use in the midst of competing interests, national standards for park overflight noise are long overdue. There is no good reason why the dispute has dragged on for over 25 years.

Although the FAA and the NPS have made important strides on park noise assessment procedures, the fact remains that we are farther from a policy resolution today than we were in 2000. In the process, more than $32 million dollars was squandered on ATMP activities without the completion of a single park study or development of standards.

There is plenty of blame to go around. The FAA has made its share of mistakes and is often too protective of commercial aviation interests. No less the Park Service, whose gamesmanship has undermined technical progress and a national agreement. Most critically, the NPS has played loose with a first rule of environmental advocacy. All good environmental policies and regulations must be constructed on solid science, not just good intentions. It is unfortunate therefore that the Park Service has pushed experimental metrics like audibility, an issue that has resurfaced again with the nation's economic recovery and reinvigorated airport planning. Good science suggests that other approaches, such as the integration of acoustic zoning with park land use management, offer a better avenue for the Park Service to obtain more control and flexibility.

Most Americans are sympathetic to the NPS mission of protecting park resources for future generations. Clearly, the NPS must share in decisions about park airspace, including the governance of air tours, the design of aircraft routes, and the latest aviation challenge—drones. But when numerous interests are at stake, no single interest can be maximized. The Park will never achieve the full autonomy it wants—park superintendents cannot be Lone Rangers. National parks exist within a larger world that needs to be reassured, especially affected businesses in aviation, that park overflight restrictions to restore natural quiet will be imposed in a balanced and objective manner.

The continued stalemate serves no worthwhile purpose. By seeking perfection, the NPS risks losing its opportunities and leverage under the increasing pressures of population growth, urbanization, and economic development. Constraining the powerful forces of aviation will only get harder with each passing year of aviation growth. Many large-scale development dreams like the Nevada heliport will be dusted off and brand new airport projects proposed. For all of us who want national parks and pristine wilderness areas protected in perpetuity, there is no more time to waste waiting for a day that will never come. We need to secure genuine safeguards now, which can always be strengthened with the aid of continuous monitoring.

CHAPTER VI

Clean Air Act: Environmental Policy At Its Best

⟜⟞

UNLIKE THE GRIDLOCK OVER PARK aircraft noise, the national experience on air quality has been a major success. The cleaner air we breathe today is attributable to the groundbreaking events of 1970, when the Environmental Protection Agency was born and major amendments to the Clean Air Act (CAA) were passed. Leading the way were Senator Edmund Muskie of Maine, considered the chief legislative architect of the CAA, and Bill Ruckelshaus, the first EPA Administrator who managed the law's initial implementation. They and their contemporaries ushered in a new era of tougher emission standards that halted open pollution of the skies, safeguarded public health, and turned the invisible air around us into a tangible asset. Their legacy is even stronger because of the flexible architecture of the CAA, which the EPA is making use of today in regulating greenhouse gas emissions.

CLEARING THE AIR FROM CALIFORNIA TO CHINA

Los Angeles epitomizes national progress on air quality through its efforts over the past 60 years to reduce ozone pollution. LA's longstanding problems with ozone, particulates, and other pollutants are a product of its large industrial and manufacturing base, second largest population in the country, and overdependence on cars. The city's predicament is complicated by local geography and weather patterns. It is surrounded on three sides by mountains, which create a bowl-like basin that traps the air and allows the sunlight to bake oxides of nitrogen (NOx) and volatile organic compounds (VOCs) into unhealthy ground-level ozone.

As early as 1903, the City of Angels reportedly experienced so much industrial air pollution that residents thought the darkness one day was due to an eclipse of the sun. A few years later, the oppressively grey and hazy conditions of the city spawned a new vocabulary word, "smog," a combination of smoke and fog.

Smog is a witch's brew of ozone precursors like NOx, VOCs, and other compounds emitted into the air by chemical and industrial facilities, oil refineries, utility power plants, cars and trucks, locomotives, ships, and other sources. Long-term exposure to ozone is linked to asthma, emphysema, and other forms of respiratory illness, particularly among children and the elderly, and to increased risk of cancer, stroke, cardiovascular disease, and premature death. Ozone also harms the natural environment by damaging the growth of trees, plants, and agricultural crops as well as lowering their resistance to disease.

The encouraging news is that the skies over LA have steadily improved since 1955, when the city began to monitor ozone. At that time, peak ozone levels were 680 parts per billion (ppb) of air volume, *nine times* above today's federal ozone standards. Over the next 15 years, the city slowly cut ozone levels by approximately 1 percent a year. This rate of improvement basically tripled with the advent of the CAA amendments of 1970. By 1996, peak ozone levels for LA had fallen to 240 ppb, nearly one-third the level of 1955. Another positive sign was declining smog alerts issued by the state of California when hourly ozone levels reached 200 ppb. The LA basin experienced 121 high smog alerts in 1977, 66 in 1987, and one in 1997, with none since then.

LA's strides in cutting air pollution continued into the new millennium and stacked up well in comparison to those of other U.S. cities. LA ozone reductions in the three decades between 1980 and 2010 more than doubled the national average of 25 percent reductions, despite a 65 percent increase in local population and a 137 percent increase in vehicle miles traveled. Still, LA had farther to come than the rest of the nation, and despite its laudable record, still has farther to go. The American Lung Association continues to rank the LA basin as having the worst air pollution in the country. In 2012, local residents experienced 116 days that exceeded the federal eight-hour standard for ozone of 75 ppb. Sharing the dubious top-10 honors with LA are five areas in the California Central Valley, also plagued by unfavorable topography and weather patterns, and metropolitan Houston, Dallas-Fort Worth, Las Vegas, and Phoenix.

On a national level, unhealthy levels of ground-level ozone continue to endanger almost 120 million Americans or 38 percent of the population living in some 50 metropolitan areas. While more work has to be done, the severity of the problem is receding. For example, the EPA reports a 68 percent decline from 1990 to 2010 in national Orange Alert Days, when the air is harmful for many to breathe. Another indicator of progress is found internationally. Whereas California ozone levels topped the entire world from the 1950s to the mid-1970s, no U.S. city now makes the world's top-10 list of cities with the worst air. Among the biggest polluters today are Mexico City, Santiago, Cairo, and Hong Kong. At the very top of the list are New Delhi and Beijing.

In the case of Beijing, it and other cities in China have experienced rapid industrialization over the past three decades, much of it with a blind eye to the environment. In the autumn of 2013, for example, 11 million Chinese living to the north of Korea in the city of Harbin experienced smog so thick that they could taste it. Visibility was down to 30 feet and the air quality index was an unprecedented 40 times worse than safe levels established by the World Health Organization. Hospitals in Harbin experienced a 30 percent increase in admissions for respiratory problems, schools were suspended, and the airport and bus lines were shut down. Chinese officials blamed the problem on a stagnant high pressure system surrounding the city in combination with more coal-burning on the first cold day of fall, agricultural burning, and vehicle exhaust.

Harbin was not the first time that the world had heard about the air pollution crisis in China. In 2008, China agreed to host the Summer Olympics in Beijing. No facades and other urban renewal measures could hide the city's hazardous air. Many athletes waited as long as they could before traveling to the city in an effort to reduce the performance effects from breathing contaminated air. For a few world-class athletes, the concerns went beyond eye irritation, scratchy throats, pulmonary congestion, and asthma attacks. They avoided the Games out of fear that the dense pollution could cause long-term damage to their lungs.

To prevent Beijing's smog from obscuring the shining image that China wanted to portray at the Games, the government imposed an extraordinary set of air quality measures in the preceding months. It closed factories, halted coal-burning and construction projects, restricted vehicle use, and even seeded the clouds to induce rainfall to control dust. The temporary measures to clear the air worked in part—emissions of sulfur dioxide, carbon monoxide, and nitrogen dioxide were cut roughly in half.

But China's Olympic-sized effort on air quality was hamstrung by the fact that half of Beijing's smog was drifting in from coal plants and inland factories located to its west. The downwind effects from these transport emissions were a stiffer challenge for the Chinese, a problem affecting the East Coast of China as it does the East Coast of the United States. Downwind air from China is also emerging as an irritant in international relations. Japan and South Korea have begun to complain about the effects of China's air pollution on their environment. And across the Pacific, here in the U.S., it is estimated that up to 25 percent of LA's particulate matter blows in via the jet stream from China.

A few hopeful signs of environmental awakening in China are starting to appear. For example, China is beginning to consider more use of renewable energy as the world's leader in solar production and installed wind power capacity. In addition, China launched an initiative in 2013 called Green Fence to improve quality control within its multi-billion dollar global salvage and recycling industry. The goal of the program is to reduce airborne releases of lead and other toxins by more closely inspecting imported plastics, scrap metal, electronics, and other waste materials to certify correct content. The additional cost of the inspections is passed back to international exporters and consumers, including the U.S., which for example, ships about half of its discarded plastic soft drink and water bottles to China for reprocessing.

Green Fence symbolizes a start to the kinds of environmental reform that China desperately needs. It is hopefully a real harbinger of things to come, and not the Harbin of 2013 with a meager government response. The only reported step that Chinese officials took for Harbin was to name and shame the city by placing it on a monthly list of China's 10 most polluted cities. But it will take more than cultural appeals and voluntary measures to improve China's air quality. Its skies have been abandoned in an economic race to expand and industrialize and it will take a monumental effort to fix China's systemic problems.

These problems were evident in May 2010, when a delegation of Chinese airport officials visited the FAA in Washington D.C. to learn about U.S. airport development. They announced that China was planning to build 90 new airports, including one state-of-the-art green airport in Kunming, the largest city in China's southern Yunnan Province above Laos and North Vietnam. We were amazed by the magnitude and pace of their plans, and curious about the one environmental specimen, but we diplomatically focused our exchange on U.S. efforts to promote clean airport technology.

Following the meeting, our office sat down to talk about our national differences in air quality management. We observed that China's lack of environmental laws like NEPA and the CAA are a major handicap. They have no backstop on pollution or a way to temper economic development with good environmental planning that contains early assessments, long-term analysis, and comparison of alternatives. We were also struck by China's reliance on math estimates as a substitute for national air quality monitoring. Without trustworthy field measurements, China lacks reliable data to pinpoint trends, defend enforcement actions, and target incentives effectively. Most importantly perhaps, China has no free press, independent courts, or citizen involvement, essential counterweights for holding government agencies and officials accountable. Thus, as imperfect as our democracy and market economics may be, the U.S. system is intrinsically better suited to balancing environmental needs than a rigid state-run system like China.

CLEAN AIR ACT

As a model of environmental lawmaking, it is useful to take a closer look at the CAA to see how it is structured and applied by federal agencies. It contains three major principles that are essential to bluer skies. The first major principle is penalties for pollution. While people and companies once polluted freely, now polluters must pay. The health-based emission standards of the CAA provide a structure that effectively monetizes the cost of specific pollutants to human health and the environment, including agriculture, forests, lakes, and wildlife.

The CAA does a remarkably good job of spreading out the costs of pollution control on an equitable basis. In industry and commerce, a higher cost on pollution forces businesses to rethink product development and to devise more efficient means of production and distribution. It leads more companies to adopt longer-term or life-cycle cost accounting and to invest in cleaner technology, including pollution control equipment, fuel-efficient vehicle fleets, and automated inventory systems.

Individual consumers also pay to control air pollution. Some of these environmental bills are paid directly in the form of household utilities and waste disposal fees. However, most of what individuals pay is embedded in the purchase price of goods and services, and paid indirectly at the point of purchase. For example, the retail price of a new car contains the cost of a catalytic converter and other automotive engineering that went into meeting national Corporate Average Fuel Economy (CAFE) and emission standards. At the gas station, consumers pay a few cents more per gallon for measures such as vapor recovery nozzles and cleaner fuel blends with ethanol and ultra-low sulfur diesel.

The second major principle of the CAA is comprehensiveness. CAA emission standards encompass all major sources of air pollution, including sources that are stationary, mobile, and natural, such as wind-blown dust. On the stationary side, emissions are controlled for point sources like factory smokestacks and area sources like industrial ponds, dry cleaning businesses, and painting shops, which are dispersed geographically but represent a collective problem. On the mobile side, emission standards cover line sources like roads and airways to complement fleet standards for cars, buses, trucks, and a wide mix of off-road vehicles and construction equipment.

A controversial aspect of source control is the air pollution that crosses state lines. Downwind states like those of the Mid-Atlantic and New England want to know why they should have to pay more for cleaner air when a major portion of their air pollution comes from other states. The main issue has been the more than 100 coal-fired power plants in the Midwest and eastern U.S. that emit large volumes of NOx and sulfur dioxide (SO_2) high into the sky, which then drift northeasterly and return to earth as acidified dust and rain droplets, commonly known as acid rain. In 1991, a coalition of 12 northeastern states and the District of Columbia formed a regional commission to advise the EPA on what could be done to reduce the damage of acid deposition to lakes, rivers, soils, and woodland ecology. The commission has served as an important counterweight to Midwestern interests and was instrumental in developing the 2011 EPA Cross-State Air Pollution Rule to reduce power plant emissions causing ozone and higher particulates in downwind states. An effective mechanism in the rule is a cap and trade credit system for NOx and SO_2, which allows owners of cleaner power plants to sell their credits to dirtier plants. As the dirtier plants become more expensive to operate, they become more likely to be closed down or converted to cleaner fuels.

The third major principle of the CAA is shared government responsibility. At the federal level, the EPA sets the pollution standards, called National Ambient Air Quality Standards (NAAQS), and maintains a national array of more than 1,000 air monitoring stations to determine if the standards are being met. EPA labels areas with substandard air quality as nonattainment areas until they are brought into compliance, at which point they are relabeled as maintenance areas and watched for 20 years to prevent backsliding.

State government is an equal partner in enforcing the NAAQS. The most important job of states is to develop remediation plans for each nonattainment area and problem pollutant. These so-called State Implementation Plans (SIPs) can include whatever set of emission control strategies the state deems appropriate, provided the EPA approves. In terms of form, SIPs are not traditional reports but a managed set of policies, regulations, future standards, modeling analysis, and other documentation that delineate the state's path to attainment.

In the event that a state fails to produce an acceptable SIP, the EPA is required to step in and produce a substitute federal plan. Breakdowns like this are rare because states can pay a hefty price for

Washington intervention. In 1994, it nearly happened in California. The problem began in the 1980s when California refused to submit SIPs for ozone nonattainment areas around Sacramento, Ventura, and Los Angeles. Under pressure of lawsuits, the EPA produced a compensatory federal plan with hard-hitting control measures. Heavy-duty trucks that violated tougher new emission standards would be heavily fined and trucks entering the state would be limited to two delivery stops. Federal highway funding for the state was at risk too. The alarmed California business community protested strenuously. In the end, the EPA and California resolved their differences, EPA rescinded the federal plan, and California prepared state plans that were eventually approved.

SIPs represent the intertwining of federal and state CAA enforcement activities. For example, the law dictates that federal projects cannot cause new, more frequent, or more severe violations of the NAAQS. As part of this requirement, all federal actions must "conform" to SIPs so as not to delay state efforts to meet the federal standards in nonattainment and maintenance areas. Federal conformity requirements are split into two parts. The first is transportation conformity, which covers the highway and transit activities of the Department of Transportation in association with metropolitan planning organizations. The second is general conformity, which covers all other federal departments and agencies, including the FAA, Department of Defense, and Department of Interior. The two regulations differ in some important ways; for example, transportation conformity is established using regional emission budgets, while general conformity is handled project-by-project.

SIPs are also integral to state management of stationary sources. Under a section of the CAA called New Source Review, states are responsible for issuing start-up permits for new and rebuilt factories, industrial boilers, refineries, power plants, and other large stationary sources. States also regulate the day-to-day operations of these facilities based on their specific pollutants, volume of releases, and how the releases are controlled. Despite the reporting and recordkeeping requirements for an operating license, called Title V, the owners of large facilities tend to like the program's one-stop accounting, especially if a facility is subject to several areas of CAA regulation. It's a popular program with states, too, because Title V annual fees make up a state's primary revenue source for air pollution control activities.

So what has the CAA meant for cleaner air? Quite a bit for the six major criteria pollutants covered by the NAAQS: ozone (O_3), carbon monoxide (CO), nitrogen dioxide (NO_2), sulfur dioxide (SO_2), lead (Pb), and particulate matter (PM). Over the three decades spanning 1980 to 2012, the measured concentrations of these pollutants dropped significantly across the country:

* Ozone, formed by complex chemical reactions of two major precursors, NOx and VOCs in the presence of sunlight, down 25 percent.
* Carbon monoxide, a colorless, odorless, and lethal gas produced by incomplete combustion of carbon fuels such as gas, oil, and wood, down 83 percent.
* Nitrogen dioxide, a NOx family member with a reddish-brown hue and sharp odor caused by high-temperature fuel combustion in power plants, industrial boilers, highway vehicles, and nonroad sources like trains, down 60 percent.
* Sulfur dioxide, an invisible gas with an acidic smell of burnt matches or fireworks that is generated by power plants and industrial processes that burn coal, oil, and gas with sulfur content, down 78 percent.

* Lead, produced by the mining industry and manufacturing of ceramics, batteries, paints, and metal alloys, and used in aviation gasoline, down 91 percent.
* Coarse particulates (PM_{10}), with diameters of less than 10 micrometers, include smoke, soot, and liquid droplets from combustion (notably diesel fuel), plus dust from construction, forest fires, and winds, down 66 percent. Combustion also produces fine particulates ($PM_{2.5}$) with diameters of less than 2.5 micrometers. These smaller particulates, which were first regulated in 1997, were down 33 percent from 2000 to 2012. Because smaller particulates penetrate the lungs more easily, making them more dangerous to human health, research is underway on the health impacts of ultra-fine particulates ($PM_{1.0}$) with diameters of less than one micrometer.

Mirroring the trend in measured concentrations is the steep decline in EPA-designated nonattainment areas between 1992 and 2013: Carbon monoxide fell from 78 areas to zero, nitrogen dioxide from 1 to zero, sulfur dioxide from 53 to 9, and lead from 13 to 5. In the case of lead, feared for its neurological risks to children, success is primarily due to the closure of lead smelters, the phase-out of leaded auto gasoline in 1995, and the strengthening of lead standards in 2008. The largest remaining airborne source of lead is piston-driven aircraft, which use lead as an octane-boosting fuel additive. Today, lead emissions from avgas are estimated to represent 45 percent of all U.S. industrial sources. The FAA is addressing the problem with a scheduled phase-out of the fuel by 2018, a schedule that the EPA has a right to accelerate if it makes a health endangerment finding.

As a result of this progress, ozone and particulates are the only criteria pollutants of broad concern today. Both pollutants are hard to control because they are caused by combustion, and in the case of ozone-contributing VOCs, found in thousands of household and commercial products such as paint, building materials, pesticides, office products, glues, cleaning supplies, and cosmetics. Yet, even nonattainment areas for ozone and particulates have fallen dramatically over the past few decades. The trouble spots for ozone have dropped from 134 to 46, despite tougher new ozone standards in 1997 and 2008, while PM_{10} nonattainment areas have decreased from 84 to 41.

With criteria pollutants largely in check, the EPA is turning more of its attention to hazardous air pollutants, otherwise known as air toxics. The agency classifies 187 of these compounds, which are known to cause cancer, birth defects, and other serious health effects. They include benzene, formaldehyde, and naphthalene, which are found in fuels, as well as dioxins, asbestos, and airborne metals like mercury, arsenic, and chromium. The EPA is planning to set standards for all air toxics but there are so many that the process will take years. Consequently, the agency is prioritizing action on these compounds by their potential health threats. Unlike the six national criteria pollutants controlled geographically, regulation of air toxics is specifically aimed at local industries and manufacturing processes that are the largest known emitters.

EPA authority to regulate air toxics expanded under the 1990 CAA amendments, a reaction in part to the terrible 1984 disaster in Bhopal, India, where the release of methyl isocyanate at a pesticide-manufacturing plant killed at least 3,800 people in the first few days and another 15,000 over time, while also injuring 550,000 people. The 1990 amendments also increased EPA authority in other areas. Among the bill's new provisions were the establishment of regional commissions, such as the 12-state northeast Ozone Transport Commission, and the phase-out of chlorofluorocarbons and other chemicals that are tearing holes in our needed layer of stratospheric ozone.

Federal requirements to analyze air toxics are evolving slowly and agencies are addressing the issue to varying degrees. At the FAA, the policy on major airport studies is to evaluate the 50 or so classified air toxics that are aviation-related. The analysis is conducted by estimating air toxic emissions as a fraction of criteria pollutants, specifically ozone-related VOCs and particulates. Generally, the FAA and other agencies simply report their numerical findings without any interpretation, citing the scientific uncertainties and lack of national standards on air toxics. This is likely to change as the health science and chemistry improve and the public demands more agency disclosure of the potential health risks.

The future of air quality contains increasingly complex scientific and regulatory challenges. More basic research is needed to understand the compound chemical reactions in the atmosphere and how to accurately assess their effects. We also need advances in health research to identify the chronic and epidemiological consequences of inhaling or ingesting toxic particles. And the political reality is that air quality is a global resource without national boundaries. As transport emissions illustrate, further progress on everything from local air quality to climate change requires greater regional and international cooperation.

While the U.S. has a long way to go to reduce its carbon footprint and high energy consumption per capita, our system of air quality management is among the best in the world. The cornerstone of the system is the durable CAA with its remarkable range, equity, enforcement measures, and adaptability. It is a model that other countries, including China, would do well to emulate.

BROKERING A DEAL ON AVIATION EMISSIONS

Every agency and industry complies with the CAA in different ways to meet its obligations under the law. In aviation, the story involves LA again and the state of California's efforts to control emissions.

In the late 1990s, the state air quality agency for the LA region, the Southern California Air Quality Management District, ordered many local industries and businesses to reduce NOx emissions, the main cause of LA's ozone. The District had avoided tangling with the aviation industry for years, but as NOx levels declined in other sectors, NOx from aviation sources were increasing as a percentage of the total. Even by aviation industry estimates, up to 15 percent of south coast ozone was attributable to aviation-related activity. Caught between federal compliance and the political perils of trying to extract further concessions from non-aviation industries, the District saw little choice but to confront aviation.

States can fulfill their air quality management needs with the help of airport emission reductions. However, states cannot regulate airport access or aircraft emissions, despite the fact that aircraft are the largest source of pollution at airports. The authority to set aircraft emission standards belongs to the EPA, which consults with the FAA and generally adheres to international guidelines established by the United Nation's International Civil Aviation Organization.

Some states and local airport authorities, unable to control aircraft operations and engine emission standards, have explored the possibility of taxing dirty aircraft types through airport emission-based landing fees. The idea of such fees has surfaced in LA, Boston, and overseas in Europe. The airline industry vigorously opposes emission fees, fearful of the cost if every nation and airport did it. In this country, the airlines and the FAA have attacked the fees on constitutional grounds, citing the foreign and interstate commerce clauses of the Constitution, which grant federal preemption over actions that restrict trade across state borders. In Europe, where the legal hurdles are not as steep, emission-based landing fees have been imposed at airports such as London Heathrow and Zurich, Switzerland, and by the European Union, which has had to suspend its fees on foreign airlines due to intense pressure from the U.S. and other countries.

Besides aircraft, another airport source of NOx is service vehicles or ground support equipment (GSE), an eclectic mix of baggage tugs, belt loaders, forklifts, fuel tankers, catering trucks, and other equipment. With aircraft emissions off-limits, the South Coast Air Quality Management District saw GSE as the next best source of NOx to pursue. Their hand was helped by California's unique legal status under the CAA. California is the only state in the union that can set its own vehicle emission standards, provided they are more stringent than EPA national standards. The state's power is magnified by its large population and economic leverage, plus the fact that the CAA allows other states with nonattainment areas to adopt California standards in lieu of national standards.

As the largest owners of GSE, the airlines feared the regulatory reach of California and the South Coast Air Quality Management District. It was clear that the costs to them could be high because GSE only contributes 12 percent or less to airport NOx levels. Thus, to obtain meaningful benefits, the state would have to require the retirement or conversion of a substantial portion of the airline's dirty gasoline- and diesel-powered GSE. The situation grew worse for the airlines when the state of Texas, facing serious ozone violations of its own, entered the fray and proposed GSE NOx reductions in the Houston and Dallas-Fort Worth areas. Following state regulatory salvos and rejoining lawsuits from the airlines, the parties in Texas sat down and agreed to voluntary airline and airport NOx reductions equal to 90 percent of their GSE emissions.

Facing the prospect of a growing state patchwork of airport regulations, the airlines came to the FAA for help. In response, the FAA and the EPA agreed in 1998 to sponsor negotiations between the airlines and states to reduce aviation-related NOx emissions. This effort became known as the Stakeholders Process. The line-up of stakeholders for the negotiation looked like a heavy-weight boxing match. In the airlines' corner were the FAA, NASA, the Defense Department, the Airlines for America association, and major aircraft and engine manufacturers led by Boeing and Pratt & Whitney. In the states' corner were the EPA, the National Association of Clean Air Agencies, and other environmental groups. The airport community also participated, represented by the Airports Council International and the American Association of Airport Executives.

The Stakeholders Process lasted six years, from 1998 to 2004. In the last year of the initiative, I had a chance to compare notes with Ceci Foster, the EPA government affairs analyst, whom I first had met at the NEPA training class at Duke University. We had crossed paths since then at various meetings and air quality conferences. One day, after a Stakeholders meeting in downtown D.C., we decided to grab some lunch on the way back to our offices.

"So how's EPA these days, Ceci?" I asked.

"Not bad," she said, "but the workload is crazy. I've asked to telecommute a couple of days a week, but no luck yet. I can understand the concerns, but working at home is so much more productive."

"If it makes you feel any better, it's the same with us," I said. But I really don't mind coming downtown. I try to break up the day by jogging on the Mall, which is where I get my best ideas—which makes me wonder, are there any left in the Stakeholders Process?"

"I don't think so," she said. "We're past being disappointed, but EPA doesn't want to be the first to back out. And the airlines won't because they're benefiting from the circus—buying time, freezing state action, and all the while complaining about how hard business is. They love to emphasize their 10-year R&D lead-times and 40-year-old aircraft—it makes new standards seem pointless. And then they tell us *everything* they're doing to help the environment. I'm getting tired of the green-washing."

"As long as I've been at FAA, the airlines have talked about their business problems. Although they did have a case after 9/11—airline activity dropped 20 percent overnight and their ops were still down 10 percent or more a year later."

"And that's why we stopped pushing for tougher aircraft emission standards after 9/11," she said.

"Incidentally, did you see any of the 9/11 research?" I shared with her that researchers at Atlanta Hartsfield had discovered a big drop in benzene and other air toxics on the days following the attack when aircraft were grounded. While there was less road traffic too, the primary influence appeared to be airport emissions.

"So after 9/11," Ceci said in reference to the 2003 resumption of the Stakeholders Process, "the only thing that kept us at the table was salvaging GSE reductions. With aircraft emissions off the table, you'd think the airlines would deal on GSE."

"I'm surprised too," I said, "especially since aircraft are a growing share of the NOx problem. I can tell you that airports would like a deal."

"I've sensed a little split in airline and airport interests at the meetings," she said.

"That's because they're separate businesses in a lot of ways," I said, noting that airports, not airlines, are the ones regulated under CAA general conformity rules and they need more help from the airlines. If the airlines were to walk away from the deal, and nothing happened on GSE, airports would be on the hook to find other more expensive ways to reduce airport emissions.

"It's frustrating," she said. "And it's not only airline intransigence. Aircraft manufacturers use the same playbook on particulates. We're still using old hokey smoke numbers to certify new aircraft engines for particulates. The science is outdated and it doesn't line up with today's standards for $PM_{2.5}$. So, how is EPA supposed to limit aircraft emissions if it's not apples to apples?"

"I get it," I said.

"It seems like an exercise in futility sometimes, doesn't it?" she said. "I'll see you at the next meeting. Catch me if I start rolling my eyes."

Not too long after my conversation with Ceci, the Stakeholders Process collapsed after a last-ditch attempt at a deal. The offer presented by the airlines featured modest new national GSE fleet standards in return for state promises not to enact new aircraft or GSE emission restrictions for 14 years. The airlines' offer was categorically rejected by the states and their allies, bringing the

Stakeholders Process to a bitter end, with recriminations on all sides.

The FAA and EPA downplayed the failure of the Stakeholders Process and tried to move on. They had been unable to shepherd any type of voluntary agreement to solve the pollution problems of aviation. If there was a winner in the process, it could only be the airlines. They had diverted the attention of state regulators for seven years and escaped without any concessions. Now they would take their chances fending off any regulatory efforts in the future, a gamble that has paid off since.

AIRPORT AIR QUALITY

Sam Jennings once told me, "I advise students to always select a few courses by professor and not by subject. In life too, sometimes the best job is the one with the best boss." His words didn't seem to register then, but I was beginning to appreciate them now when I thought about Audrey Johnson and her management style. Whenever I got anxious about going too far on an issue, Audrey would say, "Don't worry, keep going, and I'll let you know when we get into trouble."

Audrey's reassurances demonstrated trust as well as a desire to get things done. She worked hard to find the resources we needed and to run interference on senseless office drills. In return, she expected more from her staff, including teamwork and outreach to other agencies and groups.

One of her program objectives was to make sure that all of our regional environmental specialists, regardless of their area of expertise, knew the basics about airport air quality, the CAA, and how airport emissions are assessed. Consequently, Audrey asked me to run a new round of air quality training for our regions and to set up a meeting with her to discuss the syllabus.

Helping me was Dave Simms, a contractor from a small company in Virginia. Dave was tall, thin, and youthful-looking, with a small goatee and disheveled look that belied his orderly mind. I had known Dave for many years, going back to our work together on an agency air quality handbook for airports. He was a chemist by training and adept at explaining carbon chains and atmospheric composition in terms that people could understand.

Rushing into the conference room, Audrey apologized for being late. "Dave, good to see you again," she said. "It's been a wild day—like usual. I just got out of a long budget meeting down the street with Federal Highways. And it didn't get any better when someone in our group thought they were being funny and said, 'If you build a road, you go a mile; if you build a runway, you go around the world.'"

"So let's talk about the training. It's come up on the radar because we've had a few problems in the field. Part of it is staff turnover. We need to make sure that our new environmental specialists are versed in the Clean Air Act and general conformity requirements. They also need to have the latest guidance. So, let me stop there and hear what you have."

"It's still coming together," I said, "but we're thinking about a two-day class. Dave would start things off with the science, followed by my overview of the reg's. This would set up the larger discussion—how to do an air quality study. In the afternoon, to get the blood flowing, they'd do a sample computer inventory of airport emission sources. On day two, we'd show them how to do a complex dispersion analysis with weather and downwind effects. Finally, we'd wrap up with a session on guidance."

"Sounds good," Audrey said. "But tell me a little more. Dave, how are you going to handle the science?"

"The chemistry is challenging," he said, "so I'll use graphics. For instance, one slide has a transparent bubble over an airport to explain the area of a study. The top of the bubble is the 'mixing height,' which is usually about 4,000 feet depending on geography. Below that, the vertical dispersal of pollutants is restricted."

"I like your idea of trying to make it more interesting," Audrey said. "Any way to do that with the regulatory info?"

"Believe it or not," I said, "you can go online and download the game, 'Jeopardy.' They let you plug in your own questions and answers and even add the show's sound effects. So we're thinking about splitting the class up into three and having them compete for a small box of airplane-shaped paper clips."

"I've gotta see this," Audrey said. "Let me know when you pull it together. Okay, so let's talk about the nuts and bolts—doing an airport study."

Dave took the next few minutes to go over our material. He started with our top priority, general conformity analysis, which pertains only to airports located in nonattainment or maintenance areas, and only to emissions related to the proposed project, not the whole airport. He explained that the first step is to inventory emissions. For example, an inventory for a new terminal project would include emission sources from the construction phase as well as future operating conditions with aircraft, GSE, on-road vehicles, and new boiler units.

If the total *volume* of project emissions meets EPA standards for criteria pollutants, the agency's responsibilities are over. But if tonnage exceeds the minimums, it raises a red flag that area *concentrations* may also be high in violation of the NAAQS. This triggers a dispersion analysis to investigate the downwind path of project emissions. The analysis is time-consuming because it requires extensive data on arrival and departure flight paths, taxiing procedures, prevailing winds, and regional background levels. It all comes together to identify whether homes and neighborhoods around the airport may be exposed to unhealthy levels. The final report is called a "general conformity determination," which contains the detailed findings and any mitigation that may be needed.

Dave concluded by citing our take-home message for students—that the high costs for dispersion analysis, with all of its extra work and expense, make it essential to keep project emissions low with early planning and good project design. If that can't happen, the next best alternative is to petition the state to make room in their SIPs for more airport emissions. Together, these strategies have worked so well, he said, that during the first two decades of general conformity, the FAA only faced 15 general conformity determinations, less than one per year.

When Dave finished, Audrey nodded approvingly, "Good, that's how we want our folks to think, preventatively."

"After that," I said, "we'll cover the agency's new guidance on air toxics." I also mentioned our new list of exemptions for small airport jobs with minor emissions, including fencing, signage, lighting systems, and pavement markings. It was a sensitive topic because the list took one year to complete, but sat five years inside the Office of General Counsel.

"It was unfortunate," Audrey said, "but they were trying to keep us out of trouble, and you've got to remember, we were the first agency to test this provision of the Clean Air Act."

I had always assumed that agency attorneys sat on the player's bench in support of project staff—and they like to give that appearance, but it was surprisingly adversarial at times. I understood the need to protect the agency from risk and litigation, but the concerns seemed excessive in this case.

"We tried to do a lot of extra analysis," Dave said.

"We even got the letter from EPA," I added, "telling us we're doing the list correctly—making it legal. And what do our lawyers do? They complain that we're talking to EPA too much! How screwed up is that? God forbid we communicate and work things out."

"I know," Audrey said. "But they were being cautious, and the list will hardly be used. It's water over the dam." She then proceeded to shift the conversation to our grant program for improving airport air quality, called the Voluntary Airport Low Emission Program (VALE). She wanted us to help regional staff feel comfortable explaining how airports could use the funding program to buy clean vehicles and equipment. She also thought Dave should tell his VALE story about the big 2010 Philadelphia International Airport redevelopment project.

Dave's eyes lit up, "I can tell you, without VALE, Philly would have had some real trouble." He recounted that the airport was in nonattainment for several pollutants and that the proposed modernization project was going to cause substantial emissions, particularly NOx and ozone. It seemed that the only option for meeting federal and state requirements was to go onto the open market and purchase NOx offsets, which were hard to find and running $50,000 per ton. At that rate, Philadelphia would have to spend tens of millions of dollars to offset project NOx emissions, including 135 tons of excess NOx caused during construction.

"I could see it coming," Dave continued, "and I told the airport, 'you can't afford to do nothing.' They say in consulting, 'never present a problem without a solution.' So, I showed them they'd be crazy not to pursue VALE funding." In the end, Dave's efforts led to an agreement with U.S. Airways to buy over 200 electric GSE in exchange for airport and VALE funding of rechargers. VALE funding was also obtained to install preconditioned air units at 35 aircraft gates. Together, these improvements would save about 60 tons a year of NOx, and a total of 1,200 tons over 20 years. It was more than enough savings to meet the airport's requirements without purchasing NOx offsets.

"We appreciate bringing Philly along, Dave, and other airports are bound to take notice." She then thanked us for the briefing and how we planned to run the training. As we got up to leave, she turned to me and said, "And make sure you keep good records on VALE. The program's growing and we need to keep good tabs on it."

CHAPTER VII

CLEAN ENERGY: THE
OPPORTUNITY AT AIRPORTS

CONTINUED IMPROVEMENTS TO AIR QUALITY depend on the increased use of clean and renewable energy sources like solar, wind, geothermal, hydrokinetic, and biomass. These sources of energy are beginning to make major inroads into the energy economy and to attract more individual, small business, and utility-scale investors. The conversion to renewables will not happen overnight, but as wariness over carbon fuels grows, and the smart money moves to cleaner fuels, many of us may live to see renewable energy sources become the nation's and the world's leading form of energy production.

While the outlook for renewable energy is encouraging, many U.S. industries and businesses are still lagging. The airport business is a case in point despite its enormous potential. A large asset of airports is the amount of open land, much of which sits idle or is leased to agriculture. According to the U.S. Department of Interior, there are nearly 20,000 airports and landing strips in the U.S. that comprise an area larger than the state of Rhode Island. Much of the property is privately owned and goes unnoticed by the public, who fly the passenger network of 500 commercial service airports and 2,500 general aviation airports. In addition to open space, public airports have other advantages, including central operations and built-in security systems. On the demand side, airports are a microcosm of the urban environment, with a large and diverse set of building and transportation uses. All of these attributes lend themselves to renewable energy development.

Yet the potential goes largely untapped. In the years before 2000, federal interest in airport energy development fell between the cracks of the U.S. Department of Energy (DOE) and the Federal Aviation Administration (FAA). At the DOE, airports were dismissed as a small niche market, although to its credit the DOE Clean Cities Program offered airport conferences for several years to promote the use of alternative fuels. These events compensated for the lack of activity at the FAA, whose only real interest on energy was helping the airlines reduce fuel burn on international flights by optimizing daily routes based on the winds. It would not be long, however, before federal air quality requirements and changing economics would combine to expand FAA and airport energy horizons.

Several avenues exist for new energy policy. Comprehensive national legislation is ideal, but it requires strong bipartisanship. During periods of slow progress or stalemate, presidents can exert a measure of influence by setting ambitious goals for the large federal sector. For example, Presidents Bush and Obama both issued executive orders calling for increased agency use of renewable energy. Such directives by the White House make a difference because agencies have limited authority and can barely keep pace with the daily conveyor belt of reports, policy guidance, briefings, contracts, budgets, and correspondence. At the FAA, whatever could wait

another day got shoved to the side. In the process, many worthwhile ideas got shortchanged, as renewable energy would have been
without the presidential decrees.

Another avenue is targeted congressional actions that address
a particular need at agencies. This happened to the FAA in 2000
when a clean fuels pilot program popped up in our draft reauthorization bill. With some digging, we discovered that the pilot
program, which would help 10 airports purchase alternative fuel
vehicles, was the brainchild of two lobbyists from the natural gas
vehicle association, Paul Kerkhoven and Patrick Quinn. They had
persuaded two influential Members of Congress on transportation
and aviation committees to sponsor their provision: Republican
Representative Sherwood Boehlert of New York and Democratic
Senator Jay Rockefeller of West Virginia. The FAA Airports Office
expressed no objection to the provision because it had much bigger
legislative fish to fry and there was no purpose in alienating anyone
on the Hill.

Agencies respond to congressional mandates with checkered
enthusiasm. Many mandates, including pilot programs, often
receive nominal treatment, but the Boehlert-Rockefeller measure seemed to fill an important gap. The FAA had no existing
airport program on alternative fuels, which included natural gas
in this instance, and the possibilities were wide open. As such,
the proposed Inherently Low Emissions Airport Vehicle Pilot
Program, and the chain of events that followed, evolved into an
interesting case study of how programs get started in the federal
government and how advances in environmental policy come
about.

The pilot program was appealing because it addressed
the biggest barrier to alternative fuels and renewable energy

use—the lack of start-up capital. It offered 10 airports up to $2 million dollars apiece for the purchase of alternative fuel vehicles, provided that the airports matched the federal grants dollar-for-dollar with local airport revenues. The $20 million set aside for the program amounted to one-tenth of 1 percent of the FAA's $3 billion dollar annual airport budget, an easy piece to carve out.

The Office of Airports environmental division was asked to manage the pilot program and I offered to help because it represented the best job in government—handing out money—and an opportunity to get directly engaged in airport operations. I also liked the prospect of coming full circle with my former energy jobs.

It helped to have an outside frame of reference like the Franklin County Energy Conservation Task Force because big agencies and organizations often flatten people's imagination and how they perceive the possibilities. As it was, management liked my "new idea" for an interagency task force to oversee the pilot program. It made perfect sense because the new initiative was more about energy than aviation and that expertise lay elsewhere, namely at the DOE, EPA, and Federal Transit Administration.

The front office in Airports supported the pilot program but took a cautious wait-and-see approach to approving all 10 grants. We were given 17 months to construct the program, a schedule timed to the new fiscal year in the fall of 2001. This left no time to waste in developing application procedures, publicizing the program, and attracting airport interest.

Our interagency task force began by soliciting advice from vehicle manufacturers and energy associations representing the electric, natural gas, and propane industries. This led to our application procedures, which included custom software to help airports estimate project emission savings by vehicle and fuel type. The software came as an unexpected gift from our experienced Federal Transit Administration members, who financed its production.

From the 21 airport proposals submitted, the task force culled the 10 best on the basis of emission savings, cost-effectiveness, innovativeness, and other criteria. The front office approved all 10 nominations, pleased with the range of airport geography, size, and project types, which included electric ground support vehicles at Chicago O'Hare, Dallas-Ft. Worth, and Sacramento, natural gas buses and trucks at Denver, Baltimore, and Baton Rouge, propane vehicles at San Francisco, and mixed fleets at Atlanta, John F. Kennedy (JFK), and LaGuardia. We also had the participation of one or more major airline in eight of the projects: Delta, American, United, and Southwest.

The front office was also satisfied knowing that the $17.5 million dollars in requested funding ($2.5 million unrequested) would be fully matched by the participating airports, with an extra $12 million dollars coming from airport business partnerships, bringing the total investment in the pilot program to $47 million. The federal investment was leveraged further by an important stipulation: the FAA would only pay for the higher expense of alternative fuel vehicles, not their *base cost*, as determined by the retail price for the same vehicle fueled by gasoline or diesel. Everything was falling into place nicely as we looked ahead to the start of the program and airport acquisition of 2,200 alternative fuel vehicles and a sizable amount of refueling infrastructure.

9/11

Within weeks of the program launch, our optimistic estimates for the pilot program were shattered by the horrific attack of 9/11. We lost four airport projects immediately, while the other six projects barely survived the economic aftershocks of 9/11. But these remaining projects would eventually provide the FAA with useful information for incentivizing clean airport technology. Getting there, however, was anything but certain in the days following 9/11, when I decided to call Sam Jennings.

"How are you?" I asked.

"Well, I gotta say, I could be better," Sam said. "I love teaching as always, but they're ratcheting up the pressure on published research. So, I'm toying with the idea of retiring in a year or two."

"If they were smart, they'd just let you teach."

"Maybe, but I'm already thinking about new things to do," Sam said. "Now don't laugh, but I want to go into outer space. And I've got a bunch of other doozies, but that's for another time. So, how are things with you?"

"Well, that's why I called. I've been working on a green airport program. But just as we rolled it out, 9/11 occurred. Now everything's hanging by a thread."

"I have to say, I thought the FAA did a good job of reacting and grounding planes quickly. Where were you?"

"Downtown," I said. "We started hearing the news from New York and then saw clouds of smoke out the window to the southwest. A few minutes later, we learned it was the Pentagon. It would've been worse here if the passengers on the fourth plane, United Flight 93, hadn't acted. They say the plane was headed for the White House or the Capitol. Anyway, for the rest of the afternoon, we sheltered-in-place until the alert was over." As an aside, I mentioned to Sam that a participant in the pilot program, the New York and New Jersey Port Authority, which runs JFK and LaGuardia, had administrative offices in the World Trade Towers. We did not know the individuals who perished, but we heard later that some of our contract papers with the Port Authority had been discovered miles away on Long Island.

Airport activity around the country fell precipitously after 9/11. In the throes of the financial crisis, airports and airlines had to reconsider their voluntary investments in the pilot program. We certainly understood JFK and LaGuardia bowing out. But we were taken aback when Atlanta Hartsfield and Chicago O'Hare withdrew also. The other six airports were on the fence, but with some persuasion, remained in the program.

"It sounds like you did okay under the circumstances," said Sam, who had thought long and hard about the art of persuasion as a teacher. He believed that it required more than information—you had to have a vision of some kind, know your audience, and when to use techniques like humor.

"I guess in our case, it was about holding onto the vision," I said, explaining that after 9/11, FAA management was searching everywhere for unspent funds to redirect. When they asked us for a briefing on the pilot program, we knew the program was on the line. Our only chance, I said, was to defend its value to the agency—and pray for wisdom.

After a momentary pause, Sam responded, "What was it T.S. Eliot said? 'Where is the wisdom we have lost in knowledge? Where is the knowledge we have lost in information?'"

"I don't know... except top management briefings can lack all of it—they're incredibly unpredictable. With luck, you might get five minutes. And if you hand them anything, it has to be on one page." I then told him what happened—before we could even speak, management put us on our heels, demanding to know why the pilot program should not be defunded or deferred. We reacted by saying it would be a bad idea, even to back away temporarily. It would hurt the remaining participating airports and complicate our responsibility to Congress. We reported that our total grant obligations for the program had fallen 60 percent to $7 million dollars, but that the payoff in information would still be good. Finally, we mentioned the importance of preserving our reputation with the federal agencies that helped us set up the program.

"Good point," Sam said, "because you might need the trust and cooperation of these agencies in the future. It's hard to put a price tag on that."

"Fortunately, it turned out alright," I said, "but I've learned not to take communications for granted. Like a few months ago, I was speaking to a group of FAA environmental specialists on the need for outreach and public affairs, and I made a typo on my slide presentation. A *friend* of mine in the audience, who couldn't resist, raised his hand, and asked why I had left the letter 'el' off of 'public.'"

"Priceless," Sam chuckled, "but, hey, that's when you show you have a sense of humor and can laugh about yourself. Humility keeps things in perspective—it's about helping others, especially in today's competitive society with so many on the short end. But, now I'm digressing—that's a longer discussion."

"Well then, how about a visit? We can go to the old coffee shop in town and solve the world's problems. And, I want to hear more about your plans for outer space."

VALE ARCHITECTURE

The pilot program overcame its rocky start to produce valuable data and to inspire a series of clean airport initiatives at the FAA. The direct offshoot of the pilot program was a 2005 initiative called the Voluntary Airport Low Emission Program (VALE).

In the first 10 years of the VALE program, airports received $150 million dollars from the FAA to purchase clean technology, augmented by $34 million dollars in local matching funds. The funding has gone to 38 airports and 69 projects to reduce the use of petroleum products—jet fuel, oil, diesel, and gasoline—in favor of cleaner energy sources, including solar, geothermal, natural gas, and electricity.

The idea for VALE came together in autumn 2003, when the front office decided to nationalize the pilot program and make alternative energy projects eligible for funding through the FAA's large Airport Improvement Program. Doing this required legislation, which fell into the bailiwick of our resident guru on congressional airport authorizations.

Entering his office for our first get-together, I felt like I was being initiated into a secret society. Few people realize how much interaction goes on behind the scenes between the legislative and executive branches of government, particularly on agency reauthorization and appropriation bills. Now, I was getting a chance to see the game up close and witness his expert craftsmanship in drafting parts of the new FAA reauthorization.

We discussed lessons learned from the pilot program and where we could make improvements. Some issues would disappear automatically because VALE would be administered within the Airport Improvement Program. This meant that airport commitments on VALE projects would be binding. In return, airports would benefit from the standard rates for airport grants, which were substantially higher than the pilot program: large airports would receive 75 percent federal funding; small airports 90 percent.

Another funding step was to qualify VALE projects under a second multi-billion dollar airport program, called Passenger Facility Charges. These charges are collected from airline ticket taxes and treated as local airport revenues, giving airports and their airline tenants the right to decide how to spend the money, contingent on FAA approval. Most of the time, the revenues are applied to large airport capital improvements, meaning that VALE opportunities would be limited—but at least the option would be there.

In terms of policy, we believed it would be stronger to build the new program around emission reductions rather than specific alternative fuels. We also threw open the door to all kinds of infrastructure projects. One of the best available options for airports is gate electrification, which provides parked aircraft with cabin lighting, heating, and cooling. Gate plug-in services significantly cut air pollution by reducing the operation of aircraft auxiliary engines, which burn jet fuel inefficiently. Other eligible activities included underground fuel hydrant systems to eliminate fuel truck emissions, more efficient natural gas boilers and chillers for buildings, and renewable energy systems for cleaner power.

Our boldest move was to hinge VALE funding to airport emission credits. As we saw it, the program must be win-win. If the

FAA and airports were going to invest millions of dollars in clean technology, then we deserved some regulatory relief from the EPA in exchange. Consequently, we drafted a provision in the legislation to establish a new system of EPA emission credits, which airports could apply to offset emissions from any future development project. Our shorthand for the deal was "no credits, no funding." With that piece in place, our last big decision involved airport eligibility. Given the new emphasis on emissions, it made sense to target airports that had the toughest air quality requirements, those located in EPA nonattainment and maintenance areas. This limitation meant that about 150 commercial service airports, about 30 percent of the total, would be eligible for VALE.

My legislative colleague seemed to be the only person who clearly understood the structure of the reauthorization bill and how to fold our new program into it. He performed his wizardry by cross-referencing statutes, sprinkling around legal terminology, and namelessly burying the new initiative into five separate sections covering the two airport funding programs, the new emission credit system with EPA, and a special provision for vehicle retrofits, into which he tucked another all-purpose section on definitions and standards. It was a true work-of-art that I could not grasp, nor anyone else, I suspected. It was no coincidence therefore that the new program breezed through Congress unnoticed and unscathed as part of the FAA reauthorization bill of December 2003.

With only nine months from December to the new fiscal year, our preparation time for VALE was only half of what we had had for the pilot program. The deadline left no room to reconstitute the interagency working group, to collaborate closely with airport associations, or to consult with FAA general counsel. We confronted two critical paths—one was writing the program guidance and application procedures, and the other was to engage the EPA on emission credits.

Pinning the fate of the program on a credit agreement with the EPA was a gamble, particularly without any federal precedents to guide us. All of our hopes rested on our EPA liaison for air quality, an experienced manager whom we knew and liked. He needed no explanation of our legislative game of chicken. For many years, the EPA had pressed the aviation industry for emission reductions and knew how hard it was to get anything. Now, the only thing standing in the way of major investments in clean airport technology was EPA approval of emission credits.

Legally, the emission credit system had to be an amendment to the Clean Air Act, and therefore, an EPA document. While our EPA colleague was on board with airport credits, he was extremely busy and asked for a year's delay in the program. Consequently, the only hope for making our nine-month goal was to make the process easy for him. We offered to write the first draft of the credit agreement, which to our surprise, he was willing to let us do. It was a good omen—not only to stay on schedule but to make sure that the credit system fit seamlessly with FAA program guidance.

The draft credit agreement included Clean Air Act stipulations on voluntary or early action programs like VALE, followed by our prescribed procedures for calculating, issuing, and using airport emission credits. The effort culminated in August 2004, when we sat down for three days of final editing at the EPA complex in Research Triangle Park, North Carolina. From the FAA perspective, it was important to preserve the principle that one ton of emission savings was worth exactly one ton of credit. This protected airports against any proclivities to discount credits in the future. We also liked the fact that airports could apply earned credits in the early stages of project planning to avoid potential emission pen-alties. One month later, following a surprisingly smooth EPA legal review, EPA management signed and released the credit agreement, titled Guidance on Airport Emission Reduction Credits for Early Measures. With that, we rolled out the VALE program on time.

MAKING IT WORK

We were fortunate that Dave Simms, our air quality consultant, was available again to help us with VALE program guidance. He took on the toughest technical jobs and handled them in stride. In con-sultation with the EPA, he converted national vehicle emission stan-dards, based on *corporate fleet averages*, into new VALE standards for *individual vehicles* that would cover any airport combination of pur-chased equipment. He also nailed down a generous offer by the DOE Clean Cities Program to write a chapter for us on the safe handling and emission characteristics of alternative fuels. A few months into the effort, Dave and I sat down to discuss where we stood.

"It'll be interesting to see how many proposals come in," Dave said. "A lot of airports still don't know about VALE."

"Advertising has been harder than I thought," I said. "Some people think we're a ski area, and the Secretary of Transportation just mispronounced our name at a big conference in Chicago. He called us the 'Valley' program. Hell, the things you never think about in a briefing paper. But that's the least of it. I'm worried about how airports are going to perceive 100 pages of guidance… even though it's easy to apply."

Part of my concern was the amount of quantification involved, which was dictated by the introduction of emission credits. The EPA would only accredit airports if their emission savings were measurable. Another numerical linchpin was our standards for low-emission vehicles, which we set high to provide the best investment. It helped that we had ruled out partial solutions like clean diesel and low-percentage biofuel blends, which we felt would be a nightmare to track and invite more issues like the fuel vs. food debate over ethanol production from corn.

"Attention to the numbers should pay off," I said. "There's not much room for airports to play games and inflate their estimated savings."

"A lot less than highway authorities," Dave said, referring to the Federal Highway Administration's multi-billion dollar Congestion Mitigation and Air Quality program, which generalizes emission benefits in lieu of specific project data. "I think our biggest problem will be controlling the use of vehicles."

Prior to VALE, federal airport funding had been limited to fixed assets like runways and terminal buildings, with a few exceptions for mobile equipment like fire-fighting and snow removal vehicles. Now, the FAA would be financing all types of on-road and off-road vehicles, exposing the agency to potential vehicle mismanagement. To reduce the risks, we limited VALE funding to airport-owned and dedicated vehicles, ruling out regional fleets like taxis and super shuttles. We also restricted airports from selling, warehousing, or using project vehicles for personal business. Airports had to agree to operate the vehicles for their full life, affix a "VALE" sticker on vehicles for tracking purposes, and to repair or replace any equipment damaged in an accident. On top of these special vehicle conditions, airports would have to comply with some 25 standard grant assurances, including "buy American." This government-wide requirement barred airports from purchasing foreign products like the Toyota Prius and Honda Civic hybrids as airport security and service vehicles.

Our office reached out to airports, especially in the early years of the program, to help them field qualified projects that met our cost-effectiveness guidelines for emission reductions. We helped them think through siting and design issues, which are often a major challenge for alternative energy systems. Common problems included electrical service upgrades, new fueling facilities, and staff training on safety and handling procedures. In addition to technical matters, each project proposal had to run the gamut of approvals through airport operating divisions and airport boards, and in some cases, unions, airlines, and service providers.

Advancing alternative energy projects inside the FAA is no cakewalk either. The FAA regional offices are overworked and reluctant to take on anything new, especially a headquarters initiative like VALE that some perceived as nonessential to aviation. We had to convince skeptical old-liners to facilitate, not impede, regional processing of VALE applications. As a result, it took several years, and pressure from headquarters, for VALE projects to be awarded in all major regions.

Despite the difficulties, the air quality at many commercial service airports around the country is cleaner today because of VALE gate electrification, low emission vehicles, underground fuel hydrant systems, solar and geothermal installations, and other improvements. Over the lifetime of current VALE projects, a breath-taking 10,000 tons of ozone-creating NOx and VOCs will be eliminated from the air—the equivalent of taking 31,000 cars and trucks off the road each year for the next 10 to 20 years.

In addition to helping airports reduce emissions, save energy dollars, and add new revenue sources, VALE has paid off handsomely for the EPA. The availability of emission credits has enabled $184 million dollars to flow into clean airport projects, with more to come. Yet, in the first 10 years of the program, only two airports, Philadelphia and Houston, requested emission credits from the EPA and states, and only one airport, Philadelphia, used its credits in the regulatory process to support airport development.

⌣⁀

TWO DOORS OF OPPORTUNITY

Over the course of several years, the VALE program revealed where more work is needed to cut airport pollution and the best ways to do it. Two of the biggest areas of opportunity are aircraft ground support equipment (GSE) and solar energy.

As highlighted in the unsuccessful government-airline Stakeholders Process, dirty gasoline- and diesel-powered bag tugs, belt loaders, forklifts, and other GSE are a major source of airport pollution. These vehicles represent low-hanging fruit because clean options are readily available.

In the past, reliability concerns have undermined the transition to cleaner GSE. But these concerns have largely been addressed through advances in technology, such as new batteries and recharging stations that perform well in cold climates. The biggest barrier today is airline economics. As the largest owners of GSE, airlines stick with gasoline and diesel equipment because of its lower retail price. Many airlines refuse to consider purchasing alternative fuel vehicles unless they meet a short-term payback window. Anything beyond three years is often deemed risky, regardless of the longer-term savings from lower fuel and maintenance costs.

In 2009, the GSE market was showing small signs of movement, including a few airports and airlines using VALE to buy electric bag tugs and belt loaders. But there was no evidence of a broadening trend and no technology-forcing standards on the horizon. So the FAA wondered what it could do to persuade the airline industry to voluntarily abandon their older and dirtier GSE in favor of cleaner technology.

It seemed like a simple proposition but the FAA had no current data on the size and composition of the national GSE fleet. We knew precisely how many aircraft were operating at airports, but had very little clue about GSE. Some airlines were willing to offer a guess, but only a handful of them were willing to share actual data because most considered it proprietary. It soon became clear that a national inventory of equipment was needed, which the FAA proposed to do with industry through the independent National Academy of Sciences. Our goal was to obtain a total GSE count, how much of it was gasoline- and diesel-powered, and what types of government incentives could help accelerate a conversion to cleaner technology.

Often the case for change has to be made over and over again. From the time we proposed the study to the time it began, two years elapsed. The cause of the delay was stiff opposition from the powerful Airlines for America association, which alleged that the inventory was merely another attempt by the government to push for tougher GSE emission standards. It took months of cajoling to save the study, as we repeatedly stressed that our aim was to incentivize, not regulate, the airlines.

The study was completed in 2012. It reported a total of 110,000 GSE units, the breakdown by vehicle type, and the critical fact that 85 percent of the vehicles were still powered by diesel or gasoline. The findings confirmed the enormous potential for reducing airport pollution through GSE conversions. But while the study met its inventory goals, it failed to address the question of economic incentives. Time had simply run out, as the study group, with prodding from the airline association, got sidetracked writing a descriptive book about GSE types.

Cleaning up the GSE fleet continues to be the best short-term strategy for reducing airport pollution, while we wait for advances in aircraft engine technology. But the transition will remain slow and patchy until something alters the equation. It could be stronger EPA standards to reduce the air pollution caused by aviation, or the carrot of incentives. Until then, it is business-as-usual for airline purchasing departments. Their shortsighted calculus condemns us to dirtier air for decades because GSE are built to last. Ubiquitous bag tugs, for instance, average 20 years of service and are often re-engined for a second generation of use.

Compared to the challenges surrounding GSE, airport solar development is much easier because it is a land use issue under airport jurisdiction. Unlike GSE, there are no entrenched interests to overcome and no existing fleet of vehicles to retire or resell on the secondary market. Solar is all about *addition*: adding a form of energy that does not pollute, adding a new source of airport revenue, and adding a visible symbol of environmental commitment.

Airport interest in solar energy started to coalesce around 2008, led by the pioneering efforts of Denver International Airport and several California airports at Bakersfield, Fresno, Oakland, and San Francisco. These and other airports generated a wave of solar interest that soon reached the FAA. Prior to VALE, stand-alone airport solar facilities were not eligible for FAA funding. Now it was possible. Starting in 2010 and 2011, the FAA approved four solar grants, including 1 MW installations at Albuquerque International Sunport and Chattanooga Metropolitan Airport. VALE also made it possible to support other renewable energy development, including the first large airport geothermal systems in the country at Portland ME, Duluth MN, and South Bend IN, plus a small system in Rockland ME, all of which help to heat and cool airport terminals. The airport case for other renewables has been harder to make; wind power, for example, carries concerns about height obstructions, radar interference, and tower frangibility.

In addition to renewable energy use, the FAA began to look at ways to encourage all-around better airport environmental practices. Consequently, the Airports Office decided in 2010 to fund airport sustainability planning. Over the next five years, almost 50 airports took advantage of the opportunity to devise sustainability plans with various components: recycling, green building certification, water conservation, public transportation, and many other economic and community-based measures.

Meanwhile, growing airport interest in solar energy underscored the need for FAA solar guidance. The project approval process had been case-by-case so far, but moving forward, the agency wanted everyone involved in a solar project to know the requirements and procedures. We began guidance development by reaching out to our safety and compliance people, our regional offices, and the Air Traffic organization. The fact-finding process also led to experts at the DOE and Sandia National Lab, the electric utilities, airport associations, and airports around the country with solar experience. Based on this input, we proceeded to clarify FAA solar project requirements with regard to airport safety, land use compatibility, airport revenue use, and environmental compliance. We also covered major planning considerations, from solar technology—photovoltaic, thermal, and concentrated—to airport financing and electric utility agreements.

The solar guide for airports, titled Technical Guidance for Evaluating Selected Solar Technologies on Airports, was issued in the fall of 2010. It would be my last project before retiring from the government the next spring. Not a bad one to end on, I thought—helping airports to navigate the regulatory process for solar development.

Yet, even with the new guidance in place, the agency was about to learn a hard lesson on solar. DOE had learned one recently too—one garnering national headlines. The Energy Department had loaned the Solyndra Corporation $535 million to expand U.S. solar manufacturing capacity. But in 2011, unable to compete with cheaper solar panels from China, Solyndra was forced into bankruptcy and defaulted on its government loans.

Although it is unrealistic to expect perfection with any new technology, getting it right on airport solar is critical. The greatest potential safety hazard for airport solar installations is glare or glint that can temporarily blind pilots or air traffic controllers. Yet, the FAA lacked a standard method for assessing solar reflectivity at airports, a critical need that was highlighted in our solar guide. True to Murphy's Law, the problem arose in 2012 on a VALE-funded $3.5 million rooftop system on a parking garage at Manchester-Boston Regional Airport in New Hampshire. No one caught the problem in time—a quarter of the installed panels for the 530 kW system were causing glare in the nearby air traffic tower for 45 minutes at sunrise. The offending panels were immediately covered over with canvas tarps, which remained in place until 2014, when the airport and the FAA fixed the problem by reorienting the solar panels.

In response to the problem at Manchester, the FAA immediately commissioned the development of new standards and procedures for assessing airport solar glare. The effort culminated in a 2013 FAA notice in the Federal Register, the government's daily legal newspaper, requiring airports to use a reflectivity assessment tool built and tested by Sandia National Lab. With this tool, the FAA and airports should never have a similar issue. Moreover, there have been no difficulties with glare at other FAA project airports, including Albuquerque, Chattanooga, and Tucson, or with the more than 50 independently financed airport solar installations across the country.

The past several years have seen more and more private financing of solar projects, displacing the need for additional government stimulus. In states like North Carolina, progressive tax policies, combined with federal tax credits for renewable energy, are attracting large private investors. These developers are partnering with airports and other landowners to help finance, build, and operate solar facilities. At the forefront in North Carolina is one of the nation's largest electric utilities, Duke Energy, which has invested in solar farms at two airports in the state, Shelby Regional Municipal and Warren Field, in addition to other sites around the state and country.

Unfortunately, most states do not have North Carolina's prowess or sense of innovation, leaving a large majority of airports unable to attract private investment. For them, FAA grant assistance is still the key to making solar feasible, which Congress recognized in 2012 by authorizing a new FAA energy efficiency program. The new program qualified the nation's 5,000 public airports for FAA solar funding through the Airport Improvement Program, far more facilities than VALE's 150 eligible commercial service airports located in air quality nonattainment areas. Besides greatly expanding airport eligibility for solar grants, it made sense to link solar projects with energy and cost savings rather than air quality, given the fact that most of the electricity from airport solar panels flows back into the grid, offsetting emissions at regional power plants, not the airport.

The new program, however, has been slow to take hold, causing the FAA to lose momentum on solar. No FAA solar grants were issued between 2013 and 2015, although the agency reports that three airport solar projects are in the funding pipeline for 2016. Several factors may explain the slowdown, including a hefty application requirement to perform a comprehensive airport energy audit. But whatever the barriers have been, the FAA needs to renew its commitment to solar, use its leverage to attract private investment, and make it easier for airports to reap the important environmental and financial benefits of the sun.

ONE STEP LEADS TO ANOTHER

Little did the two lobbyists for the natural gas vehicle association know where their modest legislative proposal in 2001 would lead. In retrospect, their idea for the pilot program on alternative fuel vehicles jump-started a decade of FAA program building in areas of airport air quality, sustainability planning, and energy efficiency. Without their vision, it is unlikely that the FAA would have done anything like the pilot program or VALE. In all likelihood, we would have been stuck on the sidelines, unwilling to take the risks or unable to agree on a way forward.

The evolution of government planning and programming mirrors the old Chinese proverb, "A journey of a thousand miles starts with one step." The pilot program was spun off into the VALE program, which in turn provided a foundation for GSE and solar research as well as broad grant initiatives on airport sustainability planning and energy efficiency. With these measures, the FAA and the airport community are prepared for the next steps in environmental stewardship.

FAA environmental initiatives have profited from the rising tide of the environmental movement. Yet even with the growth of the movement, there is often a large gap between environmental goals and what actually gets off the ground and accomplished. Our slow national progress on renewable energy underscores how difficult the road to change can be. But the gap can be closed when people learn more, get involved, pursue new ideas, refuse to get discouraged by the unexpected, and gain the skills it takes to overcome the institutional hurdles.

CHAPTER VIII

CLIMATE CHANGE: THE INTERNATIONAL CHALLENGE

⌣⁀

CLIMATE CHANGE HAS EMERGED AS a dominant issue of our times and the central focus of the environmental movement. The new prism of climate change has transformed our concept of the planet, revealed the sweeping interdependencies of nature, and inspired increased environmental action.

Climate change differs from most environmental issues because of its global scope and ramifications to planetary survival. The world's atmosphere respects no human boundaries as concentrations of carbon dioxide (CO_2) and other greenhouse gases disperse throughout the world. For this reason, a meaningful response to the climate crisis requires international cooperation on a level never seen before.

The issue is also distinguishable by its long timescale. It has taken two centuries of industrialization for the slow-moving effects of climate change to become clearly visible. Likewise, actions today to halt and reverse global warming and other climate effects may only benefit our grandchildren and their descendants, given that greenhouse gases accumulate and persist in the atmosphere for centuries. The renowned UN-sponsored Intergovernmental Panel on Climate Change (IPCC), representing thousands of scientists from around the world, reports that about 15 to 40 percent of CO_2 emissions "will remain in the atmosphere longer than 1,000 years." Oceans are also a long-term storehouse for CO_2. Amid continuous exchange of CO_2 between air and water, scientists estimate that the oceans absorb about 60 percent of airborne CO_2, half of which penetrates the ocean surface and slowly disperses into the deep ocean over the course of a few hundred years.

CO_2 represents over 80 percent of U.S. greenhouse gases from human activity, gases which form in the atmosphere and absorb heat from infrared reflections off the earth's surface. Several years ago, U.S. scientists suggested that 350 parts per million (ppm) was a sustainable concentration of CO_2 in the atmosphere. By 2014, CO_2 levels had skyrocketed to 400 ppm, the highest level in human history, with no end in sight. According to the U.S. government's 2014 National Climate Assessment, the increase in CO_2 concentrations over the past century has caused the average temperature to rise almost 2° F, with the possibility of another 10° F increase by the end of this century. This rise in temperature, the EPA warns, could be devastating: "Small changes in the average temperature of the planet can translate to large and potentially dangerous shifts in climate and weather." Indeed, some scientists fear that we have crossed the Rubicon, the proverbial tipping point on global warming, where anything we do is too little and too late to offset years of stored CO_2 in the atmosphere.

Other greenhouse gases include methane, nitrous oxide, and fluorinated gases like hydrofluorocarbons, which also deplete the earth's protective ozone layer in the stratosphere. While methane accounts for about 10 percent of U.S. greenhouse gas emissions and is relatively short-lived in relation to CO_2, controlling methane is vital because its heat-trapping effects are roughly 25 times larger than those of CO_2.

Considering the longevity of greenhouse gases and the complexity of climate science and its consequences, climate issues present a formidable psychological challenge. Analogous to the frog's plight in a slowly boiling pot, the human species may not have the intrinsic inner tools to recognize the danger in time. We tend to ignore or discount warnings unless the consequences are immediate and direct. It is not surprising therefore that climate change ranks low among most people's top concerns when measured against other economic and social issues. Hearing the scientific call to action on climate change is even harder if people feel powerless to do anything about it individually, distrust government, or believe they have the financial ability to withstand its impacts.

Another coping strategy is climate denial, which has finally been marginalized by the scientific consensus on climate change, human causality, and growing global effects. The fifth IPCC report in 2014 drove the last nails into the coffin of climate denial by presenting multiple lines of independent evidence on climate change and its anthropogenic sources. Even before the IPCC report, U.S. public opinion was shifting quickly. Recent surveys on climate change show that more than 3 of every 4 Americans believe that temperatures are rising and that climate change will be "a serious problem for the U.S. if nothing is done."

Underlying heightened public awareness is more weather reporting on climate chaos and global weirding, growing international concern, and the consistency of scientific data pouring in from satellite imagery, ice and sediment core samples, sea level monitoring, and other sources. All of the research and publicity has made climate change part of our daily reality. As a result, we are seeing a foundation for action starting to take shape.

WARMING EFFECTS

What NASA's image of the Blue Marble did for global awareness, dramatic film footage of melting glaciers did for climate change. Watching glacial shelves tumble into the sea provided startling visual evidence of global warming to go along with everyone's anecdotal observations about warmer winters, stronger storms, and changing flora and fauna.

The so-called "evil twins" of climate change are global warming and ocean acidification, both driven by the same rapid increase in anthropogenic CO_2 emissions over the past two centuries. Global warming is the more widely researched and documented of the two primary effects, largely because it came to light first and its effects have been more apparent.

Global warming impacts range from melting polar ice caps and wildlife extinctions to extreme weather events. In the U.S., fluctuating weather patterns are caused in part by El Niño trade winds, which originate from prolonged higher surface temperatures in the Pacific Ocean off the coast of South America. Induced by climate change, El Niño is predicted to intensify during this century and bring more extreme weather, particularly to drought-stricken western states. In the East, the main concern has been storm activity and flooding, including Hurricane Katrina in 2005 and Hurricane Sandy in 2012, which caused $50 billion and $108 billion in damages, respectively.

"Climate change is about water," observed EPA Administrator Gina McCarthy. Her statement reflects IPCC predictions that global shifts in rainfall patterns will cause more frequent droughts and flooding. These conditions are expected to affect crop yields and food prices, with serious consequences for poverty, disease, and famine, all of which in turn destabilize communities and nations.

An example of how conflict can arise from climate change is the bloody Syrian civil war that began in 2011. The original cause of unrest was Syria's unexpected and severe drought from 2006 to 2010, which devastated 60 percent of the nation's farms and 80 percent of its livestock, overwhelming the government's ability to aide local farmers and starving citizens. Acknowledging the roots of the Syrian conflict, U.S. National Security Advisor Susan Rice said in 2014, "Climate change is now well understood to be a major national security issue and a source of stress on a number of underlying causes of conflict: drought, floods, food shortages, water scarcity. All of these drive increased human insecurity and poverty, and can contribute to conflict."

Global warming is also threatening wildlife. The National Academy of Sciences reports that thousands of species may not be able to adapt quickly enough. The signs of ecological stress are tangible for animals like polar bears, the iconic symbol of glacial melting, and avian populations like sea birds. Shifting bird ranges are being observed for the snowy owl, which is strangely flying south in search of food, and the chickadee, flying north for the same reason.

Another sentinel species is the monarch butterfly, which migrates 2,500 miles between Canada and Mexico annually. Scientists attribute the monarch's sudden population decline to multiple factors, including the loss of its main food source, milkweed, due to U.S. agriculture's widespread use of herbicides and the conversion of more land into cornfields for ethanol. Climate-related factors include extreme weather along migratory routes and the decline of the butterfly's small and fragile wintering grounds in the mountains west of Mexico City. About 90 percent of the world's monarch population shares this seasonal habitat, which has been reduced from hundreds of acres to a precious few due to higher temperatures and deforestation.

Global warming is also affecting insect populations, including a growing tick infestation that threatens moose by their parasitic numbers and people through a tenfold increase in Lyme disease over the past decade. Nature's adjustments to climate change are often harder to see in the plant kingdom, where native plants are becoming increasingly susceptible to invasive species and disease, such as the temperature-induced blight on eastern hemlocks.

The oceans are warming too. The IPCC reports that the vast majority of heat accumulated since 1971 is being stored in the oceans. While this helps to moderate air temperature increases and may offer us temporary reprieve from the catastrophic consequences of climate change, the ability of oceans to serve as a heat sink is not without effect. In New England, for example, warming ocean temperatures are causing rapid population increases of jellyfish and green crabs, an invasive species that feeds on clams. Commercial fishermen are also reporting large declines of cod and other ground fish, while data for the lobster industry show a northern lobster migration of 50 miles per decade into colder and deeper offshore waters, making lobsters more expensive to harvest.

∼

Ocean Acidification

The other primary effect of climate change is ocean acidification, which amplifies the problems of ocean warming. Over the past two centuries, the deeper oceans have absorbed about a third of the CO_2 produced by humans. CO_2 reacts with bicarbonate, which serves as a natural buffer against pH changes in the ocean, to create carbonic acid that lowers the pH level of water and makes it more corrosive. On the 0-14 pH scale, where a pH of 7 is neutral, oceans have historically averaged a pH of 8.2, on the basic or less acidic side of the scale. Today, that average has fallen to pH 8.1, representing a 25 percent increase in acidity on the logarithmic pH scale.

Ocean acidification is considered the biggest scientific advance in understanding climate change over the past 10 to 15 years. To find out why, I visited Dr. David Emerson, a senior marine scientist with Bigelow Laboratory for Ocean Sciences in Maine, who spoke with me about changing ocean chemistry and the growing effects of acidification.

"The oceanography community is every bit as concerned about acidification as temperature change," Emerson said. "In many cases, acidification may be a larger problem for the ocean." While the issue has not received the attention that warming has, the situation is starting to change. New research indicates that the harmful effects of acidification on the aquatic food chain are happening much faster than predicted.

Emerson described the unique physics and chemistry of the oceans and why they are becoming *sour* as well as *hot* and *breathless* due to global warming and oxygen depletion. He noted that ocean acidification is happening more uniformly than ocean warming, which displays a mosaic effect based on sea currents, thermal stratification, and the topography of continents and the ocean floor. In addition, he spoke about the pH differences between saltwater and fresh water systems, which are naturally more acidic and often fall into the pH range of 6 to 7.5. "The amazing thing about the ocean is its ability to resist changes in pH," he said. But while the oceans are well-buffered, he emphasized that they are at more risk from rising CO_2 levels because ocean organisms are less tolerant of small changes in acidity than fresh water organisms.

"The shellfish industry is going to be the most impacted—oysters, clams, mussels, mollusks," Emerson said, underscoring their delicate chemical balance by pointing out that clamshells dissolve in vinegar. He added that acidification contributes to coral reef bleaching and inhibits the growth of algae and phytoplankton, the base of the ocean food web and a vital source of the world's oxygen. "It's estimated that one out of every two breaths we take," he said, "comes from phytoplankton."

When asked about what could be done, Emerson recommended more research, including the development of more sensitive pH monitoring systems in the ocean. On the other hand, he said, the government would be wise to go slow on proposed ocean fertilization schemes to capture CO_2 from the air and sequester it in the deep ocean. One controversial geoengineering technique involves sprinkling iron on the ocean surface to induce algae blooms and the absorption of CO_2. Besides the fact that the algae are not sinking at expected rates, Emerson said that the majority of the oceanographic community opposes the idea because of its unknown side effects.

Emerson concluded by saying that "the only way to reduce ocean acidification is by reducing the amount of CO_2 in the atmosphere." But given the long odds of this happening and the longevity of CO_2, he said the real question now is how to manage the problem of climate change and how to adapt to the new realities.

BILL McKIBBEN

Greater awareness of climate effects has created a wave of interest and alarm that is re-energizing the environmental movement.

Climate activists in the U.S. are organizing communities around projects to divest in fossil fuel companies, reinvest in clean energy, and improve environmental safeguards. One of the leading organizations dedicated to the cause is 350.org, a U.S. nonprofit group with members and affiliates worldwide.

The co-founder and leader of 350.org is Bill McKibben, who burst onto the environmental scene in 1989 at age 29, with a pioneering book on climate change called *The End of Nature*. It was the first of a dozen environmental books that McKibben would author, and is Carson-esque in its lament about human mistreatment of the natural world. A Harvard graduate and former staff writer for *The New Yorker* magazine in the mid-1980s, McKibben gravitated to environmental issues in reaction to the trees-pollute-more-than-cars sentiments of the Reagan administration. He was also motivated by distinguished climatologist Dr. James Hansen, head of NASA's Goddard Institute for Space Studies from 1981 to 2013. Hansen postulated from his atmospheric studies of Venus that the Earth could experience a similar runaway greenhouse effect. He concluded that CO_2 atmospheric concentrations above 350 parts per million (ppm) were unsafe, stating, "If humanity wishes to preserve a planet similar to that on which civilization developed and to which life on Earth is adapted, ... CO_2 will need to be reduced from its current [2008] 385 ppm to at most 350 ppm, but likely less than that."

In 2008, as a resident scholar at Middlebury College in Vermont, McKibben and several of his students decided to launch a global grassroots initiative on climate change. They named the new organization 350.org after Hansen's CO_2 benchmark.

McKibben, and his well-known peer, Al Gore, published their influential books on climate change, *The End of Nature* and *Earth in the Balance*, only three years apart, yet their styles and approaches could not be more different. Whereas Gore is the consummate insider, with connections to world leaders and major corporations, McKibben is the classic outsider, leading a loose-knit coalition of citizens to change U.S. energy and environmental policy. McKibben circumvents the inside game in Washington, D.C., guiding his underdog citizen's army, like General Washington against the British, to make its presence felt by politicians and government officials.

In the spring of 2014, I spoke with Bill McKibben about his views on energy, his 350.org, and where the environmental movement was headed.

For a long time, McKibben saw his role as writing books. "I assumed someone else would take what I was doing and run with it—but that never seemed to happen. We weren't making progress in Washington, D.C. [on climate change] and writing another book was unlikely to move the needle any more. That's when we started doing 350, six or seven years ago. Since then, it's grown to dominate my schedule."

McKibben said that the organizing effort started slowly with essentially nothing—just he and seven of his Middlebury College students endeavoring to build an international network. "It was kind of witless in a certain sense. We were going to go out and organize the world. With beginner's luck in a way, we've managed to do that, or at least come closer than anybody else. It's bizarre sometimes—to wake up and realize that 191 countries have taken part, and you have lots of colleagues there, and they're doing amazing stuff. It's been very gratifying."

He believes that there is no time to lose given the severity of scientific warnings: "... the extinction in this century of perhaps half the forms of life on the planet, sea level out of control, endless extreme weather, and deaths of hundreds of millions of people, mostly in the poor world. In particular, drought has emerged as a powerful force. I also think the rate at which sea ice in the arctic is melting has proven to be a huge issue. Climate change is going to be dominant for a long time."

McKibben downplayed the scientific importance of the 2014 IPCC report: "What's interesting is how old hat it is. This is the fifth of them and basically the same one they wrote in 1995, with mild improvements in confidence levels. Basically, it's the same story I wrote in 1989 in *The End of Nature*. Our problem is not lack of knowledge about climate change at this point, we know what's going on; our problem is lack of willingness to take real action." He paused and added, "This is a systemic problem that needs to be addressed structurally and politically. What we desperately need first of all is the recognition that markets can do some of this work, but only if markets have information. Because there's no price on carbon, there's no way for markets to know anything about what's going on. And that's a huge problem. So, job one is a price on carbon."

The major barrier to carbon pricing, he said, is the power of the fossil fuel industry. He believes that despite record profits year after year, the major oil companies are not being held accountable under the polluters pay principle of U.S. environmental law. "The theory is that if anybody owns the sky, it's us, not Exxon. Why should they be allowed rent-free access to it?"

McKibben hopes that 350.org and others can at least weaken the major oil companies politically, acknowledging that it would be hard to bankrupt them in any real way. "Sometimes that means playing defense, [stopping] pipelines, things like that, and sometimes we get to play offense, as with divestments."

To ascertain 350.org's perspective on government, I mentioned President Obama's positive statements on climate science, to which he replied, "The words are great, but everybody's words on this stuff are always great. It's high time to prove he means it, actions like [stopping] the Keystone pipeline."

McKibben also questioned the president's "all of the above" energy philosophy, which supports all major types of energy development. "I think the bottom line is that it's not a philosophy at all. In any other realm of policy, he'd be laughed out of the room. If he announced he was going to have an 'all of the above' foreign policy, like England and North Korea the same, everybody would say that's ridiculous. And this is ridiculous."

As McKibben's words implied, the Obama administration had some fence-mending to do with the environmental community. Likewise, various sectors of the energy industry, particularly coal, were critical of the president's policies. Besides losing market share to cleaner natural gas, coal companies were facing tougher EPA emission standards for power plants, rendering new coal-fired plants virtually impossible to build without a system of underground carbon sequestration. I asked McKibben about that: "[Carbon sequestration] is possible to do theoretically and in practice. The problem is that it is incredibly expensive. Just think of the volumes involved," he said, explaining that carbon and oxygen atoms interact during combustion such that each rail carload of coal burned requires sequestration of two and a half of carloads of CO_2. "The physical engineering is so enormous that the expense of burning coal [becomes] ridiculous." Sequestration, he added, "... is just the bone they keep trying to throw to the coal industry—to pretend that we're still going to be burning coal in a little while, which if we have any sense, we're not."

I wondered what we thought about other proposed geoengineering fixes, like pumping aerosols or sulfur dioxide into the atmosphere to cool it. "All the studies show its side effects are likely to be much larger, on an order of magnitude comparable to climate change," he said. "It just strikes me as the kind of solution that addicts come up with to avoid dealing with the fact that they've got a real problem. We know what the problem is, we know basically what the solution is—get off fossil fuel. Geoengineers are [offering] one more attempt to not do it."

McKibben also shared his views on nuclear energy as a carbon-free alternative. He made it clear that he does not see nuclear hazards on the same scale as climate change. "I don't think they're comparable risks," he said, but added, "I'm unconvinced that nuclear is going to ride to our salvation. The numbers I've seen indicate it takes a long time to build and that the cost is enormous. Unfortunately, we don't have as much money around as we used to. I think where the world really wants to go is in the direction of what the engineers call 'distributed generation,' instead of big centralized power plants, nuclear or otherwise. An energy system that looks more like the internet does—widely distributed, everybody putting in and taking out."

With the inference to renewables, I asked if there were any silver bullets like solar? No, McKibben responded, "We already had our magic fuel—that was fossil fuel. It was great stuff, easy to get at, easy to transport around, rich in BTUs—one-for-one, nothing energy denser or as useful. The only problem is it's destroying the planet. I think our task is, and our hope is, that there's enough silver buckshot lying around that if we carefully picked up each piece, we might be more or less okay. I don't think we're going to [live our lives doing] exactly the same things we've done for the last 40 years. [For example] I don't see any energy solution that allows everybody to fly constantly at the drop of a hat."

We then turned to the topic of international cooperation and he shared a few of his thoughts: "We're eventually going to have to get some kind of global agreement. We just think that the forces on the other side [fossil fuel industry] are so strong that, for the moment, that's not really possible."

"If it were," I said, "what would the framework look like?"

"I've always said that the best plan is 'fees and dividends.' That's where you put a serious tax on things and then refund the money straight to citizens. You'd pay European prices at the pump and you'd get a check every month. Most people would come out ahead. I think that's highly doable politically. The problem is that it gets more difficult each year because the fee you need to put on gets steeper because the cuts need to get steeper. So we just keep getting behind the 8-ball, which worries me."

Concerning the ability to verify a new international agreement, McKibben said, "It shouldn't be beyond our abilities to enforce. We've got a pretty good handle on the movement of fossil fuel around the world and how much is produced, and where, and so forth. So if we had the will, there would be the way. Look, unfortunately, we're really good at surveillance now. This stuff is pretty easy to surveil. It comes in large quantities."

"Speaking of surveillance," I said, "how damaging were Edward Snowden's revelations that the National Security Agency wiretapped the 2009 international climate change conference in Copenhagen?"

"I gotta say, I take that stuff really seriously," he said. "I think it's outrageous. Copenhagen, piped like that, is a bad thing. The whole point is trying to build some trust there, and that was not happening. Yes, they [NSA] apparently had every delegation completely bugged. There's a lot of money at stake. The fossil fuel industry is the richest industry in our world."

Addressing what has been the greatest international impediment—the global economic disparities between nations and the demands on richer nations to assume historic responsibility for climate change, McKibben stated, "Inequality makes things very hard [and] is a serious obstacle. It's obvious what needs to be done. We need to take some small portion of the wealth that we have piled up burning fossil fuel and transfer it, mostly in the form of technology north-to-south, so that countries can develop without going through the carbon phase—too late for China, maybe not too late for India."

McKibben expressed uncertainty about hopes for an international agreement: "It depends on whether we get anything done within countries beforehand. And that really means the U.S. and China. So it's one of the reasons that I think Keystone [pipeline] is important. We give Obama some kind of bargaining chip about leaving carbon in the ground."

With regard to Keystone, I wondered if McKibben agreed with climatologist Dr. James Hansen, who is quoted as saying, "Tar sands equals game over."

"I really respect Jim Hansen. If you do the numbers, there is a huge concentration of carbon up in Alberta. If you were able to get everything that was economically recoverable, added in the tar sands in Alberta and burned it, you'd run the atmospheric carbon concentration to about 540 ppm. So that would, obviously, be yes, game over. The only problem with saying that is that there are eight or nine other deposits of carbon, maybe more, around the world that are equally as large [as Alberta] and that we have to work just as hard to keep in the ground. Operations of fossil fuel companies are not the problem. The problem is that these guys have five times as much carbon in their proven reserves as scientists think would be safe to burn."

Nearing the end of our talk, I asked McKibben what people could do. He said that while everything helps, the most important thing is to organize. "By yourself, you can't do too much, but if you come together with people, you can do a lot." He sees a rising *fossil fuel resistance* that "fights on local grounds but also comes together around big climate fights, like Keystone." He also mentioned efforts by 350.org to encourage financial divestiture from fossil fuel companies, which is showing signs of progress among a growing number of churches, schools, and municipalities. "The more colleges and churches that say we don't want to be associated with you [fossil fuel companies], the weaker they become. That's what happened around apartheid a generation ago—that's the hope here."

⌒

SOUTH PORTLAND TAR SANDS BLOCKADE

The controversy over the proposed Keystone XL pipeline brought the issue of climate change to the doorstep of average Americans. The oil industry wanted the pipeline to expand production of Canadian tar sands and deliver it to the U.S. gulf coast for refining and export. The environmental community, led by Bill McKibben and 350.org, opposed Keystone because of the large carbon footprint of tar sands manufacturing, and turned the project into the nation's defining issue on climate change.

The proposed route for the Keystone pipeline covered 1,179 miles from Alberta, Canada, through Montana and South Dakota, to southern Nebraska. The 36-inch pipeline was slated to carry 830,000 barrels of oil sands a day, approximately one-third of all U.S. crude oil imports from Canada, our nation's largest foreign oil supplier since 2004.

The oil companies needed Keystone to expand their lucrative Alberta tar sands mining operations, which had evolved over 40 years and were expected to last another 50 to 60 years with known reserves. The oil industry touted the project's contribution to secure and affordable energy and to thousands of new jobs in the U.S. and Canada, while the environmental community used the issue to confront indifference over climate change and to call for full carbon accounting of tar sands extraction.

Environmental concerns about mining Alberta tar sands include damage to the boreal forests of Canada, which like the Amazon rainforest, serve as the lungs of the earth to collect and store carbon. The extensive deforestation, strip mining, and high-pressure steam injections to heat and release the underground oil combine to emit three times more CO_2 than conventional drilling. Local impacts include vast tailing ponds of toxic slurry created during the mining process. In the U.S., states and communities worry that a pipeline spill could contaminate the Great Plains Ogallala aquifer, which provides drinking water to millions of people.

Environmental opposition to Keystone delayed the project for years. During this time, the oil companies and Canadian government made contingency plans in search of other pipeline routes and shipping ports. Reaching the Pacific from Alberta with a western pipeline expansion ran into stiff opposition, and a proposed new pipeline to the northwest across the Canadian Rocky Mountains would be expensive.

The most economical path was to the east, taking advantage of the existing pipeline to Montreal and its connection to ExxonMobil's Portland-Montreal pipeline, a combination of 24-inch and 18-inch diameter underground pipes built during World War II to bring oil from the U.S. to Canada. Since the war, the Portland-Montreal system has operated in one direction only, with arriving ocean tankers at South Portland, Maine, off-loading oil, which is then pumped across Maine, New Hampshire, and Vermont and over the Canadian border to Montreal. However, with Canada's metamorphosis from oil importer to exporter, ExxonMobil proposed reversing the flow of one of the pipelines to carry Alberta tar sands from Montreal to South Portland, where the product would be loaded onto tankers and shipped to refineries around the world.

In 2013, the tar sands proposal turned South Portland into a battleground between Big Oil and the city's 25,000 residents. South Portland is located across the Fore River from Portland, the state's largest city, and is known as an oil depot and shipping center as well as a working waterfront for fishermen. But it is also a gentrifying coastal community with quaint neighborhoods, parks, clean beaches, lighthouses, and summer tourism.

Many citizens of South Portland were concerned about the health, safety, and environmental risks associated with tar sands and did not want their city to become known as the "tar sands capital of the U.S." They had heard about the 2010 pipeline break in Michigan that dumped 843,000 gallons of tar sands into the Kalamazoo River, the largest inland oil spill in U.S. history, contaminating 35 miles of the river and causing health problems in nearby communities. Four years later, the party responsible, a Canadian energy company called Enbridge, had still not finished the Kalamazoo cleanup, incurring EPA fines for failing to complete the job in three years. The billion dollar cleanup has been particularly onerous because diluted pipeline tar sands, called bitumen or dilbit, are heavier than regular oil and have to be dredged from the bottom of the river.

South Portland residents were also concerned about air quality. To make tar sands viscous enough to slide through pipes, natural gas liquids and volatile chemicals such as benzene, toluene, and xylene are added to the sticky tar sands mixture of raw petroleum, sand, and water. At the end of the pipeline, these toxic chemicals are burned off prior to loading the crude oil onto ships. ExxonMobil contended that the construction of two 70-foot smokestacks in South Portland would provide the safety margin for the burning operation, but these assurances were met with skepticism by many residents.

To fight the tar sands proposal, a small group of concerned citizens in South Portland banded together with state environmental organizations in the spring of 2013 to draft a city ordinance blocking tar sands. They collected thousands of signatures, enough to put the ordinance on the ballot for the upcoming election in November, and proceeded to mount a grassroots campaign to secure the vote.

In the fall of 2013, I spent a few weekends in South Portland canvassing door-to-door with the Protect South Portland citizen's coalition. Walking into their converted storefront, one immediately felt a semblance of order behind the chaotic bustle. After signing in, I and other volunteers received 20 minutes of training on tar sands, the ordinance, and how to talk with local residents about the issue. We were handed three-hour canvassing assignments with street maps and a computerized list of residents by name, address, age, and party affiliation. Some people tackled their assignment alone, while others of us, new to the area, teamed up to knock on doors. This day, our street lists contained undecided voters, which offered an opportunity to hear the concerns of people and hopefully sway a few minds.

The biggest complaint about the ordinance was that it was written too broadly and could inadvertently restrain the growth of existing petroleum and waterfront businesses. Indeed, writing the ordinance had been tricky. Pipeline regulation is a federal activity, off-limits to local government, and tar sands could not be barred indiscriminately. The ordinance therefore had to thread the needle of home rule and local zoning authority over new types of business activity.

The pro-tar sands coalition consisted of the oil companies, backed by the national American Petroleum Institute, business groups, and local labor unions, all of which promoted the job benefits of the project. However, the oil industry forces knew that they were up against Yankee antipathy toward outside interests and Mainers' passionate pride in their state's natural beauty. They therefore made a calculated decision not to wage the fight over tar sands, but around what they deemed was a *poorly written ordinance* that would limit current businesses and their handling and distribution of home heating oil, gasoline, jet fuel, and other refined products.

The character of the campaign became "fear vs. fear"—the loss of a clean environment versus the loss of jobs, tax revenues, and new business. The similar slogans of the two sides only helped to confuse voters: "Protect South Portland" versus "Save the Waterfront."

The oil industry used its large war chest to hire a top team of lobbyists, lawyers, advertising consultants, and foot soldiers to run their pseudo-grassroots "astroturf" campaign. On the other side, citizens favoring the ordinance received back-up support from several state environmental groups: Environment Maine, the Natural Resources Council of Maine, and the state chapter of 350.org. Both sides waged a spirited campaign with repeated rounds of canvassing and phone-calling, and a plethora of lawn signs, newspaper editorials, endorsements, and media events. As the November finish line approached, I talked with a supporter on the phone who barked angrily that if he got one more call from us about the ordinance, he was going to switch his vote!

Election Day in South Portland finally arrived. I joined many other volunteers in the push to get out the vote. At the campaign office, we sat on a motley array of chairs that lined the walls of the crowded storefront room, and used our cell phones to call supporters who had not voted. Our calling lists were updated every hour, as real-time information trickled in from our precinct monitors at the polling stations. We told those we contacted that every vote counted and that it was going to be extremely close.

And indeed it was. The election hinged on just 192 votes, 4,453 to 4,261, reflecting a 45 percent turnout for the city in an off-year election. The oil industry had won by a whisker, despite far outspending the citizens' coalition at a rate of $168 for each industry vote. When the results were tallied by 9 pm, the leaders of the ordinance campaign, visibly shaken, addressed the storefront faithful, endeavoring to put the best face on the disheartening results, thanking workers, and vowing to continue the fight.

The election would have been a spectacular victory for the oil companies and their backers except for one thing—their disingenuous tactics. Having challenged the ordinance on technical grounds, many of their voters simply wanted a better worded ordinance. Knowing this, the city council interpreted the vote as a *rejection* of tar sands, and voted 6 to 1 a month later to slap a six-month moratorium on related development, an action that the oil industry charged was unconstitutional and vowed to take to court. In January 2014, the city council followed up by appointing a professional panel to draft a better defined restriction on tar sands, surgically constructed around local air quality and land use authority. Six months later, the council adopted the revised ordinance on the same 6 to 1 vote, barring the bulk loading of crude oil onto marine tank vessels, and effectively banning tar sands from South Portland. In early 2015, the industry made good on its pledge to sue, a case that is expected to last years.

Against all odds, a handful of concerned citizens had built an adept organization within a year, taken on Big Oil, and led the city and the state to a historic victory over the proposed eastern route for Alberta tar sands. If Canada and the oil industry wanted an eastern port, they would now have to go north around the United States to the city of Saint John in the coastal province of New Brunswick.

The oil industry received another blow when President Obama rejected the Keystone pipeline in November 2015. The decision was anticlimactic and largely symbolic given the alternatives for moving tar sands from Alberta and crude oil from the large Bakken oil fields of North Dakota. In addition to the existing network of Midwest pipelines, the industry can use rail transportation, which does not require presidential approval or massive new infrastructure. Unfortunately, every method of transport carries risk. Following a recent series of oil car derailments and explosions, the federal government has proposed tougher standards, including notification to local communities along the routes.

While there is no pleasing conservatives whose mantra is "Drill, baby, drill," the president placated his Keystone critics with his "all of the above" energy policy that rewards the fossil fuel industry in other areas, such as natural gas fracking and offshore oil drilling. On the environmental side, the American public submitted an extraordinary 2.5 million comments on the Keystone EIS. By saying no to Keystone, he appeased the environmental community, which made the pipeline its rallying cry, and added a feather to his mixed environmental legacy.

More importantly perhaps, the president had to reject Keystone if the U.S. hoped to lead the international community toward a comprehensive climate change agreement. His decision gave the

U.S. greater credibility and leverage to persuade other nations to act: Australia to curtail open pit uranium mining, Brazil to protect the Amazon rainforest, the Philippines to stop deforestation for palm oil production, and emerging nations everywhere to avoid the environmental mistakes made by the industrialized world.

GOVERNMENT ACTION

Climate change is a classic *tragedy of the commons*, where the resource at risk is not a cattle pasture overused by farmers, but the world's atmosphere overused by all of us in the form of an inverted sink for carbon emissions. Each person, business, and industry plays a minor part, burning only a tiny fraction of the world's carbon output. Yet together, our actions represent the environmental equivalent of death by a thousand cuts. We all contribute to the build-up of CO_2 and other greenhouse gases that warm the earth and acidify the oceans, disrupting the delicate equilibrium and causing harmful effects like sea level rise, extreme weather, habitat destruction, and biological extinctions. Putting it in a philosophical context, Mahatma Gandhi said it best, "Earth provides enough to satisfy every man's need, but not every man's greed." Climate change is showing us where the new line is.

While many in society can ignore the issue of climate change, and continue to put the global commons at risk, government cannot. It needs to assess the environmental and economic risks systematically and then act to protect the long-term public interest. The most important government challenge is managing the earth's atmosphere for what it is, a limited natural resource, and restricting the self-interest of individuals, corporations, and nations to degrade the resource.

Meaningful reductions in carbon emissions will require a sustainable and comprehensive international framework with binding agreements on emission reduction targets, timetables, and enforcement mechanisms. Without an enforceable global treaty, it is hard to imagine that individual nations will voluntarily scale back on energy consumption, significantly invest in energy efficiency and clean technology, or supply poorer nations with financial and technical aid to leapfrog the dirty 20th century path to industrial growth.

While the unilateral actions of nations are also critical to solving the climate crisis, the U.S. coal export business illustrates the larger challenge. Between 2000 and 2013, U.S. coal consumption declined 15 percent due to tougher federal emission standards and utility plant conversions to cleaner burning natural gas. Yet coal production in the U.S. remained relatively level during this period as a result of a 100 percent increase in U.S. coal exports, which hit an all-time high in 2012. Thus from the standpoint of climate change, the U.S. coal industry has been exporting CO_2 emissions like second-hand smoke, and causing as much global greenhouse pollution as if the coal were burned domestically.

As Bill McKibben indicated, developing an effective global strategy for pricing carbon will require leadership from the U.S. and China, which surpassed the U.S. as the world's largest CO_2 emitter in 2007, as well as other large carbon contributors like the European Union, Russia, India, and Japan. On a per capita basis, the U.S. remains a large CO_2 emitter, but so are many other countries that need to come clean, including Australia, Canada, Saudi Arabia, and several small but wealthy nations of the Middle East.

Government regulation is often a response to abuse or the potential for it. In the case of climate change, the abuse has become apparent, making it time for the international community to rein in the muscular fossil fuel industry and impose a higher price on carbon that reflects the true costs of CO_2 and other greenhouse gases to the natural environment and to humanity in the form of sickness, poverty, conflict, property damage, and other effects.

Solving the climate dilemma will require more than small adjustments. For its part, the U.S. government is beginning to take major steps that send the right signal to energy markets. In 2014, for example, the EPA proposed new regulations for power plants, the largest source of U.S. greenhouse gas emissions, to reduce CO_2 emissions by 30 percent in 2030 from 2005 levels. As the EPA does with criteria pollutants like ozone and particulates, it is giving states the flexibility to produce their own CO_2 action plans, using strategies built around energy efficiency, renewable energy use, and coal plant conversions to natural gas.

The EPA has also proposed new regulations to curb methane emissions from municipal landfills and numerous elements of the oil and gas industry, including oil drilling, gas pipeline leaks, and hydraulic fracturing, a mining technique now used on a massive scale by oil shale and natural gas companies in the U.S., Canada, and China. From a climate perspective, like the example of U.S. coal exports, heat-trapping methane released from natural gas production and transport cancels out some of the emission benefits of burning natural gas instead of oil and coal.

But government has other jobs in addition to regulating. It must also soften the economic impacts of climate change, ranging from extreme weather events like Hurricane Sandy, which scoured New Jersey coastal communities, to long-term economic dislocations and disproportionate impacts that raise issues of climate justice. The poor will invariably feel the consequences of climate change more keenly, including higher prices for food, energy, shelter, and other necessities. Sorting out these and other matters of economic fairness will be complex and demanding.

Government also has responsibilities to advance climate science by supporting further research, data collection, policy development, and programming. For example, the EPA has developed 30 or more scientific indicators of climate change to improve monitoring, while the U.S. Department of Agriculture recently set up several clearinghouses around the country to coordinate climate change research for farming, ranching, and forestry.

In addition to correcting market signals on the supply side, including turning off the spigot of tax subsidies to the oil industry, we need to send the right signals to consumers, such as cutting government subsidies for flood insurance that obscures the risk of sea level rise. The *inconvenient truth* about climate change is that it will force lifestyle changes. However, it remains to be seen how much change is required and how much of it can be tempered by better science and engineering in areas like green architecture, smart grids and battery technology, public transportation, telecommunications, and renewable energy.

We are also seeing better environmental practices being adopted into the mainstream of U.S. manufacturing and services. More companies are going green as a smart business strategy because more consumers are willing to pay for environmental responsibility: organic and locally grown foods, biodegradable and recyclable household products, and energy-saving appliances. So too, businesses are adjusting to the fact that more of today's college graduates are expressing interest in working for environmentally responsible companies.

Avoiding a global tragedy of the commons requires action in all directions. But the universal scope of the problem puts the greatest burden on government. The enormous challenge is twofold. The first, as Al Gore and others have imparted, is the need to reorganize society around environmental stewardship and less around political, economic, and religious doctrines. The second is making the necessary investments in climate change prevention despite inherent uncertainties about the effectiveness of such investments. Because of these uncertainties and the time it will take to see a turnaround in climate change, it also makes sense to consider reasonable interim measures for adaptation.

⟡⟶

ACCEPTING ADAPTATION

Only a few years ago, discussion of adaptation was considered giving up or a dangerous diversion from addressing the human causes of climate change. Today, *prevention* and *adaptation* have emerged as independent strategies to pursue, both reasonable in their own right.

In many ways, adaptation is more actionable than prevention because it involves local application of improved techniques for civil engineering, agriculture, forestry, and other fields. For example, the city of Miami is proposing to spend $400 million on storm water improvements at Miami Beach, a barrier island only 4 to 5 feet above sea level, to offset the risk of future flooding from sea level rise. This investment is considered a small sum to protect Miami Beach real estate and over $9 billion in annual tourism. In Miami and elsewhere, communities are considering new zoning restrictions on the size and location of coastal development and new building codes that heighten structures for better storm resistance. Similarly in transportation planning, expected sea level rise and storm surges are now a design factor in the siting and construction of new roads, rail lines, and runways.

Climate change, like any change, reshuffles the cards of misfortune and favor. While ocean communities may pay a price for seawalls and other expensive measures to fight beach erosion and storm surges, farmers may benefit from warmer summers and longer growing seasons. On a global scale, the melting Arctic ice is opening up a new sea lane above Canada that could reduce shipping distances between Europe and China by 40 to 50 percent. A downside may be the Panama Canal's loss of commerce.

While adaptation affirms the underlying truth of climate change, it should not condition us to accept climate change as unstoppable. Planning the future too optimistically around adaptation carries substantial risk. Misplaced optimism over adaptation might undermine the moral imperatives of climate justice in places like Bangladesh, where millions of people live at sea level without the means to relocate or rebuild. Second, it may weaken the urgency to act collectively, ultimately costing us more with each passing year of inaction and the accumulation of greenhouse gases. For these reasons, adaptation should not become an excuse to delay or sidestep preventative measures, or a subterfuge like geoengineering with cures worse than the disease.

The challenge is to hold governments accountable for devising policies, programs, and regulations that move us in the right direction, slowing the human causes of climate change and moving us toward a sustainable future. Actions are needed on all levels to meet the greatest environmental threat we have ever faced. And above all, as former astronaut and U.S. Senator Bill Nelson said about his environmental revelation in seeing Earth from outer space—it will take nothing less than a new perspective on the unity of nature and the human spirit.

CHAPTER IX

SUSTAINABLE CHOICES

THE ENVIRONMENT IS UNDER STRESS from human activity around the world. In the words of Al Gore, the human species has become "a sufficiently powerful force of nature to reshape the ecological system of our planet." Yet we also possess the collective power to address the causes of pollution, restore balance, and put ourselves on a sustainable path.

Building a sustainable future requires a change in perspective and a willingness to put a higher premium on environmental protection, beginning with price controls on carbon to arrest the human causes of climate change. Although such controls will make fossil fuels more expensive, they avoid the worse fate of doing nothing about carbon pollution. What is more, they will deliver immediate benefits to human health and open up new energy and economic opportunities.

Needed changes will take time, but there is reason for optimism. The environmental movement has grown from the bottom up into a mature and durable force, characterized by decentralized leadership and widespread involvement by individuals, communities, businesses, churches, schools, and nonprofit organizations. People everywhere are coming to the same realization that protecting the air and water, climate, and biodiversity is more than a moral concern—it is the most rational thing we can do, like a stitch in time.

Preceding chapters have highlighted individuals who have made major contributions to environmental awareness and the environmental movement. Some of these leaders made their contributions inside the system, pulling for change, while others made it from the outside, pushing for change. They came from many professional walks of life: politician Teddy Roosevelt, scientist and author Rachel Carson, publisher Stewart Brand, federal executives Bill Ruckelshaus and Russell Train, and writer and organizer Bill McKibben. Besides such well-known figures, we have considered the impact that citizens groups can have on the course of events, including the 1977 Seabrook nuclear power plant occupation and present-day blockades of tar sands production to stem greenhouse gases.

As the range of leadership shows, environmental stewardship is interdisciplinary and extraordinarily complex. Every major environmental issue is a dynamic nexus of science, economics, and politics that carries an assortment of trade-offs and alliances. It may not be clear who the good guys and bad guys are, if indeed there are any, or whether we possess adequate information to make good decisions. In some cases, the best interests of the public may be ambiguous and the full consequences of action uncertain.

Appreciating these complexities led us to discussions about the National Environmental Policy Act, the Clean Air Act, and various forms of energy production. With regard to NEPA, we took a thorough look at its central role in the environmental process and how to improve it. On air quality, we saw how public policy can succeed when the national commitment is there, in contrast to the elusiveness of an agreement on park overflight noise. In the energy sector, we explored issues surrounding the use of fossil fuels, nuclear power, and renewables and how to reduce our energy footprint.

Despite the complex issues and the government's multi-layered roles and responsibilities for dealing with them, many people still view the government simplistically. Those who do, often view it negatively. This is not to say that skepticism about government is unwarranted. History is replete with examples of cover-ups, foot-dragging, and poor decision-making. As we have seen on the environment, it took citizen action on nuclear power to force more rigorous government oversight. It took visionaries like Rachel Carson to expose the indiscriminate use of pesticides, agitators like Stewart Brand to pry loose more space photos of Earth, and intellectuals like Bill McKibben to help us respond to climate change. Their success in raising environmental awareness is a strong reminder that our representative government *follows* public opinion.

Many successful environmental reforms start locally. Moving the system to act often begins with concerned citizens, who battle the odds, organize their neighbors, and enlist the support of civic groups, schools, churches, and political parties. As these grassroots initiatives take hold and expand, they influence local, state, and federal government planning and decision-making.

Environmental advocacy is always stronger when citizens know how the government operates. South Portland, Maine, is a good example of effective advocacy because the community carefully researched what was allowed under their home rule charter and what was cordoned off to the federal government. In this regard, we have examined the government's tools, including legislation, research, and program development as well as the surprising berth that agencies possess to set the agenda and interpret mandates. In the process, we visited some of the problems that arise within agencies, between agencies, and between government and industry when it comes to environmental policymaking.

Despite the variability and complexity of environmental issues, one lesson stands out. Those who know more about government and how it works are in better position to amplify the scientific, political, and moral arguments for the environment and make themselves the most effective players in the room.

BACK TO THE LOCAL CAFÉ

Sam was on the return leg of a trip and it was great to see him. His last visit had been years ago, when we were chatting about Seabrook. Since then, Sam had retired from teaching and caught the travel bug.

With rain in the forecast, we decided to go to the old coffee shop for the afternoon. We found a table and some comfortable chairs, grabbed a few refreshments, and plunked down. We reminisced about his teaching days and joked about the short shelf life of college credentials. In the working world, it's all what you know and how well you do your job. That got Sam ruminating about the ingredients of success. As if leaning on his lectern again, he wanted to know how I felt about the public service spirit in Washington.

"It goes mostly unspoken," I said, "but I saw lots of smart and ambitious people in federal service who didn't reach the top because they didn't have that spirit."

Sam cited the old refrain that our laws are only as good as the people who administer them. "The problem today," he said, "is that public servants, including teachers, are held in such low esteem that good people are getting scared away from these careers—I'd hear it from my students."

"Feds have been treated like a punching bag for so long, it's a given," I said. "All you can do is ignore it and deal with the realities." But I quickly added that the realities weren't always much better, as when important actions were stymied by paperwork and lengthy coordination. One could only accept the fact that the system was intended to be slow to gather a complete picture, find errors, and avoid other pitfalls.

"For what it's worth, I've found that going slow isn't always bad," said Sam, who observed that sacrificing some efficiency, especially taking more time to consult with people, can be more effective in the end. He emphasized its importance in academia, which made him curious again about successful personal qualities in government.

It varies, I said, but management will often recognize someone as a capable team player and groom them for the next level. I also noted that people tend to self-select under the "two-track theory" of becoming a manager or a scientific expert. On the managerial track, the theory holds that managing is managing, and that top federal managers will excel in any agency or area of work. While the theory contains an element of truth, the most successful and well-liked managers tend to be the ones who stay tethered to their technical expertise, while the best scientists tend to be good communicators with crossover managerial skills. "The problem with managing," I continued, "is that your time gets eaten up by meetings and administration. That's why I liked the project side better—it offered more contact with environmental scientists and enthusiastic younger people."

"Let's stop there for a second," said Sam, who had read a recent poll showing that the younger generation is less interested in the environment than their parents. "What's going on? Today's young adults have been reared on the environment since they were knee-high."

"Maybe it's the polling question. I've heard that millennials don't like to be called environmentalists because they think the term is loaded. If not that, maybe a little fatigue from hearing so much about the environment or the size of the problems."

"They're not the only demographic to worry about," Sam said. "A lot of working class people consider the environment a rich man's issue."

Sam knew he was getting to the heart of environmental opposition. Poor communities have a hard time seeing the environment as their fight too. Project proponents understand that and often try to drive a wedge through communities by citing the loss of jobs and tax revenue if their proposal is rejected. Those with the courage to stand up for the environment are automatically attacked as NIMBYs, obstructionists, or anti-business and anti-growth.

"It seems only natural to discount environmental issues if you think your current or future job is at stake," Sam added.

I acknowledged that environmental considerations can sometimes alter a business deal and affect some people's financial interest. It can also cost more upfront to go green. However, the economic arguments against environmental caution are often shortsighted. Where would the fishing and lumber industries be without the conservation of marine fisheries and forestlands? And what about the emerging renewable energy industry, which is quickly expanding, generating well-paying jobs, increasing competition, and holding prices down, all of which boost the economy?

"Still," Sam said, "the environment is a long-term issue and sacrificing for the future can get abstract."

"But that's it," I said. "Managing natural resources and finding the right balance requires the longer view. And the environment can't protect itself—it's up to us."

"I don't disagree, but it helps me see why some people, especially those who are struggling, oppose stronger environmental rules," Sam said. "Just one more thing the government is doing to them."

"There's so much talk these days about cutting government rather than making it better. It's toxic," I said. "No one disagrees that the government has problems." I had seen a few of them first-hand, like too much wasteful outsourcing, secrecy, and political decision-making. But I couldn't buy the shop-worn platitudes about government being too big, uncaring, or better managed like a corporation. Such myths erode respect for civil servants and our environmental laws by association. Eventually the problems reach the surface, like the broken federal appropriations process and government shutdowns. Under the circumstances, it's a miracle that federal agencies do as well as they do.

Sam agreed that a lot of anti-government rhetoric is just that; then suggested it was time for the private sector to do more for the environment. But he cautioned against relying too much on corporate America: "Where was Detroit when Toyota was pioneering the hybrid?"

It reminded me of Sam's old class on organizational development and his "3-C" matrix. The first C stood for *culture*: was an organization receptive or hostile to its social responsibilities? The second was *commitment*: did the organization take real steps to meet them? And the third was *control*: were effective systems in place to ensure accountability?

"Okay," he tested, "how would FAA stack up?"

I started by citing the FAA's dedication to safety. But on the environment, I could only give the agency a passing grade, although I gave the Airports Office higher marks for understanding that airports need to work with local communities. I also recalled the Airports management once asking the office to brainstorm what airports *should* look like in the future. The environmental list included universal airport sustainability plans, 100% recycling, green buildings, intermodal transportation, total gate electrification, and solar power. Indeed, a few of the ideas worked their way into our office goals and programs.

But I had to admit how unusual this exercise had been. Normally, we were bogged down in our routine environmental duties and reacting to each day's problems. I drew an analogy to the whole environmental movement and how much energy since the 1980s had gone into managing existing laws and defending them against attack.

We discussed why that was, including the formidable power of the oil industry, which continues to enjoy big federal subsidies in the form of tax depletion allowances, master limited partnerships to avoid corporate taxes, loan guarantees, low royalties on federal land leases, and other breaks. We also shared our disappointment over the Obama Administration's decisions to deregulate oil and gas exploration off the coast of Alaska and along the Eastern Seaboard. Hadn't we learned anything in the Gulf with Deepwater Horizon? We both shuddered at the thought of blasting the Atlantic floor with low-frequency sound cannons to locate oil deposits. According to the U.S. Bureau of Ocean Energy Management, this sound will be heard underwater for *thousands* of miles and harm thousands of sea creatures, including the hearing of whales and dolphins.

"It's hard not to lose faith these days," Sam bemoaned, "when there's irreversible harm to wildlife and habitat."

"And we keep letting it happen by downplaying the risks," I said, citing the cleanup costs of accidents and malfeasance like Deepwater Horizon and Love Canal, plus other back-end costs like the $500 million dollar decommissioning of Maine Yankee nuclear power plant in 1996, with its ongoing price tag of $9 million a year to store and protect 1,400 spent fuel assemblies. That price tag will soon be dwarfed by numerous other decommissionings, like the San Onofre nuclear plant in southern California. Dismantling the plant will take two decades and $4.4 billion dollars."

"I'd really get depressed if there wasn't some good news once in a while," Sam said. "I've read that the ozone layers over the poles are recovering, and bald eagles and condors are coming back. I know too, from visiting Costa Rica, that their big effort at reforestation is working.

"And I'll add one to the list—the IPCC's scientific professionalism," referring to the International Panel on Climate Change. "By the way, ever hear of Jairam Ramesh?" I asked. Sam shook his head. Ramesh was a leader of India's Congress Party and the former environmental minister of India from 2009 to 2011. He gained a reputation for halting billions worth of highway, dam, coal mining, and hillside housing projects that threatened healthy forests and India's environmental laws. Industry and business attacked him viciously, but he never wavered, saying, "We cannot afford to pollute our way to prosperity."

"Haven't heard many politicians say that," Sam said.

I added that Ramesh also wanted a positive environmental agenda for his country, which he framed around a proposed cap on carbon emissions. It was a good example, I thought, of how climate change had created a rallying point for environmental action.

It all came back to the basics for Sam—education. "Pardon my teaching bias," he said, "but if citizens are informed, they'll be able to sort through the trade-offs and competing claims. And better educational training leads to the innovation we need."

"How about this idea," I said, "making Earth Day a national holiday? Or setting an ambitious goal for solar, like we did for putting a man on the moon: 30 percent of our electricity from solar by 2030, then 10 percent more each decade as the technology improves until we reach 90 percent by 2090?"

Sam leaned back and wondered, "90 percent?"

"Right, solar has everything," I said, citing its attributes: a proven technology, flexible in terms of siting and end uses, low maintenance, increasingly economical, resistant to monopoly, and best of all low-impact, even compared with other renewables. "You'll never hear about solar spills," I joked.

"I guess the issue is cloudy days and winters," Sam said.

"Solar has current limits, but not as many as some think," I said, referring to the energy establishment's penchant for talking down solar potential. Their standard refrain is scalability—that solar and renewables will always be a niche market, never able to satisfy a sizable percentage of the nation's energy demand.

"And you're saying it's a failure of imagination?" Sam asked.

"Absolutely—you taught me to look out for that." I noted that the electric grid already provides the bridge to a solar future. But taking full advantage of it requires changes to the utility business. The roadblocks to independent power production and net metering have to be removed in order to facilitate individual and collective investments in solar. It had been decades since the utility issue had come up in Franklin County, but maybe now was the time to reinvent the utilities to better reflect the public interest on renewable energy. Looking farther into the future, new breakthroughs in energy storage and battery technology would enable a grid-less system. We'd be able to store electricity on-site and solve weather and seasonal issues.

"It's hard to imagine being totally independent of the grid," Sam said. "I suppose it would feel like a final mortgage payment to the bank. But let's be real, solar has been around for decades and hasn't taken off yet."

"I think it shows the critical role of public policy in energy development," I said. "Solar will never emerge in a big way if we let the utilities dictate, or keep propping up fossil fuels and high-risk operations like fracking and offshore oil drilling. It doesn't have to be this way. Look at what Germany is doing with solar energy and renewables. I don't know the whole story, but I've heard they've made some big strides."

"So hey, let's do this," Sam said, "why don't we go grab another cup of coffee and search the Net on that."

⌣‿⌐

SOLAR EXPERIMENT IN GERMANY

As our search revealed, Germany has become a trailblazer in Europe and around the world in renewable energy development, particularly solar photovoltaics (PV). After two decades of progress, Germany has more installed PV capacity than any other country, including the U.S., which has 27 times more land and four times more population. The Germans have built over 1 million solar installations, which together account for approximately 7 percent of Germany's electricity production. On some sunny days, their solar capacity can satisfy as much as 50 percent of the country's demand for power.

Germany's bold steps on solar and other renewables are matched by their resolve to use less coal and nuclear power. For example, Germany retired eight of 17 nuclear power plants in 2011 after Japan's Fukushima nuclear plant disaster and vowed to shut down the rest by 2022. Furthermore, the major German engineering corporation that built the plants, Siemens, announced its exit from the nuclear industry.

Germany's solar experiment offers a model for other industrialized nations. Its success is all the more remarkable because of its limited solar access. Germany's northern latitudes, which are above the continental U.S., receive about one-third less sun than our northern states and less than half of what falls on our solar-friendly southwest.

Yet what the Germans lack in solar radiation, they make up for with keen understanding of economics. Despite less sunshine at northern latitudes, solar energy can be an effective choice even there because of higher heating and energy costs. The Germans also calculated the economic and national security risks associated with foreign oil imports. They were unwilling to cede too much control over supply and prices, or become prey to the environmental costs of oil spills and nuclear accidents.

The German formula includes attractive economic incentives for renewables. Their landmark Renewable Energy Sources Act of 2000 obligates electric utilities to enter into long-term contracts with homeowners and other third-party producers, who are paid for their electricity with feed-in tariffs that exceed the retail rate for electricity and reflect the production costs of different renewable energy technologies. The program's effect on household electricity bills has been a drop in the bucket, but the results have been dramatic. Germany's solar PV capacity has effectively doubled every 18 months from 1990 to 2012, representing an almost 59 percent annual growth rate.

In contrast, the U.S. addiction to fossil fuels has barely changed over the years, despite advances in renewable technology and a long line of presidential energy proclamations from Richard Nixon's "Project Independence" to Jimmy Carter's "moral equivalent of war" to George W. Bush's "Freedom Car." In 1950, the United States obtained 8 percent of its energy from renewable sources, chiefly hydroelectric power and biomass. In 2012, over 60 years later, the total share for U.S. renewables was roughly 10 percent, a bump of only two percentage points. Of that total, solar energy is a small component—about one-half of 1 percent of the nation's energy consumption. The statistics suggest that U.S. commitment to renewable energy development, particularly solar, has been long on words and short on results.

Besides Germany, other countries around the world outperform the U.S. in energy production from renewables, including Italy on solar PV, China on wind power, and China and Brazil on hydropower. Our international rankings decline more when production is measured on a per capita basis, and they are not likely to improve soon. Other large oil importers like Japan and India are on a faster track to renewables, attracted by the benefits of lower imports, more stable energy prices, and new business opportunities. The same is true in Europe, where the European Union has set a renewable energy goal of 20 percent of *total energy consumption* by 2020. The U.S. boasts a similar timeframe and 20 percent target for renewables, but our goal, by contrast, pertains only to *federal government use of electricity.* Indeed, even if the goal applied to the nation as a whole, electricity use only represents about 40 percent of U.S. total energy consumption.

Despite the barriers, the U.S. solar industry remains poised for a major breakthrough. Prices on panels have fallen 75 percent in recent years and the federal government continues to offer a tax break for solar. Another economic inducement has been third-party financing. Solar leasing companies can virtually eliminate the start-up costs for businesses and homeowners that want to go solar but cannot afford to buy a system. These investors make solar easy by handling the design, permitting, installation, and maintenance.

So what is holding solar back? The solar revolution confronts a three-part challenge involving U.S. energy supply, energy demand, and public policy. On the supply side, the U.S. is blessed with more solar potential than Germany but it goes untapped because conventional fuels hold the inside track. These advantages have been boosted by recent oil discoveries and increased natural gas production from fracking, which have made solar and other energy alternatives more expensive by comparison. On the demand side, solar economics have been affected by falling U.S. energy consumption since 2000, due in part to energy efficiency improvements like higher-mileage vehicles and more efficient heating, cooling, and lighting systems. Reduced demand puts a downward pressure on energy prices, making it harder for new entrants like solar. Finally, in terms of public policy, the U.S. tax code is weighted heavily in favor of fossil fuels, fortifying the competitiveness of the oil industry. All of these factors combine to delay the inevitable dawning of the solar age.

TAKING SOCIAL RESPONSIBILITY

"You've got to hand it to the Germans for turning a million consumers into producers," Sam said.

"Makes me wonder," I said, "what if everyone could invest in their electric utility and renewable energy production, like owning shares in a utility solar farm?"

"There'd probably be takers," Sam said. "People are willing to spend to help the environment if they have reasonable choices." His comment brought us around again to the thousand and one ways to help the planet, like using public transportation, buying local, and eating less meat. The latter subject on diet shot us online again to learn that cattle farms use five times the energy and 25 percent more land than other animal husbandry.

"Usually one lifestyle change leads to more," I said. "I'm hopeful, but it's not easy when you consider how quickly the environment and habitat can be damaged, and how long it takes to restore it."

Sam smiled and sang, "*You don't know what you've got 'til it's gone,*" a verse from Joni Mitchell's tune, "Big Yellow Taxi."

"It's funny," I said. "Our family used to go to the Delaware shore for a week in the summer. The kids loved a mini-golf place called Paradise. One summer we got there, only to discover that Paradise had gone out of business and had been paved over—into a parking lot for a new store."

"I don't think Joni had mini-golf in mind," Sam said, "but it shows how little control we have sometimes."

"I'd guess that's why people get discouraged," I said, "along with the slow pace of change, including economic policy."

"Don't get me started," said Sam, who believed it was high time for a stiff tax on luxuries like private jets, yachts, and vacation homes. He condemned the growing income inequality in America and the lack of individual and corporate responsibility, including environmental. Too many businesses, he said, see it one way—environmental regulations as an impediment to growth. They and their government lobbyists want everyone to get out of their way. They fail to recognize or appreciate the many benefits provided by the public sector, including security and safety, roads and transportation, an honest legal system with patent and trade protections, a strong middle class and educated workforce, and a clean environment.

"This one takes the cake," I said. "Local businesses in my community are complaining about a proposal to charge customers a paltry 5 cent fee for plastic bags and Styrofoam boxes that blow around, clog storm drains, and harm waterfowl. And the businesses get to keep the 5 cents."

"It often gets around to ethics," Sam said, "but like they say, you can't legislate morality. And morality can get a little muddy on issues like the environment, where we might not even be aware of the damage we're doing."

"In what sense?" I asked.

"Well... millions of people try to do everything in their daily life to save energy and do the right thing, and then they blindly invest their money in polluting companies, undoing everything they're trying to do personally."

"Divestment," I said. "It's starting to gain attention."

"It should be, because anyone who plays the market without understanding and screening their investments is part of the problem—unknowingly," said Sam, who believed that it wasn't hard these days to do the research on socially responsible mutual funds and other investments. It seemed even easier for large institutions with specialists who manage college endowments, pension plans, and other major investments. If people and organizations had sound advice about the available options, he believed they would scrub their portfolios.

"So why don't we go back online," I said, "and see who's divesting for environmental reasons."

~

FINANCIAL DIVESTITURE

When we searched on fossil fuel divestiture, we found several firms advertising green investment services along with a bevy of stories about the fast-growing divestiture movement among municipalities, religious institutions, colleges and universities, and foundations. The West Coast was setting the trend for municipalities—Seattle, Portland, San Francisco, Oakland, and other cities in California being among the first to act. In Oakland, the city council unanimously voted to divest from any company "whose primary business or enterprise is extraction, production, refining, burning and/or distribution of any fossil fuels."

Within the religious community, the World Council of Churches is one of the biggest organizations to divest from fossil fuels. The Council represents over 300 churches and 500 million Orthodox Christians worldwide, including Baptists, Lutherans, and Methodists. Other religious bodies taking action are Philadelphia Quakers, the Unitarian General Assembly, and the Union Theological Seminary. In the Catholic church, it remains to be seen what effect Pope Francis' 2015 encyclical on rescuing the planet from climate change will have on Catholics and church decisions.

Of the first dozen colleges and universities divesting from fossil fuels, the most well-known, Stanford University, purged coal-mining companies from its $18.7 billion endowment. Stanford trustees used the rationale of not causing "substantial social injury" as the basis for their decision.

Also extricating themselves from fossil fuel companies and reinvesting in clean energy are some of the world's largest public financial institutions such as the World Bank and the European Investment Bank, along with a number of private foundations, including the Rockefeller Brothers Fund, Wallace Global Fund, and Russell Family Foundation.

Yet for every organization that has navigated the internal debate and divested, there seemed to be a failed attempt somewhere else. Institutional opposition to divestment revolves around three basic concerns. First is the argument that it will hurt an institution's bottom line. However, the research shows that green investments can be as lucrative as fossil fuel stocks. Moreover, the financial risk in divesting is generally small because energy firms are only a fraction of the holdings in a diversified portfolio. Advocates of divesting also point out that coal and other fossil fuel stocks may be over-valued today in light of growing international efforts to control greenhouse gases and convert to cleaner technologies. In the final analysis, the earnings debate often hides a more human issue—as a fiduciary matter, financial committees do not like having their hands tied in any way.

The second argument against divestment is that it makes little difference in the battle against climate change. While true now, the argument fails to recognize that moral progress is possible over time, like the successful boycott of South African companies in the 1980s to end apartheid. It is doubtful that fossil fuel giants will be humbled by divestment directly, but money diverted from their coffers represents a substantial sum for capitalizing clean energy projects. By reinvesting in renewable energy systems, the competi-tive stakes are raised and the entire energy industry is stirred to adopt better environmental practices.

The third argument is the proverbial slippery slope. Institutional gatekeepers say that if they agree to divest for environmental rea-sons, they will be inundated by other demands. However, it is hard to equate climate change with other causes. It stands out as a sci-entific issue of global proportions, and few issues have such mass appeal. If the problem does happen, institutions are always free to set up protective thresholds.

While financial managers want to be persuaded on their terms, ethics is still at the heart of the divestment debate. In the case of colleges and universities, students are asking school administrators and trustees why their institution's financial practices are divorced from its educational purposes and larger social obligations. Given the global scientific consensus, students can make a compelling argument that continued institutional investment in fossil fuel companies is the epitome of arrogance. As Bill McKibben says, "If it's wrong to wreck the climate, then it's wrong to profit from that wreckage."

TIME TO GO

"Changing the establishment always takes time," Sam said. "Divestiture won't be any different."

"Maybe it'll catch on," I said, "and buying solar panels. Both are important steps that individuals can take."

"It may surprise us, you never know," Sam said. "In any event, add divestment specialist to hundreds of new and promising environmental careers today."

"I only wish things were happening faster," I said, referring to the fact that Al Gore, Bill McKibben, and the scientific community had to talk up climate change for three decades before the EPA enacted its first strong carbon regulations. But with that said, I still had faith in utilizing government to greater effect.

"Save those thoughts for later," Sam said, "it's probably time for us to be going. And it's stopped raining."

"It's been fun," I said, "just like your classes used to be."

"Thanks," he said, "but the tires are getting a little thinner."

"You haven't lost a step. And no one touched more students than you," I said.

"Well, I hope so, otherwise I didn't do my job." Looking out the café window onto the street, we noticed a couple of joggers go by. Never one to miss a teaching moment, Sam remarked, "Remember what I said years ago about jogging and health. It requires a certain mindset. It's less about speed and distance. Just stay at it for half an hour and you'll do it your whole life."

ACKNOWLEDGMENTS

⌒

THREE YEARS AGO, IT WAS audacious to think that I could pull my loose ideas together and overcome years of ingrained technical writing for the government to offer a book of general interest on a popular topic like the environment. I had a good share of discouraging moments and doubts along the way but I was fortunate to have the support of family, friends, and colleagues to help me through.

While the opinions expressed in the book are mine, I am indebted to many talented individuals for their contributions. These reviewers steered me in the right direction, sharpened my approach and writing style, got me over the bumps, and offered needed encouragement.

In the area of air quality, I'd like to thank Darcy Zarubiak and Mike Kenney for lending their scientific and regulatory expertise, which included fact-checking, sorting out timelines, and clarifying technical issues. The same support came from Bob Miller on matters of acoustics and aircraft noise and from Steve Barrett on solar and renewable energy.

Helping me with the inside look at government and how the government applies environmental laws and regulations were three savvy and dedicated pros: Ed Melisky, Ralph Thompson, and Bill Brennan. Ed Melisky is a leading expert on the National Environmental Policy Act and other environmental statutes. Ralph Thompson shared his extensive knowledge of airport and environmental planning, including air quality and noise evaluations. And last but not least, Bill Brennan offered valuable insights into national energy policy and federal management. Bill, who is the author of five books, also encouraged me to write when it was just a pipedream and provided helpful advice on the mechanics of publishing.

I am especially grateful to Bill McKibben, who gave me a personal interview on a full range of climate-related issues. Likewise, David Emerson shared his thoughts with me on ocean acidification. I could not have written the chapter on climate change without their offerings. In addition, I'd like to thank Annie Cheatham for her observations about Al Gore when he first came to Congress and joined the House Congressional Clearinghouse on the Future, an organization that Annie directed and where I worked one summer as an intern.

I'd also like to express appreciation to my good friends Charles Behling and Larry Checco, for their broad reviews and recommendations. They knew the direction I wanted to go and provided the reassuring wind in the sails when I needed it.

Presenting the material in the best of form would have been impossible without my editors, and I was blessed to have two of the best. Mara Ranville provided a strong sounding board from an environmental standpoint, sharpening both the message and the writing style. Anne McManus, my dear friend and neighbor, was by my side from the start, and provided invaluable organizational advice and skillful copy editing. She opened my eyes in many ways to what needed improving—things I would have never seen.

Finally, my wife Marcia and children Alexandra and Tyler, to whom I owe so much, were my bedrock supporters day in and day out. Tyler was also my ace twentyish editor in the hole, helping to keep the writing and examples more youthful and contemporary. And essential to everything were the contributions of my accomplished and energetic wife, Marcia, who offered the wonderful balance of strong critiques with eternal patience and support.

SOURCE NOTES

I. CITIZEN ACTION: THE PROTEST AT SEABROOK

1 We were told: Anna Gyorgy, *No Nukes: Everyone's Guide to Nuclear Power* (Boston, South End Press, 1979), 398.

2 The president's message: "Thompson Looking for Funds to Pay Costs of Seabrook Protest," *Hartford Courant*, AP, May 5, 1977, 12.

2 The protest was led by the Clamshell Alliance: Gyorgy, *No Nukes*, 396.

2 They also required each participant to join an "affinity group": Gyorgy, *No Nukes*, 388-389, 397.

The Occupation

4 It was an empty landscape: Gyorgy, *No Nukes*, 398. Photo by Lionel Delevingne.

6 "In America": Robbie Leppzer and Phyllis Joffe, Directors, *Seabrook 1977* (Turning Tide Productions, 2007, remastered 80-min. CD of 1978 VideoNewsReal).

6 "When the police come": Leppzer and Joffe, *Seabrook 1977*.

7 The arrest of 1,4,14 protestors: Shel Horowitz, "Peace, Gentleness, Community," *Peace Work Newsletter*, 54 (June 1977): 3.

Live Free or Die

7   When I looked around the bus: "Many N-Power Foes Remain in Custody," *Hartford Courant*, AP, May 4, 1977;

Arnie Alpert, "The 1977 Seabrook Occupation: Discipline, Humor, and the Power of Nonviolence," PeaceWork Magazine, Issue 375 (May 2007).

7   Handling legal matters: John Kifner, "Atom Plant Protest is Being Prolonged," *New York Times*, May 5, 1977;

"A Power Problem in New Hampshire," *New York Times Editorial*, May 7, 1977.

8   Over 600 people: Alpert, "The 1977 Seabrook Occupation: Discipline, Humor, and the Power of Nonviolence";

John Kifner, "Arrested Nuclear Foes Vow to Keep Movement Going," *New York Times*, May 8, 1977, 18.

10   "The planning that went into the operation": Leppzer and Joffe, *Seabrook 1977.*

10   Around New England: John Kifner, "New Hampshire's Governor Asks Public for Funds to Help Pay Cost of Jailing Protesters," *New York Times*, May 7, 1977;

"CPI Inflation Calculator," (used to assess inflation from 1977 to 2013), accessed December 7, 2013, http://data.bls.gov/cgi-bin/cpicalc.pl.

Sam Jennings

13   Actually, only about 100 plants operate: Larry Copeland, "New reactors OK'd for first time since '78," *USA Today*, February 10, 2012, 3A. The Nuclear Regulatory Commission approved two additional units at the Vogtle site near Augusta, Georgia.

14   Silkwood allegedly got run off the road: "Karen Silkwood Biography," Bio., accessed December 7, 2013, http://www.biography.com/people/karen-silkwood-9542402.

14 After TMI, the nuclear industry did its best: "14-Year Cleanup at Three Mile Island Concludes," *New York Times Archives*, August 15, 1993, accessed February 17, 2013, http://www.nytimes.com/1993/08/15/us/14-year-cleanup-at-three-mile-island-concludes.html?pagewanted=print&src=pm.

14 But then, the Japanese earthquake and tsunami struck: "Contamination Continues from Fukishima Disaster," *PBS Newshour Broadcast*, July 26, 2013; accessed March 14, 2015, http://www.pbs.org/newshour/bb/environment-july-dec13-fukushima_07-26/;

     "Fukushima Accident," World Nuclear Association, accessed July 31, 2015, http://www.world-nuclear.org/info/Safety-and-Security/Safety-of-Plants/Fukushima-Accident/.

14 "We're also hearing new revelations": Kate Brown, *Plutopia: Nuclear Families in Atomic Cities and the Great Soviet and American Plutonium Disasters* (Oxford University Press, 2013). Note: the author attended Dr. Brown's presentation of her book and findings at Bowdoin College in Maine on September 26, 2013.

15 Since that time: "Official: Waste a Risk at Vermont Yankee," *Portland Press Herald*, AP, April 19, 2013, C6.

II. CHRONICLE OF THE MODERN ENVIRONMENTAL MOVEMENT

Theodore Roosevelt: Resource Conservation

19 To become the youngest president at 42: Patricia O'Toole, *When Trumpets Call: Theodore Roosevelt after the White House* (New York, Simon & Schuster, 2005).

19 As president, the multi-faceted Roosevelt: "Roosevelt is Awarded the Nobel Peace Prize," accessed August 18, 2015, http://www.theodorerooseveltcenter.org/Blog/2010/December/10-Roosevelt-is-Awarded-the-Nobel-Peace-Prize.aspx.

19   "I always believe in going hard at everything": "Theodore Roosevelt: Icon of the American Century," The Smithsonian National Portrait Gallery, accessed January 24, 2013, http://www.npg.si.edu/exh/roosevelt/trintro2.htm.

20   His unassailable standing as an outdoorsman: "Theodore Roosevelt: The Father of Conservation," National Park Service, accessed April 1, 2015, http://www.cr.nps.gov/logcabin/html/tr5.html.

20   Roosevelt's zeal: "Theodore Roosevelt and the National Park System," The National Park Service History E-Library of January 16, 2003, accessed January 24, 2013, http://www.nps.gov/history/history/hisnps/npshistory/teddy.htm.

20   He also doubled the number of national parks: Ken Burns, "The National Parks: America's Best Idea," The National Parks Film Project, WETA, 2009, accessed January 25, 2013, http://www.pbs.org/nationalparks/people/historical/roosevelt/.

21   Describing the presidency as a "bully pulpit": "Theodore Roosevelt and the Environment," PBS American Experience (n.d.), accessed January 25, 2013, http://www.pbs.org/wgbh/americanexperience/features/general-article/tr-program/.

21   He also used an Executive Order: "Theodore Roosevelt: Icon of the American Century, Rough Rider in the White House 1901-1909," The Smithsonian National Portrait Gallery, accessed January 24, 2013, http://www.npg.si.edu/exh/roosevelt/trintro2.htm.

21   Roosevelt's entourage: "Roosevelt African Expedition Collects for Smithsonian Institution," Smithsonian Institution Archives, accessed January 26, 2013, http://siarchives.si.edu/collections/siris_sic_193.

21   His animal kill included nine rare white rhinos: Edmund Morris, *Colonel Roosevelt* (New York, Random House, 2011) paperback edition, 25.

21   Roosevelt stoutly defended the hunt: O'Toole, *When Trumpets Call: Theodore Roosevelt after the White House,* 67.

Rachel Carson: Web of Life

22 Rachel Carson served: William Souder, *On a Farther Shore: The Life and Legacy of Rachel Carson* (New York, Crown Publishers, 2012), 86.

22 Carson's literary and scientific achievements: Linda Lear, *Rachel Carson: The Life of the Author of Silent Spring,* (New York, Henry Holt & Company, 1997), Chapters 2-4.

23 In the 1940s, women scientists: Linda Lear, *Rachel Carson: Witness for Nature.* (New York, Henry Holt, 1997), 79-82.

23 She considered herself a scientist: Caula A Beyl, "Rachel Carson, Silent Spring, and the Environmental Movement", Reading 31-3, History of the Organic Movement, (1991). Reference to 1962 Life Magazine article), accessed February 4, 2013, https://hort.purdue.edu/newcrop/Hort_306/reading/Reading%2031-3.pdf.

23 She also earned praise: Lear, *Rachel Carson: The Life of the Author of Silent Spring,* 107;
    Mark Madison, "Rachel Carson and the Fish and Wildlife Service," National Conservation Training Center, May 21, 2009, accessed February 15, 2013, http://training.fws.gov/History/ConservationHeroes/Carson.html.

23 By 1951, Carson had released her second book: "Rachel Carson (1907-1964)," U.S. Fish & Wildlife Service, accessed February 15, 2013, http://www.fws.gov/northeast/rachelcarson/carsonbio.html. Other sources for NY Times bestseller list are: Amazon Books description of *The Sea Around Us,* accessed February 5, 2013, http://www.amazon.com/gp/reader/0195069978/ref=sib_dp_pt/177-1739083-2812501#reader-link; and J.J. Lewis, "About.com: Women's History," http://womenshistory.about.com/od/carsonrachel/p/rachel_carson.htm.

23 With her success: Lear, *Rachel Carson: The Life of the Author of Silent Spring,* 233.

24 It was an immediate bestseller: Diana Post, "Celebrating Rachael Carson (1907-1964) in Her Centennial Year," Rachel Carson Council, Inc., brochure, March 2007.

24 Her writing brought several serious issues to light: Rachel Carson, *Silent Spring* (Boston/New York, Mariner Book/Houghton Mifflin Co., 1962), Chapter 3: Elixirs of Death, 7-8, 15.

24 Carson wrote *Silent Spring* because: Lear, *Rachel Carson: The Life of the Author of Silent Spring*, 452.

25 Carson knew all about the military's DDT: Linda Lear, "Introduction to *Silent Spring* by Rachel Carson," Houghton Mifflin 40th Anniversary Edition, 2002.

25 A pesticide trade association: Lear, *Rachel Carson: The Life of the Author of Silent Spring*, 428.

25 The assault came from all sides: Lear, *Rachel Carson: The Life of the Author of Silent Spring*, 429.

26 Carson's message emerges like the sun: Robert Stone, "Earth Days," PBS-WGBH American Experience video, 2009, accessed February 15, 2013, http://www.pbs.org/wgbh/americanexperience/films/earthdays/player/.

Lady Bird Johnson: America the Beautiful

27 Claudia Alta Taylor Johnson: "Lady Bird Johnson: General Biography," The National First Ladies' Library, First Ladies Research, accessed January 11, 2013, http://www.firstladies.org/biographies/.

28 Her trademark cause was "beautification": J. Wilson, "East Texas wildflower," *Austin American-Statesman*, July 13, 2007, Lady Bird Johnson Commemorative Section, 2.

28 Announcing the program: "Lady Bird Johnson: General Biography".

28 "Where flowers bloom so does hope": Jone Johnson Lewis, "Lady Bird Johnson Quotes," about education, accessed August 18, 2015, http://womenshistory.about.com/od/quotes/a/ladybirdjohnson.htm.

29 She also deplored the growth of billboard advertising: "Lady Bird Johnson: General Biography".

29 The Highway Beautification Act passed: "Lady Bird Johnson: General Biography".

29 The business case for beautification: "Lady Bird Johnson: General Biography".

30 The First Lady also left a lasting imprint on the nation's capital: "Lady Bird' Johnson," National Park Service, National Register of Historic Places, Lady Bird Johnson Park, accessed February 15, 2013, http://www.nps.gov/history/nr/feature/highlight/ladybirdjohnson.htm.

Stewart Brand: The Blue Marble

31 As astronaut Cernan observed: Carolyn McDowell, "Apollo, from Earth to the Moon: Imagination and Knowledge," The Cultural Concept Circle, December 21, 2011, accessed January 14, 2013, http://www.theculturecon-cept.com/circle/from-the-earth-to-the-moon-apollo-imagination-knowledge.

32 Brand used an early satellite picture of Earth: Stewart Brand, "Photography Changes Our Relationship to Our Planet," Smithsonian Institution Archives article (n.d), accessed January 16, 2013, http://click.si.edu/Story.aspx?story=31.

32 Brand was delighted: Brand, "Photography Changes our Relationship to Our Planet".

32 Brand believed that if people saw a color photograph: Brand, "Photography Changes our Relationship to Our Planet".

33 The modern international realities: Marshall McLuhan and Quentin Fiore, *The Medium is the Massage*, (New York, Bantam Books, 1967).

Gaylord Nelson and Dennis Hayes: Earth Day

34 Commenting on the social acceptance of environmental ethics: "William D. Ruckelshaus: Oral History Interview," U.S. Environmental Protection

Agency, interviewed January 1993 by Dr. Michael Gorn, 202-K-92-0003, accessed January 8, 2013, http://www.epa.gov/aboutepa/history/publications/print/ruck.html.

34   Earth Day was the brainchild: Senator Gaylord Nelson, "How the First Earth Day Came About," Wilderness Society interview, Envirolink, accessed January 9, 2013, http://earthday.envirolink.org/history.html.

35   Indeed, it was a real blaze: Jonathan H. Adler, "Fables of the Cuyahoga: Reconstructing a History of Environmental Protection," *Fordham Environmental Law Journal*, Vol. XIV (October 16, 2003): 89-146, accessed January 10, 2013, http://law.cwru.edu/faculty/adler_jonathan/publications/fables_of_the_cuyahoga.pdf.

35   A few months after Nelson's invitation: Stephanie Strom, "Earth Day Extravaganza Sheds its Humble Roots," *New York Times*, April 22, 1990, accessed January 11, 2013, http://www.nytimes.com/1990/04/22/us/earth-day-extravaganza-sheds-its-humble-roots.html.

36   The first Earth Day: "William D. Ruckelshaus: Oral History Interview".

36   Although Earth Day was enormously popular: "News Coverage of the first Earth Day" (NBC broadcast by Frank Blair, April 22, 1970), accessed January 7, 2013, http://www.nbcnews.com/video/icue/29901277#29901277.

36   But the environmental movement was here to stay: Strom, "Earth Day Extravaganza Sheds its Humble Roots";
     "Earth Day History," Earth Day New York, accessed January 9, 2013, http://www.earthdayny.org/about/history.html;
     "Earth Day: The History of a Movement," Earth Day Network, accessed October 23, 2012, http://www.earthday.org/earth-day-history-movement.

37   His legacy is also shaped: Senator Gaylord Nelson, *Beyond Earth Day: Fulfilling the Promise* (Madison, University of Wisconsin Press, 2002), accessed January 8, 2013 http://uwpress.wisc.edu/books/2095.htm.

Russell Train and Bill Ruckelshaus: Law of the Land

38 Influential articles and books: Garrett Hardin, "Tragedy of the Commons," *Science Magazine*, 1968, Vol. 162, 1243-1248;

Dr. Paul Erlich, *The Population Bomb* (New York, Ballentine Books, 1968).

39 Russell Train, an environmental advisor: Keith Schneider, "Russell E. Train, Conservationist Who Helped Create the E.P.A., Dies at 92," *New York Times: Environment*, September 17, 2012, accessed December 12, 2012, http://www.nytimes.com/2012/09/18/science/earth/russell-e-train-92-dies-helped-create-the-epa.html?pagewanted=all.

39 Russell Train was a moderate Republican: "Russell Train Obituary," *The Associated Press*, September 18, 2012, accessed December 10, 2012, http://www.legacy.com/ns/obituary.aspx?n=russell-train&pid=159965167.

39 In 1968, Train chaired: Schneider, "Russell E. Train, Conservationist Who Helped Create the E.P.A., Dies at 92".

40 Some 40 years later: U.S. Representative John Dingell, "This World is Not Ours," The Huffington Post, April 22, 2012, accessed December 13, 2012, http://www.huffingtonpost.com/rep-john-d-dingell/earth-day-2012_b_1437710.html.

41 The EPA, which opened its doors: "The Guardian: Origins of the EPA," U.S. Environmental Protection Agency, Spring 1992, accessed March 30, 2015, http://www2.epa.gov/aboutepa/guardian-origins-epa.

41 The first EPA administrator: "The Guardian: Origins of the EPA," accessed December 17, 2012.

41 Ruckelshaus and Train worked well together: "William D. Ruckelshaus: Oral History Interview," U.S. Environmental Protection Agency, interviewed January 1993 by Dr. Michael Gorn, 202-K-92-0003, accessed January 8, 2013, http://www.epa.gov/aboutepa/history/publications/print/ruck.html.

42 Ruckelshaus respected Train's knowledge: "William D. Ruckelshaus: Oral History Interview".

43 Had the Endangered Species Act existed earlier: Elizabeth Kolbert, *The Sixth Extinction: An Unnatural History*. (Picador, Henry Holt and Company, 2014);
Barry Yeoman, "Why the Passenger Pigeon Went Extinct," *Audubon Magazine,* May-June 2014, accessed December 6, 2014, http://www.audubonmagazine.org/articles/birds/why-passenger-pigeon-went-extinct.

44 Since the 1920s: "Love Canal," U.S. Environmental Protection Agency, Region 2 Superfund, accessed February 5, 2014, http://www.epa.gov/region2/superfund/npl/lovecanal/.

46 It had been a rocky environmental road: Tim Radford, "Do Trees Pollute the Atmosphere?" *The Guardian*, News/Science, (May 13, 2004), accessed March 25, 2014, http://www.theguardian.com/science/2004/may/13/thisweekssciencequestions3.

46 In addition to his political savvy: "William D. Ruckelshaus: Oral History Interview".

47 When Ruckelshaus departed the EPA in 1985: Phil Wisman, "EPA History (1970-1985): William D. Ruckelshaus (2nd term)," U.S. Environmental Protection Agency, November 1985, accessed December 15, 2012, http://www2.epa.gov/aboutepa/epa-history-1970-1985.

Al Gore: Global Reality

47 His active participation in the Clearinghouse: Annie Cheatham, email to author, February 4, 2013.

48 The Clearinghouse arose: "Congressional Clearinghouse on the Future," Wilson Center Science and Technology Innovation Program, October 1, 2002, accessed January 27, 2013, http://www.wilsoncenter.org/article/congresional-clearinghouse-the-future.

48 Gore used his soapbox: "Congressional Clearinghouse on the Future."

49 The resulting Kyoto Protocol: "Status of Ratification of the Kyoto Protocol," United Nations Framework Convention, accessed August 18, 2015, http://unfccc.int/kyoto_protocol/status_of_ratification/items/2613.php

49 After his razor-thin loss in the presidential contest: "Al Gore: New Thinking on the Climate Crisis," TED talks, March 2008, accessed January 7, 2013, http://www.ted.com/talks/al_gore_s_new_thinking_on_the_climate_crisis.html.

50 Echoing Rachel Carson: Al Gore, *Earth in the Balance: Ecology and the Human Spirit* (New York, Plume, 1992), 2.

50 Gore's special contribution: "Testimony of the Honorable Al Gore before the U.S. Senate Environment and Public Works Committee, March 21, 2007", Washington D.C.

50 In *Earth in the Balance*, Gore warns: Gore, *Earth in the Balance: Ecology and the Human Spirit*, 269.

51 Because climate change is a global problem: "Al Gore: New Thinking on the Climate Crisis," TED talks.

III. EARLY DAYS OF DOE AND LOCAL ENERGY CONSERVATION

55 There was a lot to learn: Terry Fehner, Historian, U.S. Department of Energy, email to author with attached table on DOE staffing history from 1978 to 1989, August 28, 2015.

55 Immediately following President Reagan's January inauguration: "Timeline of Events: 1981 to 1990," U.S. Department of Energy, Office of Management, accessed March 23, 2013, http://energy.gov/management/timeline-events-1981-1990.

Quicksand
Franklin County Energy Conservation Task Force

58 The agency's case: President Jimmy Carter, April 18, 1977 televised address to the nation, accessed February 22, 2013, http://millercenter.org/ scripps/archive/speeches/detail/3398.

58 Patterned after the 1930s Work Progress Administration: "The Comprehensive Employment Training Act," Advisory Commission on Intergovernmental Relations, June 1977, accessed August 22,2015, http://webcache. googleusercontent.com/search?q=cache:UwthS5cjwgYJ:www.library.unt. edu/gpo/acir/Reports/policy/A-58.pdf+&cd=4&hl=en&ct=clnk&gl=us; "CETA Training Programs – Do They Work For Adults?" A study by the U.S. Congressional Office and the National Commission for Employment Policy, July 1982, xv.

60 Only 65,000 people lived in Franklin County: "Franklin County Energy Profile, 1975-1979," Franklin County Energy Conservation Task Force, Office of County Commissioners, 1979, 15.

60 Franklin County was 73 percent forested: "Franklin County Energy Profile, 1975-1979," 8.

61 Besides renewables: "Yankee," accessed August 18, 2015, http://www.yankeerowe.com. The Yankee Rowe nuclear power station was decommissioned in 1992;
"Northfield Mountain," accessed August 18, 2015, http://www.gdfsuezna. com/northfield-mountain. The facility was the largest of its kind when built in 1972.

61 From the energy survey: "Franklin County Energy Conservation Survey," Franklin County Energy Conservation Task Force, Office of County Commissioners, 1978, 2-3.

61 From doing the fact book: "Franklin County Energy Profile, 1975-1979".

62 There was also much to discover from the county's history of hydropower: "Franklin County Energy Profile, 1975-1979." See comparison of kilowatt hour sales (millions) by town in Franklin County, 14.

62   When the local newspaper reported the story: "Franklin County Dam
      Inventory," Franklin County Energy Conservation Task Force, Office of
      County Commissioners, 1979. This source also applies to the following
      discussion on the power potential of the 125 unused sites.

62   The research set the stage: "Franklin County Energy Goals and Policy
      Document 1980-1985," Franklin County Office of Commissioners,
      October 30, 1979, 38.

63   Nor did it help when the university: "Groundwork: Energy Planning in
      Franklin County," U.S. Department of Energy, Region I (PO #PM-357),
      1980, 27.

63   In his August 1979 syndicated column: Ronald Reagan, August 17, 1979 syn-
      dicated column, King Features Syndicate Inc., appearing in *The Greenfield
      Recorder*, "Reagan Praises County Energy Study," August 24, 1979.

64   Franklin County benefited: "Groundwork: Energy Planning in Franklin
      County".

Going to DOE
Reduction in Force
Good Advice
Dusk 'til Dawn

71   In May 1982, President Reagan renewed his assault: "Timeline of Events:
      1981 to 1990."

IV. THE NATIONAL ENVIRONMENTAL POLICY ACT

Homestead Hurricane

75   Hurricane Andrew slammed into the south Florida coast: "Hurricane
      Facts," *Sarasota Herald-Tribune*, September 24, 1994, accessed April 25,
      2013, http://news.google.com/newspapers?id=mCAfAAAAIBAJ&sjid=P
      30EAAAAIBAJ&pg=3668,3958333&dq;

"Hurricane Andrew: South Florida and Louisiana August 23-26, 1992," U.S. Department of Commerce, National Disaster Survey Report, November 1993, accessed August 18, 2015, http://www.nws.noaa.gov/om/assessments/pdfs/andrew.pdf.

75 South of Miami and midway to the Keys: Kathy Lohr, "A City Leveled by Hurricane Andrew Rebuilds, Again," *National Public Radio*, August 23, 2012, accessed April 24, 2013, http://www.npr.org/2012/08/23/159921591/a-city-leveled-by-hurricane-andrew-rebuilds-again;

"Census 2010 and 2000 Interactive Map, Demographics, Statistics, Quick Facts," Census Viewer, Moonshadow Mobile, Inc., accessed on May 1, 2013, http://censusviewer.com/terms-of-use/;

Christiana Lilly, "Hurricane Andrew: 20 Facts You May Have Forgotten," *HuffPost Miami*, August 24, 2012, accessed on April 24, 2013, http://www.huffingtonpost.com/2012/08/21/20-facts-hurricane-andrew-anniversary_n_1819405.html.

76 A few miles northeast of Homestead: "Final Supplemental Environmental Impact Statement: Disposal of Portions of the Former Homestead Air Force Base, Florida (Summary)" U.S. Department of the Air Force and Federal Aviation Administration, December 2000, 8-10;

William Booth and Mary Jordan, "At Least 10 Killed; City Under Curfew," August 25, 1992, *The Washington Post*, A01, accessed April 25, 2013, http://www.washingtonpost.com/wp-srv/weather/hurricane/post-stories/andrew.htm.

76 Feeling the legal and political pressure: "Final Supplemental Environmental Impact Statement: Disposal of Portions of the Former Homestead Air Force Base, Florida (Summary)" 1-7.

77 We agreed to help knowing the technical challenges: "Ambient Sound Levels at Four Department of Interior Conservation Units," Federal Aviation Administration, June 1999, Report No. AEE-99-02, DOT/VNTSC/FAA-99-3 (317 pp.).

78 The FAA and the Air Force published: "Final Supplemental Environmental Impact Statement: Disposal of Portions of the Former Homestead Air Force Base, Florida (Summary)" 4; Jim DeFede, "Collision Course," *Miami New Times*, New Times, Inc., November 23, 2000.

78 Meanwhile, the presidential election of 2000: DeFede, "Collision Course".

79 The ploy would have succeeded: DeFede, "Collision Course".

80 McGinty met with a select group: DeFede, "Collision Course." This source also applies to the subsequent discussion of criticism about Gore's public neutrality.

80 The electoral goal of the Nader campaign: Jonathan Chait, "Crashing the Party: How to Tell the Truth and Still Run for President," *The American Prospect*, October 15, 2002 book review of "Nader: Crusader, Spoiler, Icon" by Justin Martin, accessed April 30, 2013, http://prospect.org/article/books-review-1.

81 Nader received 97,488 votes in Florida: "2000 Presidential General Election Results," Florida Board of Elections, accessed April 19, 2013, http://uselectionatlas.org/RESULTS/state.php?year=2000&fips=12&f=0&off=0&elect=0.

81 The Air Force signed: "Homestead SEIS Newsletter," U.S. Air Force and Federal Aviation Administration, February 2001, 7th Issue, 1.

The NEPA Process

82 NEPA has been battle-tested since 1970: Lynton Caldwell, "Environment: A New Focus for Public Policy?" *Public Administration Review*, American Society for Public Administration, 1963, 132-138.

82 Caldwell served as an advisor: Senator Richard G. Lugar, "Tribute to Lynton Caldwell," December 7, 2006, Senate Vol. 152, No. 134, S11493, accessed May 3, 2013, http://capitolwords.org/date/2006/12/07/S11493-3_tribute-to-lynton-caldwell/.

83 Caldwell also helped to draft the goals: "Regulations for Implementing the Procedural Provisions of the National Environmental Policy Act," Council on Environmental Quality, Executive Office of the President, November 29, 1978, reprint of 43-FR 55978-56007.

84 Draft EISs are also reviewed: "Environmental Impact Statement (EIS) Rating System Criteria," U.S. Environmental Protection Agency, National Environmental Policy Act, accessed May 11, 2013, http://www.epa.gov/compliance/nepa/comments/ratings.html.

84 In the end, the project agency: "Order 1050.1E," Federal Aviation Administration, 2004, chapter 5, section 512b, 5-21.

EPA Insights
NEPA-Like States

88 Seeing the benefits of NEPA: "State Environmental Planning Information," Council on Environmental Quality, Executive Office of the President, National Environmental Policy Act, State Information, February 14, 2013, accessed April 23, 2013, http://ceq.hss.doe.gov/state_information/states.html.

89 Because Maine has no NEPA-like law: Chandler E. Woodcock, Commissioner, State of Maine, Department of Inland Fisheries and Wildlife, letter to Dr. Jake A. Plante and Ms. Marcia Harrington, January 30, 2012; "Head of Maquoit Restoration Project Full Proposal," Maine Natural Resources Conservation Program, Maine Department of Inland Fisheries and Wildlife, September 2011. Proposal submitted to the Nature Conservancy in Maine.

89 The project was supported by a $425,000 grant: "Head of Maquoit Restoration Project Full Proposal"; Stewart Fefer, Project Leader, U.S. Department of the Interior, U.S. Fish and Wildlife Service, letter to Alex Mas, Project Manager for the Nature Conservancy in Maine, September 12, 2011;

Michael Chelminski, Stantec Consulting Services, Inc., letter to Steve Walker, Maine Department of Inland Fisheries and Wildlife, June 21, 2011;

"Permit-by-Rule," Natural Resources Protection Act, Maine Department of Environmental Protection, October 2008, accessed May 13, 2012, http://www.maine.gov/dep/land/nrpa/ip-pbr.html.

89   It all unraveled quickly: Alex Lear, "Brunswick, Topsham natural resource projects receive funds," *The Mid-Coast Forecaster*, January 13, 2012, Vol. 8, No. 2, 2.

Six Areas for Reform

91   NEPA founders did not intend for this to happen: "Regulations for Implementing the Procedural Provisions of the National Environmental Policy Act," Council on Environmental Quality, Executive Office of the President. November 29, 1978, reprint, Sec. 1502.7, 11.

91   Thus, when CEQ added climate change: Nancy H. Sutley, "Draft NEPA Guidance on Consideration of the Effects of Climate Change and Greenhouse Gas Emissions," Memorandum for Heads of Federal Departments and Agencies, Council on Environmental Quality, Executive Office of the President, February 18, 2010, 4-6.

91   Department of Transportation records indicate: "Typical Length of Time Required to Complete NEPA," Federal Highway Administration 1999 survey, presentation slide #4, accessed February 9, 2000, http://www.fhwa.dot.gov/environmental/slide4.htm.

91   Increasing EIS times and expense: Personal communications with Jessica Aresta-DaSilva, U.S. Environmental Protection Agency, headquarters, September 2013, and Timothy L. Timmerman, Associate Director, EPA Office of Environmental Review, New England-Region 1, July 23, 2013. Sources also include EPA national EIS database, including table on all

EIS's filed since January 2004, special query, accessed May 9, 2013, http://www.epa.gov/compliance/nepa/eisdata.html.

93   An illustration is the U.S. Department of Interior's: Blake Androff and David Quick, "Obama Administration Approves Roadmap for Utility-Scale Solar Energy Development on Public Lands," U.S. Department of Interior press release, October 12, 2012, accessed May 21, 2013, http://www.doi.gov/news/pressreleases/Obama-Administration-Approves-Roadmap-for-Utility-Scale-Solar-Energy-Development-on-Public-Lands.cfm.

94   *"The proposed Intercounty Connector"*: "Final Environmental Impact Statement for the Intercounty Connector," Federal Highway Administration and Maryland State Highway Administration, January 3, 2006, Section A: Project Purpose, I-1.

94   Federal highway and state transportation planners: Lindsey McPherson, "Agreement advances ICC interchange in Laurel," Laurel Leader, affiliate of the Baltimore Sun, accessed August 18, 2015, http://archives.explore-howard.com/news/83058.

94   Seeking to neutralize the opposition: "Vision 100 – Century of Aviation Reauthorization Act," Federal Aviation Administration, Title III: Environmental Process, December 2003.

95   Rarely do politics infect the NEPA process: Personal records as a charter and 4-year member of the Montgomery County ICC Citizens Advisory Committee.

95   At one controversial FAA public hearing: Personal conversation with FAA colleague about the New York and New Jersey Airspace Redesign Project, public hearing on Draft Environmental Impact Statement, circa 1990.

96   At another memorable event: Personal conversation with FAA colleague, circa 2008.

96 Litigants under NEPA have to prove: "Legal Theory Lexicon," Standards of Review, accessed May 24, 2013, http://lsolum.typepad.com/legal_theory_lexicon/2006/08/standards_of_re.html.

97 The FAA happens to enjoy: Charles Prock and Patrick Wells, "Current Legal Issues," Federal Aviation Administration, 2010 Recurrent Environmental Training presentation, Palm Coast Florida, February 9-11, 2010.

99 The lack of accountability: Nancy H. Sutley, "Draft Guidance for NEPA Mitigation and Monitoring," Memorandum for Heads of Federal Departments and Agencies, Council on Environmental Quality, Executive Office of the President, February 18, 2010, 3-4.

Putting it in Perspective

100 This was tried in 2015 by the oil industry: "President Vetoes Congress's Keystone Pipeline Bill," Earthjustice, February 24, 2015, accessed May 21, 2015, http://earthjustice.org/news/press/2015/president-vetoes-keystone-pipeline.

V. COMPETING PUBLIC INTERESTS: QUIET PARKS VS. OPEN SKIES

Echoes of the Canyon

102 Managing airspace over national parks: Judith Cummings, "Air Crash Kills 25 at Grand Canyon," *New York Times*, June 19, 1986, accessed June 12, 2013, http://www.nytimes.com/1986/06/19/us/air-crash-kills-25-at-grand-canyon.html;

Penny Pagano, "Prompted by Crash Fatal to 25: FAA Proposes Flight Ban Below Grand Canyon Rim," *Los Angeles Times*, December 6, 1986, accessed on August 18, 2015, http://articles.latimes.com/1986-12-06/news/mn-1657_1_grand-canyon.

102 Following the accident: "Special Flight Rules Area in the Vicinity of Grand Canyon National Park: Actions to Substantially Restore Natural Quiet," U.S. Department of the Interior, National Park Service, Draft EIS (DES 10-60), February 2011, Vol. 1, 131; "The National Parks Overflight Act of 1987," Public Law 100-91, 1987, Sec. 3: Grand Canyon National Park.

103 Anything less they contended: "An Act to Establish a National Park Service and For Other Purposes (Organic Act)." August 25, 1916, 16 U.S.C. §1.

The Cultural Divide
Acoustics and Analysis

107 Earlier in the year, the president had issued a memorandum: "Additional Transportation Planning to Address Impacts of Transportation on National Parks," April 22, 1996, Federal Register, Vol. 61, No.81, April 25, 1996, 18229-18230.

107 The AEE Director quickly set up: "Noise Limitations for Aircraft Operations in the Vicinity of the Grand Canyon National Park, NPRM," Draft Environmental Assessment, Federal Aviation Administration, Air Traffic Airspace Management, December 1996.

108 To jumpstart the effort: "Draft National Park Overflights Rule: Noise Research Plan," Federal Aviation Administration, Office of Environment and Energy, February 1998 (90 pp.).

109 The meeting went well: "Draft Research Plan Outline for Air Tour Overflights of National Parks," April 1998. Three-page agreement between the Federal Aviation Administration and the National Park Service. The Park Service commonly used "draft" in document titles, but both agencies considered the research agreement final. The FAA research

commitments in the agreement, which were the most expensive and time-consuming, were executed faithfully by the FAA.

109 The FAA conducted its first dose-response study: "Development of Noise Dose/Visitor Response Relationships for the National Parks Overflights Rule: Bryce Canyon National Park Study," Federal Aviation Administration, Office of Environmental and Energy, July 1998, Report No. AEE-98-01, DOT/VNTSC/FAA-98-6 (230 pp.).

111 While natural sounds: "Comparative Noise Levels," Hartsfield Atlanta International Airport EIS Fifth Runway Extension, September 2001, Figure 4-2;

"Noise Level Comparison," Taos Regional Airport EIS, September 2012; "Understanding Highway Noise," *The Washington Post* (n.d.), with multiple sources: the Federal Highway Administration, D.C. Public Works Department, Maryland Highway Administration, and Virginia Department of Transportation.

114 Given the unproven accuracy: J.R. Hassel and M. Zaveri, *Acoustic Noise Measurements* (Bruel & Kjaer, 1979) 4th edition, 33.

114 Moreover, the FAA wanted to put more of the focus: "Aviation Noise Research Conducted by FICAN Member Agencies," Federal Interagency Committee on Aviation Noise, November 1998. Committee conversations with Robert A. Lee, Chief, Noise Effects Branch, U.S. Air Force Armstrong Laboratory, pertaining to Air Force research findings on animals.

Ranger Talk

115 "I wanted to tell you": Jon Pietrak, FAA Office of Environment and Energy, Noise Division, email to author, May 20, 2002. The offset of 15-20% in overlook and short-hike conditions was observed in the 1997 and 1998 studies, which were published in 1998 and 2005, respectively.

115 "Let's suppose we drew a line": "Study of Visitor Response to Air Tour and Other Aircraft Noise in National Parks," Federal Aviation Administration,

January 2005, Volpe National Transportation Systems Center, Report No. DTS-34-FA65-LRI., Sec. 4.0, 27-28.

116 "However, it does serve to sensitize people": "Report on Effects of Aircraft Overflights on the National Park System," Report to Congress, National Park Service, July 1995, 22-23, 60, & chapter 6. Prepared pursuant to Public Law 100-91: The National Park Service Overflights Act of 1987.

117 "On the other hand, the research was showing": "Special Flight Rules in the Vicinity of the Rocky Mountain National Park," Federal Aviation Administration, Air Traffic Airspace Management, February 1997, subheading "FAA Authority to Manage the Airspace".

117 *"A civilization which destroys"*: Edward Abbey, *Desert Solitaire* (New York, McGraw-Hill, 1968), 211.

117 These findings showed that Time Above: "Study of Visitor Response to Air Tour and Other Aircraft Noise in National Parks," 22, 62 (Table E-6).

The Plan Unravels

119 In the winter of 1999, the White House launched: Gore response to on-line question from Gloria Sodaro: "What is the status of the reinventing government effort?" Gore 2000 Town Hall website, accessed April 8, 1999, http://www.algore2000.com/townhall/index.html.

121 In the first instance of guidance: "Director's Order #47: Soundscape Preservation and Noise Management," National Park Service, December 1, 2000.

121 The final validation report was issued in 2003: "Findings and Recommendations on Tools for Modeling Aircraft Noise in National Parks," Federal Interagency Committee on Aviation Noise, February 2005, 2. FICAN review of Grand Canyon National Park model validation study findings.

122 The NPS claimed: Howie Thompson, "Air Tour Management Plan Program," The George Wright FORUM, 2004, Vol. 21, No. 1, 26-28.

Mr. Thompson served in the National Sounds Program Office of the National Park Service;

William Withycombe, Regional Administrator for the FAA Western-Pacific Region, "Congressional testimony before the Committee on Energy and Natural Resources, Subcommittee on National Parks, July 22, 2004";

"Memorandum of Understanding Between the Federal Aviation Administration and the National Park Service: Implementation of Air Tour Management Planning as Directed by the National Parks Air Tour Management Act of 2000," signed by FAA Administrator Marion C. Blakey and NPS Director Fran P. Mainella, effective January 27, 2004.

123 In 2006, the needs assessment: Barry Brayer, Manager, "National Parks Air Tour Management Plan Program (ATMP)," Federal Aviation Administration, Western-Pacific Region, FAA Environmental Forum presentation, May 2006.

123 The downhill slide continued: William C. Withycombe, Regional Administrator for the FAA Western-Pacific region, Congressional testimony before the Committee on Energy and Natural Resources, Subcommittee on National Parks, July 22, 2004.

The Airports Office Flies Direct

124 She complained that the Park Service: "Notice of Recommendation from the Aircraft Noise Model Validation Study," National Park Service, November 7, 2003, Federal Register Notice, Vol. 68, No. 216, 63131-2. This source illustrates Park Service pressure to use the audibility metric and related tools.

125 The first opportunity: "Final Environmental Assessment (EA) for Proposed Airport Improvements at Flagstaff Pulliam Airport," Prepared for the City of Flagstaff, Arizona and approved by the Federal Aviation Administration, June 2006.

126 Immediately, our scientific doubts about audibility were confirmed: Jon M. Woodward, Landrum & Brown, Inc., memo to FAA review team on the St. George Replacement Airport EIS audibility analysis for Zion National Park, circa 2006.

127 We could not believe our damn luck: Environmental Impact Statement (EIS) and Record of Decision (ROD) for the Proposed Replacement Airport and Associated Airport-Related Development: St. George, Washington County, Utah, 2006.

Cal Black
Analytical Integrity

129 After our experience at St. George: Environmental Impact Statement (EIS) and Record of Decision (ROD) for the Proposed Horizon Air Operations Specifications Amendment: Service to Mammoth Yosemite Airport, Mammoth Lakes, Mono County, California, 2008.

130 In trying to diagnose the mechanics of audibility: FAA Office of Environment and Energy, Noise Division, hand-delivered analysis to author, June 2010. One-page table of results on a sensitivity analysis of audibility using one operation (B737-800).

131 An exchange later in the day: Author's notes and FAA Airports Office trip report on FAA and NPS Parks Noise Criteria Workshop: "Human Response to Aviation Noise in Protected Natural Areas," Cambridge, MA, October 28-29, 2008.

132 Another weakness of the regional analysis: "Report to Congress: Non-Military Helicopter Urban Noise Study," Federal Aviation Administration, December 2004 (71 pp.);

Vince Mestre, et al., "Assessing Community Annoyance of Helicopter Noise," National Academies, Airport Cooperative Research Program, August 4, 2014, Report No. ACRP 02-48.

132 An example of this was on Long Island: FAA issue paper on proposed legislation: "Controlling Helicopter Noise Pollution in Residential Areas," S. 223, Sec. 740. Additional sources: Federal Register Notice on FAA Proposed Rule, Vol. 75, No. 101, May 26, 2010; and internal agency meeting notes of April 26-28, 2011.

132 Inexplicably however, the Park Service never did submit: "Final Environmental Assessment: Proposed Southern Nevada Regional Heliport," Clark County, Nevada, October 2008.

132 The FAA immediately ordered: Author conversation with colleague in the FAA Office of Airports, Financial Assistance Division, 2010.

VI. CLEAN AIR ACT: ENVIRONMENTAL POLICY AT ITS BEST

Clearing the Air from California to China

136 As early as 1903: "The Southland's War on Smog: Fifty Years of Progress Toward Clean Air," May 1997, accessed October 1, 2013, http://www. aqmd.gov/news1/archives/history/marchcov.html#The%20Arrival%20 of%20Air%20Pollution.

136 A few years later: "Smog," The Free Dictionary, Farlex, accessed October 3, 2013, http://www.thefreedictionary.com/smog.

137 The encouraging news: "The Southland's War on Smog: Fifty Years of Progress Toward Clean Air".

137 Another positive sign was declining smog alerts: "Fact Sheet: Reducing Emissions from California Vehicles," California Environmental Protection Agency, Air Resources Board. February 23, 2004, 2.

137 LA's strides in cutting air pollution: "US EPA Region 9 Air Quality Trends, 1976-2012: Air Quality8-Hour Ozone Design Value Concentrations by Nonattainment Area," accessed October 11, 2013, http://www.epa.gov/ region9/air/trends/o3.html;

"Air Quality Trends," U.S. Environmental Protection Agency, Percent Change in Air Quality table, accessed October 7, 2013, http://www.epa.gov/airtrends/aqtrends.html;

"California's Progress Toward Clean Air: A Report by the California Air Pollution Control Officer's Association," April 2013, Executive Summary, 5.

137 Still, LA had farther to come: Liz Neporent, "Los Angeles Tops 'Dirty Air' List for 13ᵗʰ Time in 14 Years," April 24, 2013, accessed October 11, 2013, www.abcnews.go.com/blogs/health/2013/04/24/los-angeles-tops-dirty-air-list-for-13th-time-in-14-years/ with cross-reference to the American Lung Association, http://www.stateoftheair.org/2013/states/;

"Classifications of 8-Hour Ozone (2008) Nonattainment Areas," U.S. Environmental Protection Agency, Green Book, July 13, 2013, accessed October 14, 2013, http://www.epa.gov/airquality/greenbk/hnc.html;

"Historic Ozone Air Quality Trends: Ozone, 1976-2013," South Coast Air Quality Management District, Number of Basin-Days Exceeding Health Standard Levels, accessed July 24, 2015, http://www.aqmd.gov/home/library/air-quality-data-studies/historic-ozone-air-quality-trends;

"National Ambient Air Quality Standards (NAAQS)," U.S. Environmental Protection Agency, Air and Radiation, accessed October 11, 2013, www.epa.gov/air/criteria.html.

137 For example, the EPA reports: Alison Davis, Senior Advisor for Public Affairs, U.S. Environmental Protection Agency, email to author, October 29, 2013, in reference to Air Quality Index ozone data from 100 "Trend Sites." See Office of Air Quality Planning and Standards.

138 Another indicator of progress is found internationally: Douglas McIntyre, "The 10 Cities With the World's Worst Air," *Daily Finance*, November 29, 2010, accessed October 13, 2013, www.dailyfinance.com/2010/11/29/10-cities-with-worlds-worst-air/.

138 In the case of Beijing: Jason Samenow, "Chinese city shut down by off-the-charts pollution," *The Washington Post*, October 21, 2013, accessed October 22, 2013, www.washingtonpost.com/blogs/capital-weather-gang/wp/2013/10/21/chinese-city-shut-down-by-off-the-charts-pollution/; Eyder Peralta, "Chinese City of 11 Million Paralyzed by Off-The-Charts Smog," *NPR News*, October 21, 2013, accessed October 22, 2013, www.npr.org/blogs/thetwo-way/2013/10/21/239262731/chinese-city-of-11-million-paralyzed-by-off-the-charts-smog.

138 Harbin was not the first time: "Henin trying to manage asthma, might skip Olympics," ESPN.com news services, August 4, 2008, accessed August 19, 2015, http://sports.espn.go.com/sports/tennis/news/story?id=3095205

139 To prevent Beijing's smog: "Beijing Olympics Provides Rare Window into Air Pollution's Effect on Health," University of Rochester Medical Center, May 15, 2012, accessed October 15, 2013, www.urmc.rochester.edu/news/story/index.cfm?id=3501.

139 Downwind air from China: Laurie Garrett and Jane C.S. Long, "The great smoke-out," *Los Angeles Times*, October 7, 2007, accessed October 1, 2013, http://articles.latimes.com/2007/oct/07/opinion/op-garrett7/2; Jim Yardley, "China's Next Big Boom Could Be the Foul Air," *New York Times*, accessed June 15, 2015, http://www.nytimes.com/2005/10/30/weekinreview/chinas-next-big-boom-could-be-the-foul-air.html.

139 A few hopeful signs: "Global Wind Statistics," Global Wind Energy Council, February 2, 2015, accessed August 19, 2015, http://www.gwec.net/wp-content/uploads/2015/02/GWEC_GlobalWindStats2014_FINAL_10.2.2015.pdf; Ucilia Wang, "Guess Who Are The Top 10 Solar Panel Makers in the World," *Forbes*, December 3, 2014, accessed April 19, 2015, http://www.forbes.com/sites/uciliawang/2014/12/03/guess-who-are-the-top-10-solar-panel-makers-in-the-world/.

139 In addition, China launched an initiative in 2013: "China Cracks Down on Waste Imports," *Portland Press Herald*, AP, October 4, 2013, A2.

140 The only reported step that Chinese officials took: Ramy Inocencio and Feng Ke, "China to shame worst-polluting cities over and over in push for green action," *CNN*, September 19, 2013, accessed October 22, 2013, www. cnn.com/2013/09/19/business/china-shame-worst-air-polluting-cities/.

Clean Air Act

141 As a model of environmental lawmaking: "Air and Radiation," U.S. Environmental Protection Agency, accessed October 21, 2013, http:// www.epa.gov/air/index.html.

142 The second major principle: Gary Jensen, "Clean Air Act Success Story: Continuing Reductions in Transportation Emissions," TR News, Transportation Research Board, July-August, 2003, Issue No. 227, 4.

142 A controversial aspect of source control: Phone conversation with Ozone Transport Commission staff, Washington, D.C., October 25, 2013. The staff identified a meeting of May 7, 1991 as the OTC starting date; "The Plain English Guide to the Clean Air Act," U.S. Environmental Protection Agency, April 1993, EPA 400-K-93-001, Acid Rain, 14-15.

143 The commission has served: Dina Cappiello and Sam Hananel, "Downwind pollution limits upheld," *Portland Press Herald*, AP, April 30, 2014, A3; "Cross-State Air Pollution Rule (CSAPR)," U.S. Environmental Protection Agency, accessed August 19, 2015, http://www.epa.gov/crossstaterule/ basic.html.

143 The third major principle of the CAA: "Air Quality Index: A Guide to Air Quality and Your Health," U.S. Environmental Protection Agency, OAQPS, August 2009, Report No. EPA-456/F-09-002, 3.

143 In the event that a state fails: Susan L. Mayer, "California Air Quality FIP – A Fact Sheet", *ENR*, April 13, 1995, ENR No. 95-491, accessed

October 18, 2013, http://digital.library.unt.edu/ark:/67531/metacrs175/ml/1/high_res_d/95-491_1995Apr13.html;

"A Summary: Transportation Programs and Provisions of the Clean Air Act Amendments of 1990," U.S. Department of Transportation, Federal Highway Administration, October 1992, PN #FHWA-PD-92-023, 17.

144 SIPs are also integral to state management of stationary sources: "Air and Radiation," U.S. Environmental Protection Agency, accessed October 21, 2013, http://www.epa.gov/air/index.html.

145 So what has the CAA meant: "Air Quality Trends," U.S. Environmental Protection Agency, accessed October 23, 2013, www.epa.gov/airtrends/aqtrends.html;

"Voluntary Airport Low Emission Program Technical Report," Federal Aviation Administration, Office of Airports, December 2, 2010, Appendix A: Glossary of Terms.

146 Combustion also produces fine particulates: "Air Quality Trends".

146 Mirroring the trend: "Green Book: Summary Nonattainment Area Population Exposure Report," U.S. Environmental Protection Agency, July 31, 2013, accessed October 21, 2013, http://www.epa.gov/oaqps001/greenbk/popexp.html.

146 In the case of lead: "Impact of Lead Emission Standards on General Aviation," Federal Aviation Administration, Office of Environment and Energy briefing paper to the Office of Airports, March 23, 2011;

Memo from Ralph Thompson, Manager, Federal Aviation Administration, Airport Planning and Environmental Division, to Regional Airports Division Managers, "Interim Guidance on Mitigating Public Risks Associated With Lead Emissions from Avgas," June 19, 2013.

146 Both pollutants are hard to control: "An Introduction to Indoor Air Quality: Volatile Organic Compounds (VOCs)," U.S. Environmental Protection Agency, accessed December 12, 2013, http://www.epa.gov/iaq/voc.html.

147 Yet, even nonattainment areas for ozone and particulates: Gary Jensen, "Air Quality and Transportation," Federal Highway Administration, *Public Roads*, July/August 2003, accessed October 21, 2013, http://www. fhwa.dot.gov/publications/publicroads/03jul/10.cfm; "Green Book: Summary Nonattainment Area Population Exposure Report".

147 EPA authority to regulate air toxics: Edward Broughton, "The Bhopal disaster and its aftermath: a review," BioMed Central, May 10, 2005.

148 Federal requirements to analyze air toxics: "Guidance for Quantifying Speciated Organic Gas Emissions from Airport Sources," Federal Aviation Administration, Office of Environment and Energy, September 2, 2009, Version 1.

Brokering a Deal on Aviation Emissions

149 Even by aviation industry estimates: "Regulatory Brief: FAA/ EPA Stakeholder Meetings on Air Quality," Aircraft Owners and Pilots Association, accessed September 26, 2013, http:// www.aopa.org/Advocacy/Regulatory-,-a-,-Certification-Policy/ Regulatory-Brief-FAA-EPA-Stakeholder-Meetings-on-Air-Quality.

150 Some states and local airport authorities: "Aircraft Emission Charges Zurich Airport," Zurich Airport, Switzerland, Emission Charges brochure, July 2010, accessed October 31, 2013, http://www.zurich-airport. com/the-company/noise-policy-and-the-environment/air-quality; "Towards a sustainable Heathrow—a focus on air quality," Heathrow Airport, England, accessed October 31, 2013, http://www.heathrowairport.com/about-us/community-and-environment/sustainability/ environment/air-quality; "Reducing emissions from aviation," European Commission, Climate Action, accessed April 24, 2015, http://ec.europa.eu/clima/policies/ transport/aviation/index_en.htm.

150 Besides aircraft, another airport source of NOx: Barbara Schussman and Marc Bruner, Bingham McCutchen LLP, "State and Local Air Quality Regulation of Airports," *Airport Air Quality: Approaches, Basics and Challenges*, University of California Berkeley, Institute of Transportation Studies, 2005, 25-29.

150 It was clear that the costs: Jim Humphries, CH2M HILL, Inc., "Aircraft Ground Support Equipment," *Airport Air Quality: Approaches, Basics and Challenges*, 60.

151 The situation grew worse for the airlines: Schussman and Bruner, "State and Local Air Quality Regulation of Airports," *Airport Air Quality: Approaches, Basics and Challenge.*

151 Facing the prospect: Bryan Manning, "Voluntary Aviation Emissions Reduction Stakeholder Process," U.S. Environmental Protection Agency, slide presentation to Airport Air Quality Symposium, March 1-2, 2001.

152 "Although they did have a case after 9/11": Barbara De Lollis, "Flights increase, but some sites see more than others," *USA Today*, Business Travel, May 7, 2002, 9B.

152 "Incidentally, did you see any of the 9/11 research?": "Aviation and the Environment," U.S. Government Accountability Office, September 13, 2010, Report No. GAO-10-50, 8;

Che Smith, Nagambal Shah, and Monica Stephens, "Investigating the Effects of Airplane Emissions on Atlanta's Air Quality Before and After 9/11/01," Spellman College, slide presentation at AWMA SASS Annual Meeting, November 4, 2004;

Michael Kenney, Deborah Dutcher Wilson, and Wayne Arner, "Air Quality Around Our Nation's Airports During the Aftermath of the September 11, 2001 Attack on America," URS Corporation, (n.d.), Paper No. 42735.

Airport Air Quality

156 "The top of the bubble": "Air Quality Procedures For Civilian Airports and Air Force Bases" (Air Quality Handbook), Federal Aviation

Administration, Office of Environment and Energy, with U.S. Air Force Armstrong Laboratory, Tyndall Air Force Base, April 1997, Report No. FAA-AEE-97-03.

156 If the total *volume* of project emissions: "Air Quality Procedures For Civilian Airports and Air Force Bases".

157 Together, these strategies have worked so well: Darcy Zarubiak, air quality expert for Leigh Fisher, Inc., phone conversation with author, September 26, 2013.

157 "After that," I said, "we'll cover the agency's new guidance": "Guidance for Quantifying Speciated Organic Gas Emissions From Airport Sources," Federal Aviation Administration, Office of Environment and Energy, September 2, 2009, Sec. 2.1, 13-15;

"Federal Presumed To Conform Actions Under General Conformity," Federal Aviation Administration, Office of Airports, Federal Register, Final Notice, July 30, 2007, Vol. 72, No. 145, 41565-41580.

158 "We even got the letter from EPA": Tom Coda, Manager for General Conformity, U.S. Environmental Protection Agency, letter to author, FAA Airports Office, regarding February 12, 2007 Federal Register Draft Notice for the FAA Presumed to Conform List, April 9, 2007.

158 Dave's eyes lit up: "Air Quality Technical Report: Philadelphia International Capacity Enhancement Program," Federal Aviation Administration, Revised Draft, March 24, 2010, 3-35.

158 "I could see it coming": "Draft General Conformity Determination," Philadelphia International Airport Capacity Enhancement Program, Federal Aviation Administration, April 27, 2010.

VII.   CLEAN ENERGY: THE OPPORTUNITY AT AIRPORTS

160 A large asset for airports is the amount of open land: Travis L. Devault, et al., "Airports Offer Unrealized Potential for Alternative Energy

Production," *Environmental Management*, U.S. Department of Interior, No. DOI 1007/s00267-011-9803-4, copyright: Springer Science and Business Media, LLC, January 14, 2012.

160 Much of the property: "Report to Congress: National Plan of Integrated Airport Systems (NPIAS) 2009-2013," Federal Aviation Administration, 2014, Ch. 1.

161 For example: Presidents Bush and Obama: Steve Barrett, "Renewable Energy as an Airport Revenue Source," National Academies, Airport Cooperative Research Program, 2015, Report No. ACRP 01-24, 41. Citations include E.O. 13423 (2007), E.O. 13514 (2009), and the December 5, 2013 Presidential Memorandum, "Federal Leadership on Energy Management," issued by the White House Office of the Press Secretary.

162 This happened to the FAA in 2000: "Inherently Low-Emission Airport Vehicle Pilot Program," Wendell H. Ford Aviation Investment and Reform Act for the 21st Century (AIR-21), 49 U.S.C §47136, April 2000.

162 They had persuaded two influential members: "Final Report: Inherently Low Emission Airport Vehicle Pilot Program," Federal Aviation Administration, Office of Airports, January 2006, 1.

163 It offered 10 airports: "Inherently Low-Emission Airport Vehicle Pilot Program."

163 Our interagency task force began: "Report to Congress: Inherently Low-Emission Airport Vehicle Pilot Program," U.S. Department of Transportation, Federal Aviation Administration, November 2001 (50 pp.).

164 From the 21 airport proposals submitted: "Report to Congress: Inherently Low-Emission Airport Vehicle Pilot Program".

164 The front office was also satisfied: "Report to Congress: Inherently Low-Emission Airport Vehicle Pilot Program," Ch. 4.

164 Everything was falling into place: "Report to Congress: Inherently Low-Emission Airport Vehicle Pilot Program," 22.

9/11
VALE Architecture

168 In the first 10 years: "Voluntary Airport Low Emission Program," Federal Aviation Administration, Office of Airports, accessed February 18, 2015, www.faa.gov/airports/environmental/vale/. See Summary of Airport Projects and Contacts.

171 The draft credit agreement: "Guidance on Airport Emission Reduction Credits for Early Measures Through Voluntary Airport Low Emission Programs," U.S. Environmental Protection Agency, Office of Air and Radiation, Air Quality Strategies and Standards Division, September 2004.

Making it Work

173 "I'm worried about how airports": "Voluntary Airport Low Emission Program: Technical Report," Federal Aviation Administration, Office of Airports, December 2, 2010, Ver. 7, Report No. DOT/FAA/ AR-04/37.

174 Over the lifetime of current VALE projects: "Estimated VALE Program Emission Reduction Benefits: Cars and Trucks Off-the-Road Equivalent (CORE) Values," Federal Aviation Administration, Office of Airports, software application based on EPA MOBILE 6.2 emission factors for all vehicle types.

Two Doors of Opportunity

177 The study was completed in 2012: "Airport Ground Support Equipment (GSE) Inventory and Emission Reduction Strategies, Tutorial, and GSE Database," Transportation Research Board, Airport Cooperative Research Program, June 2012, Report No. ACRP 02-16.

179 The solar guide for airports: "Technical Guidance for Evaluating Selected Solar Technologies on Airports," Federal Aviation Administration, Office of Airports, November 2010 (150 pp.).

179 DOE had learned one recently too: Joe Stephens and Carol D. Leonnig, "Solyndra solar company fails after getting federal loan guarantees," *The Washington Post*, August 31, 2011, accessed August 20, 2015, http://www.washingtonpost.com/politics/solyndra-solar-company-fails-after-getting-controversial-federal-loan-guarantees/2011/08/31/gIQAB8IRsJ_story.html.

179 True to Murphy's Law: "Work Underway to Correct Glare from Solar Panels: Manchester-Boston Regional," *Aviation Emissions Report*, February 18, 2014, Vol. 6, No., 15, 109.

180 The effort culminated: "Interim Policy, FAA Review of Solar Energy System Projects on Federally Obligated Airports," Federal Aviation Administration, October 23, 2013, Federal Register Notice, Vol. 78, No. 205, 63276-63279.

180 Moreover, there have been no difficulties: Steve Barrett, "Renewable Energy as an Airport Revenue Source," National Academies, Airport Cooperative Research Program, 2015, Report No. ACRP 01-24, Appendix A: List of Airport Solar Projects.

180 The past several years have seen: Steve Barrett, "Renewable Energy as an Airport Revenue Source," Appendix D.

180 For them, FAA grant assistance is still the key: "The Federal Aviation Administration Modernization and Reform Act of 2012," February 14, 2012, Section 512.

180 The new program qualified the nation's 5,000 public airports: "Report to Congress: National Plan of Integrated Airport Systems (NPIAS) 2009-2013".

181 No FAA solar grants were issued between 2013 and 2015: Patrick Magnotta, FAA Office of Airports, Planning and Environmental Division, email to author, August 20, 2015.

VIII.   CLIMATE CHANGE: THE INTERNATIONAL CHALLENGE

183 The issue is also distinguishable by its long timescale: "Climate Change 2013:   The Physical Science Basis," Intergovernmental Panel on Climate Change, Fifth Assessment Report, Summary for Policymakers, 2013, 26; "How does the IPCC work?" Intergovernmental Panel on Climate Change, accessed June 22, 2014, http://www.ipcc.ch/organization/organization_ structure.shtml#authors.

184 Oceans are also a long-term storehouse for CO_2:   "Climate Change 2013: The Physical Science Basis," 6;

"Carbon is Forever," *Nature Reports: Climate Change*, November 20, 2008, accessed March 13, 2014, http://www.nature.com/climate/2008/0812/ full/climate.2008.122.html.

184 CO_2 represents over 80 percent of U.S. greenhouse gases: "Climate Change: Overview of Greenhouse Gases," U.S. Environmental Protection Agency, July 21, 2015, accessed August 21, 2015, http://www.epa.gov/climatechange/ghgemissions/gases/co2.html;

"Climate Change 2013: The Physical Science Basis," 11.

184 According to the U.S. government's 2014 National Climate Assessment: Justin Gillis, "U.S. Climate has already changed, study finds, citing heat and floods," *The New York Times*, May 7, 2014, A1.

184 This rise in temperature: "Climate change is happening: Our Earth is warming," U.S. Environmental Protection Agency, Climate Change: Basic Information, accessed March 20, 2014, http://www.epa.gov/ climatechange/basics.

184 Other greenhouse gases: "Climate Change: Overview of Greenhouse Gases," U.S. Environmental Protection Agency, accessed March 13, 2014, http://www.epa.gov/climatechange/ghgemissions/gases.html.

184 While methane accounts for about 10 percent: Juliet Eilperin, "White House outlines strategy on methane gas," *Portland Press Herald* (reprint *The Washington Post*), March 29, 2014, A5.

185 Even before the IPCC report: "Larger share of Americans worried about climate change," *Portland Press Herald*, AP, December 15, 2012; Jon Krosnick, "Climate Change and Clean Energy – A Survey of US Public Attitudes," Resources for the Future, March 11, 2014 seminar presentation, accessed July 17, 2014, http://www.rff.org/Events/Pages/Climate-Change-and-Clean-Energy%E2%80%94A-Survey-of-US-Public-Attitudes.aspx.

Warming Effects

186 In the U.S., fluctuating weather patterns are caused in part by El Nino: Tom Arup, "Major El Nino events likely to double in next century," *The Sydney Morning Herald*, January 20, 2014, accessed August 21, 2015, http://www.smh.com.au/environment/climate-change/major-el-nino-events-likely-to-double-in-next-century-20140119-312sy.

186 In the East: David Porter, "Hurricane Sandy Was Second-Costliest in U.S. History, Report Shows," Huffpost Green, AP, April 14, 2013, accessed August 21, 2015, http://www.huffingtonpost.com/2013/02/12/hurricane-sandy-second-costliest_n_2669486.html.

186 "Climate change is about water": Gina McCarthy, Administrator, U.S. Environmental Protection Agency, C-SPAN broadcast of speech to National Press Club, Washington D.C., September 20, 2013.

186 These conditions are expected: Elaine Kurtenbach, "Costs of climate change steep, tough to tally," *Portland Press Herald*, AP, April 4, 2014. Author references conference summary report of the Intergovernmental Panel on Climate Change, which met in Yokohama Japan the same week.

187 An example of how conflict can arise from climate change: Al Gore, Vice President, "The Turning Point: New Hope for the Climate," *Rolling Stone Magazine*, June 18, 2014.

187 Acknowledging the roots of the Syrian conflict: "Years of Living Dangerously," *Showtime*, TV interview of Susan Rice, U.S. National Security Advisor, by author Thomas Friedman of The New York Times,

April 6, 2014, accessed April 25, 2014, http://yearsoflivingdangerously. com/stories/.

187 Global warming is also threatening wildlife: "Scientists concerned by sudden warming changes," *Portland Press Herald*, AP, December 4, 2013, A5. Reference to National Academy of Sciences report, "Abrupt Impacts of Climate Change: Anticipating Surprises".

187 The signs of ecological stress: Jeff Thaler, "To dismiss climate change is to ignore its insidious effects in Maine," *Portland Press Herald,* September 27, 2013, A10.

187 Shifting bird ranges: "Snowy Owl," National Wildlife Refuge Association, accessed May 4, 2014, http://refugeassociation.org/wildlife/birds/snowy-owl/; Sandy Bauers, "Chickadee in the coal mine?" *Maine Sunday Telegram* (reprint *The Philadelphia Inquirer*), March 30, 2014, G1.

187 Another sentinel species is the monarch butterfly: Deirdre Fleming, "Butterfly survey taking flight," *Portland Press Herald,* May 5, 2014, B11; Tim Johnson, "Monarch butterfly has friends in high places," *Portland Press Herald*, McClatchy, February 21, 2014, A4.

188 Global warming is also affecting insect populations: Patrick Whittle, "Maine moose hunters find parasite thinning the herd," *Maine Sunday Telegram*, AP, September 21, 2014, B6; Alan Caron, "Is the real question how to adapt to climate change?" *Portland Press Herald*, February 21, 2013, A9.

188 Nature's adjustments to climate change: "Global Warming and Eastern Hemlock Forests," National Wildlife Federation, accessed May 5, 2014, https://www.nwf.org/Wildlife/Threats-to-Wildlife/Global-Warming/ Effects-on-Wildlife-and-Habitat/Eastern-Hemlock-Forests.aspx.

188 The oceans are warming too: "Climate Change 2013: The Physical Science Basis," 6.

188 In New England: Mary Pols, "As jellyfish appear in waves, questions follow," *Portland Press Herald*, July 16, 2014, A1;

Personal notes from "Climate Solutions Expo and Summit," Panel presentation: Fisheries, Augusta, Maine, March 12, 2014.

Ocean Acidification

188 The other primary effect of climate change: "Ocean Acidification: Carbon Dioxide is Putting Shelled Animals at Risk," *National Geographic*, accessed April 10, 2014, http://ocean.nationalgeographic.com/ocean/critical-issues-ocean-acidification/.

189 Ocean acidification is considered the biggest scientific advance: Bill McKibben, personal interview with the author, March 4, 2014.

189 To find out why: Dr. David Emerson, Bigelow Laboratory for Ocean Sciences, Boothbay, Maine, personal interview with the author, April 22, 2014.

189 New research indicates: Craig Welch, "Research suggests acid rain already harming sea creatures," *Portland Press Herald*, McClatchy, May 6, 2014, A7.

Bill McKibben

191 The co-founder and leader of 350.org: "Bill McKibben," accessed August 21, 2015, http://www.billmckibben.com/bio.html;

"Hansen to Hand Over Reins of Goddard Institute for Space Studies Director," National Aeronautics and Space Administration, Research news, April 2, 2013, accessed August 21, 2015, http://www.giss.nasa.gov/research/news/20130402/.

191 Hansen postulated: James Hansen, et al., "Target atmospheric CO2: Where should humanity aim?" *Open Atmospheric Scientific Journal*, October 31, 2008, Vol. 2, 217-231, accessed March 25, 2014, http://benthamopen.com/ABSTRACT/TOASCJ-2-217.

192 In the spring of 2014, I spoke with Bill McKibben: Bill McKibben, personal interview with the author, March 4, 2014.

South Portland Tar Sands Blockade

198 The proposed route for the Keystone pipeline: "U.S. Imports by Country of Origin," U.S. Energy Information Administration, April 29, 2014, accessed May 14, 2014, http://www.eia.gov/dnav/pet/pet_move_impcus_a2_nus_epc0_im0_mbblpd_a.htm;

"Crude Oil Imports Into the U.S. by Country of Origin: 1980 to 2009," U.S. Census Bureau, Statistical Abstract of the United States, Energy and Utilities, 2011, Table 932, 589, accessed May 14, 2014, https://www.google.com/search?q=U.S.+oil+imports+from+1990+to+2010+by+nation&ie=utf-8&oe=utf-8&aq=t&rls=org.mozilla:en-US:official&client=firefox-a&channel=sb;

Curtis Tate, "Rail industry jumps in to ship oil," *Maine Sunday Telegram*, March 9, 2014, B7;

Matthew Daly, "Proposed oil pipeline clears key environmental hurdle," *Portland Press Herald*, January 1, 2014, C7.

199 The oil companies needed Keystone: Neela Banerjee, "For locals, oil sands exact heavy cost," *Portland Press Herald*, Tribune Washington Bureau, October 24, 2013, A2.

199 Environmental concerns about mining Alberta tar sands: Banerjee, "For locals, oil sands exact heavy cost".

200 In 2013, the tar sands proposal: Matt Byrne, "Oil lobbyists threaten suit against S. Portland," *Portland Press Herald*, December 12, 2013, C1.

200 Many citizens of South Portland were concerned: "Tar Sands Facts," Natural Resources Defenses Council. July 2013, (4 pp.);

Jordan Schneider, Emily Figdor, and Taryn Hallweaver, "Inside the Big Oil Playbook: Strategies and Tactics Used in the Industry's Battle to Ship

Tar Sands Oil Out of Casco Bay," Environment Maine Research and Policy Center, June 2014, (31 pp.);

Kirk Johnson and Dan Frosch, "A Pipeline Divides Along Old Lines: Jobs Versus the Environment," *The New York Times*, September 28, 2011, accessed August 21, 2015, http://www.nytimes.com/2011/09/29/us/rancor-grows-over-planned-oil-pipeline-from-canada.html.

200 Four years later, the party responsible: "EPA's Response to the Enbridge Oil Spill," U.S. Environmental Protection Agency, accessed May 9, 2014, http://www.epa.gov/enbridgespill/.

200 The billion dollar cleanup: Schneider, Figdor, Hallweaver, "Inside the Big Oil Playbook: Strategies and Tactics Used in the Industry's Battle to Ship Tar Sands Oil Out of Casco Bay";

"Tar Sands Facts".

203 The election hinged on just 192 votes: Matt Byrne, "Ordinance targeting tar sands oil defeated," *Portland Press Herald*, November 6, 2013, A1.

203 The oil industry had won by a whisker: Schneider, Figdor, Hallweaver, "Inside the Big Oil Playbook: Strategies and Tactics Used in the Industry's Battle to Ship Tar Sands Oil Out of Casco Bay".

203 Knowing this, the city council interpreted the vote as a *rejection*: Matt Byrne, "Council passes moratorium on tar sands oil," *Portland Press Herald*, December 17, 2013, A1.

203 In January 2014, the city council: Matt Byrne, "S. Portland council picks 3 to craft oil sands ordinance," *Portland Press Herald*, January 24, 2014, C1.

204 Following a series of recent oil car derailments: Curtis Tate, "Rail industry jumps in to ship oil".

204 On the environmental side, the American public: Emily Atkin, "Delaying the Keystone XL Decision Wasn't All About Politics," ClimateProgress, April 22, 2014, accessed May 15, 2014, http://thinkprogress.org/climate/2014/04/22/3429089/keystone-delay-politics/.

Government Action

205 Climate change is a classic *tragedy of the commons*: Garrett Hardin, "Tragedy of the Commons," *Science Magazine*, 1968, Vol. 162, 1243-1248.

206 Between 2000 and 2013, U.S. coal consumption: "Coal Overview: 1949-2012," U.S. Department of Energy, Energy Information Administration, Annual Energy Review, Table 6.1, accessed March 30, 2014, http://www.eia.gov/totalenergy/data/annual/#coal.

206 As Bill McKibben indicated, developing an effective global strategy: John Vidal and David Adam, "China overtakes US as world's biggest CO_2 emitter," *The Guardian*, June 19, 2007, accessed March 20, 2014, http://www.theguardian.com/environment/2007/jun/19/china.usnews/print; "Each Country's Share of CO_2 Emissions," Union of Concerned Scientists, November 18, 2014, accessed August 21, 2015, http://www.ucsusa.org/global_warming/science_and_impacts/science/each-countrys-share-of-co2.html#.VdeOjJdiO_R.

206 On a per capita basis: "Carbon dioxide emissions (CO_2) metric tons of CO_2 per capita," United Nations Statistics Division, July 6, 2015, accessed August 21, 2015, http://mdgs.un.org/unsd/mdg/SeriesDetail.aspx?srid=751.

206 Solving the climate dilemma: Juliet Eilperin and Steven Mufson, "EPA to propose cutting coal plant emissions," *Portland Press Herald* (reprint *The Washington Post*) June 2, 2014, A3.

207 The EPA has also proposed new regulations to curb methane: "Rule and Implementation Information for Standards of Performance for Municipal Solid Waste Landfills," U.S. Environmental Protection Agency, August 14, 2015, accessed August 21, 2015, http://www.epa.gov/ttnatw01/landfill/landflpg.html;

Gardiner Harris and Coral Davenport, "E.P.A. Announces New Rules to Cut Methane Emissions, *The New York Times*, August 18, 2015, accessed August 21, 2015, http://www.nytimes.com/2015/08/19/us/epa-announces-new-rules-to-cut-methane-emissions.html;

Sara Sjolin, "China's shale ambition: 23 times the output in 5 years," Market Watch, February 12, 2015, accessed August 21, 2015, http://www.marketwatch.com/story/chinas-shale-ambition-23-times-the-output-in-5-years-2015-02-11.

208 Government also has responsibilities to advance climate science: "Climate Change Indicators in the United States," U.S. Environmental Protection Agency, accessed June 18, 2014, http://www.epa.gov/climatechange/science/indicators/;

Josh Lederman, "Bid to tackle extreme weather involves seven 'climate hubs'" *Portland Press Herald*, AP, February 6, 2014, A5.

208 So too, businesses are adjusting: Rebecca VanderMeulen, "The Science of Saving the World: College Majors Go Green!" CollegeXpress, Science and Engineering, accessed March 24, 2014, http://www.collegexpress.com/interests/science-and-engineering/articles/careers-science-engineering/science-saving-world/.

Accepting Adaptation

209 In many ways, adaptation is more actionable: "Senate holds Miami Beach hearing on climate change," AP, April 22, 2014, accessed May 19, 2014, http://www.naplesnews.com/news/2014/apr/22/senate-holds-miami-beach-hearing-on-climate/.

210 On a global scale, the melting Arctic ice: Paul Koenig, "LePage points to climate change as plus for Maine," *Portland Press Herald*, December 6, 2013, D6.

210 And above all, as former astronaut and U.S. Senator Bill Nelson said: "Senate holds Miami Beach hearing on climate change".

IX. SUSTAINABLE CHOICES

211 The environment is under stress: Al Gore, Vice President, "The Turning Point: New Hope for the Climate," *Rolling Stone Magazine*, June 18, 2014.

Back to the Local Café

215 "Let's stop there for a second": Martha Irvine, "Younger generation shows less concern for environment," *The Washington Post*, AP, March 16, 2012, Sec. A.

218 We discussed why that was: Robert J. Seeber, "Anti-wind power column ignores subsidies for other energy sources," *Maine Sunday Telegram*, July 21, 2013, Sec. E.

218 We both shuddered at the thought: Jason Dearen, "Seismic Shift in Oil Exploration," *Portland Press Herald*, AP, July 19, 2014, D5.

219 And we keep letting it happen: Paul Josephson, "Renewables a far better power option than small nuclear stations," *Portland Press Herald*, July 13, 2015, A6;

Eric Russell, "Feds to pay Maine Yankee for nuclear waste storage," *Portland Press Herald*, November 16, 2013, B2.

219 That price tag will soon be dwarfed: "Dismantling of nuke plant will cost about $4.4 billion," *Maine Sunday Telegram*, AP, August 3, 2014, A7.

219 "I'd really get depressed": Seth Borenstein, "Ozone layer recovering, study finds," *Portland Press Herald*, AP, September 11, 2014, A3;

Justin Gillis, "Restored Forests Breathe Life Into Efforts Against Climate Change," *The New York Times*, December 24, 2014, A1.

219 "By the way, ever hear of Jairam Ramesh": Rama Lakshmi, "Environmental protection efforts rile pro-development forces in India," *The Washington Post*, January 4, 2011, A7.

221 "I think it shows the critical role": Juliet Eilperin and Steven Mufson, "U.S. lifts ban on deep-water drilling: Environmentalists Dismayed," *The Washington Post*, October 13, 2010, A1.

Solar Experiment in Germany

221 As our search revealed: Dr. Harry Wirth, "Recent Facts about Photovoltaics in Germany," Fraunhofer ISE, May 19, 2015, accessed August 22, 2015, http://www.ise.fraunhofer.de/en/publications/veroeffentlichungen-pdf-dateien-en/studien-und-konzeptpapiere/recent-facts-about-photovoltaics-in-germany.pdf;

Alan Caron, "For Solar Power, Maine doesn't lack sun as much as imagination," *Portland Press Herald*, December 5, 2013, A11.

222 Germany's bold steps on solar: "Nuclear Power in Germany," World Nuclear Association, August 2015, accessed August 22, 2015, http://www.world-nuclear.org/info/Country-Profiles/Countries-G-N/Germany/;

"Response to Fukushima: Siemens to Exit Nuclear Energy Business," Spiegel Online International, September 19, 2011, accessed August 22, 2015, http://www.spiegel.de/international/business/response-to-fukushima-siemens-to-exit-nuclear-energy-business-a-787020.html.

222 Germany's solar experiment: Caron, "For Solar Power, Maine doesn't lack sun as much as imagination";

"Technical Guidance for Evaluating Selected Solar Technologies on Airports," Federal Aviation Administration, Office of Airports, November 2010, Figure 9: Photovoltaic Solar Resources, 14. Original source noted is the National Renewable Energy Laboratory.

222 The German formula includes attractive economic incentives: Toby D. Couture, et al., "A Policymaker's Guide to Feed-in Tariff Policy Design,"

National Renewable Energy Laboratory, Report No. NREL/TP-6A2-44849, July 2010, accessed August 22, 2015, http://www.nrel.gov/docs/fy10osti/44849.pdf;

Amory B. Lovins, "Germany's Renewables Revolution," Rocky Mountain Institute, April 17, 2013, accessed on August 22, 2015, http://blog.rmi.org/blog_2013_04_17_germanys_renewables_revolution;

Thomas Neider, "Zeitreihen zur Entwicklung der erneuerbaren Energien in Deutschland," Bundesministerium fur Wirtschaft und Energie, February 2015, accessed August 24, 2015,

http://www.erneuerbare-energien.de/EE/Redaktion/DE/Downloads/zeitreihen-zur-entwicklung-der-erneuerbaren-energien-in-deutschland-1990-2014.pdf?__blob=publicationFile&v=3.

223 In contrast, the U.S. addiction to fossil fuels: Steven Mufson, "Obama seeking one-third cut in oil imports by 2025," *The Washington Post*, March 31, 2011.

223 In 1950, the United States obtained 8 percent: "Primary Energy Production by Source," U.S. Department of Energy, Energy Information Administration, Monthly Energy Review, December 2013, accessed July 21, 2014, http://www.eia.gov/totalenergy/data/monthly/previous.cfm#2013; "U.S. Energy Facts—Energy Explained, Your Guide to Understanding Energy," U.S. Department of Energy, Energy Information Administration, accessed January 13, 2014, http://www.eia.gov/energyexplained/index.cfm?page=us_energy_home.

223 Of that total, solar energy is a small component: Chenda Ngak, "Powering the Future: What will fuel the next thousand years?" CBS News, August 26, 2013, accessed July 21, 2014, http://archive-e.blogspot.com/2013/08/powering-future-what-will-fuel-next.html. Primary CBS source is the U.S. Energy Information Agency.

223 Besides Germany, other countries around the world: "Renewables 2013 Global Status Report," REN21: Renewable Energy Policy Network for

the 21st Century, 2013, accessed January 11, 2014, http://www.ren21.net/ren21activities/globalstatusreport.aspx.

223 Other large oil importers like Japan and India: "Imports of Crude Oil including Lease Condensate 2012," U.S. Energy Information Administration, accessed August 22, 2015, http://www.eia.gov/beta/international/rankings/#?prodact=57-3&cy=2012&pid=57&aid=3&tl_id=3-A&tl_type=a.

223 The same is true in Europe: "What Do We Want to Achieve?" European Commission, Renewable Energy, accessed January 13, 2014, http://ec.europa.eu/energy/renewables/index_en.htm.

224 The U.S. boasts a similar timeframe: "Obama: Triple renewable sources for electric power," *Portland Press Herald*. December 6, 2013, A-3.

224 Indeed, even if the goal: "Energy vs. Electricity and why we care," Next Generation Nuclear Power (NGNP) Alliance Blog, February 25, 2013, accessed January 13, 2014, http://blog.ngnpalliance.org/energy-vs-electricity-and-why-we-care/. Primary source is Energy Information Administration data analyzed by Lawrence Livermore National Laboratory.

224 Prices on panels have fallen 75 percent: "Lawmakers should pass solar power rebate bill," *Portland Press Herald,* March 4, 2014, A8.

224 On the demand side: "Total Energy: Annual Energy Review," U.S. Energy Information Administration, September 27, 2012, Table 1.5: Energy Consumption, Expenditures, and Emissions Indicators Estimates, 1949-2011, accessed July 18, 2014, http://www.eia.gov/totalenergy/data/annual/showtext.cfm?t=ptb0105.

Taking Social Responsibility

225 The latter subject on diet: Seth Borenstein, "Raising beef is by far the worst for environment," *Portland Press Herald*, July 22, 2014, A7. Additional

references are Michael Pollan, *The Omnivore's Dilemma: A Natural History of Four Meals*, 2006, and Richard North, *The Real Cost,*1986.

Financial Divestiture

227 The West Coast was setting the trend: "Oakland City Council Votes to Divest from Fossil Fuel Companies," 350.org, June 18, 2014, accessed July 23, 2014, http://350.org/press-release/oakland-city-council-votes-to-divest-from-fossil-fuel-companies/.

228 Within the religious community: Adam Vaughn, (2014, July 11). "World Council of Churches pulls fossil fuel investments," *The Guardian,* July 11, 2014, accessed August 2, 2014, www.theguadian.com/environment/2014/jul/11/world-council-of-churches-pulls-fossil-fuel-investment;
Bill McKibben, "We Want People to Change Their Minds," Huffington Post: The Blog, July 10, 2014, accessed August 2, 2014, www.huffington-post.com/bill-mckibben/we-want-people-to-change-b-5574066.html;
Kelley Bouchard, "Pope's plea on climate 'crisis' applauded by some Mainers," *Portland Press Herald*, June 19, 2015, A1.

228 Of the first dozen colleges and universities: Michael Wines, "Stanford to Purge $18 Billion Endowment of Coal Stock," *The New York Times*, May 7, 2014, A13.

228 Also extricating themselves from fossil fuel companies: John Schwartz, "Rockefellers, Heirs to an Oil Fortune, Will Divest Charity of Fossil Fuels," *The New York Times*, September 21, 2014, accessed September 25, 2014, www.nytimes.com/2014/09/22/us/heirs-to-an-oil-fortune-join-the-divestment-drive.html;
"Divestment Goes Mainstream as Major Funds Kick the Fossil Fuel Habit," EcoWatch, February 3, 2014, accessed July 22, 2014, http://ecow-atch.com/2014/02/03/divestment-mainstream-kick-fossil-fuel-habit/.

228 However, the research shows that green investments: Stephanie R. Leighton, "Getting out of fossil fuel investments a wise approach for state," *Portland Press Herald*, January 9, 2014, A8.

229 The second argument against divestment: Leighton, "Getting out of fossil fuel investments a wise approach for state".

230 As Bill McKibben says: "Fossil fuel divestment campaign," Climate Science & Policy Watch, December 21, 2012, accessed September 1, 2015, http://www.climatesciencewatch.org/2012/12/21/fossil-fuel-divestment/.

Made in the USA
Middletown, DE
04 August 2020